Don Quixote's Delusions

Don Quixote's Delusions

TRAVELS IN CASTILIAN SPAIN

Miranda France

THE OVERLOOK PRESS
WOODSTOCK & NEW YORK

First published in the United States in 2002 by
The Overlook Press, Peter Mayer Publishers, Inc.
Woodstock & New York

WOODSTOCK:
One Overlook Drive
Woodstock, NY 12498
www.overlookpress.com
[for individual orders, bulk and special sales, contact our Woodstock office]

NEW YORK:
141 Wooster Street
New York, NY 10012

⊗The paper used in this book meets the requirements for paper
permanence as described in the ANSI Z39.48-1992 standard.

Library of Congress Cataloging-in-Publication Data
France, Miranda.
Don Quixote's Delusions : Travels in Castilian Spain / Miranda France.
p. cm.
Includes bibliographical references and index.
1. Castilla-La Mancha (Spain)—Description and travel. 2. Castilla y León
(Spain)—Description and travel. 3. France, Miranda, 1966—Journeys—Spain—
Castilla-La Mancha. 4. France, Miranda, 1966—Journeys—Spain—Castilla y
León. 5. Cervantes Saavedra, Miguel de, 1547-1616. Don Quixote. I. Title.
DP302.C553 F73 2002   946'.2—dc21   2002070408

Manufactured in the United States of America
ISBN 1-58567-292-0
1 3 5 7 9 8 6 4 2

'The day before yesterday we were poor and now we are not, and the bonanza seems to have gone to our heads.'

ROSA MONTERO

'When Don Quixote went out into the world, that world turned into a mystery before his eyes. That is the legacy of the first European novel to the entire subsequent history of the novel.'

MILAN KUNDERA

To my mother and father

CONTENTS

1 A Dead Man in Madrid   1
2 The Taxi-Driver's Cousin's Friend   17
3 Don Quixote's Delusions   30
4 Transvestites, Anarchists and
    a Peruvian Poet   46
5 Double Lives and Double
    Cheeseburgers   55
6 Is *Anything* Real?   71
7 Pastoral Scenes in Avila   91
8 Love in a Cold Climate   109
9 A Question of Faith   129
10 Is Burgos Boring?   154
11 A Little Place in La Mancha   176
12 Which Are You? Quixote or Sancho?   194
13 An Angel in Segovia   206
14 New Life in Castile   222

Further Reading   236
Index   238

ACKNOWLEDGEMENTS

For help in Spain I would like to thank Teresa Amina, Martin and Erin Brau, Javier Corcuera, Bill Schomberg and Miren Valero. For tracking down medical and psychoanalytical studies on Don Quixote, I am grateful to Professor Hugh Freeman and Dr Matthew Hotopf. Professor Edward Riley, an eminent Cervantine scholar, gave me valuable pointers. For help and advice generally, I thank Diana Beatty, Sara Lodge, John Stonehouse, Professor Philip Swanson and especially my husband Carl Honoré.

I am grateful to Penguin Books for permission to quote passages from *Don Quixote*, translated by J. M. Cohen.

CHAPTER ONE
A Dead Man in Madrid

This book starts with a funeral and ends with a christening, although neither of those events turned out to be quite what it seemed.

The funeral took place in a chapel in Madrid, and was presided over by a priest with a streaming cold. The chapel was inside one of the city's oldest convents, home to a declining population of elderly nuns. It was a closed order, so although the women were present, they were nowhere to be seen. Four ceremonial candles stood guard around the coffin, which was draped in purple, signifying the status of the deceased. About fifty men and women were gathered towards the front of the chapel where storage heaters had been placed to comfort the mourners.

The women were mostly stocky inside close-fitting clothes, like small pieces of upholstered furniture, and they had hairstyles that might have been made by the same, helmet-shaped mould. Some of the men had their coats draped around their shoulders as if they had never lost the medieval habit of cape-wearing. Outside it was a pleasant, spring evening, but the warmth did not penetrate the convent's stone heart. The ancient buildings of Castile are designed to cling on to cold even in the hottest summer.

I was sitting at the front of the chapel, close to the coffin. Like most of those present, I was an admirer of the dead man, though none of us could really say we knew him. So much of his life was shrouded in mystery, and now that all of him was shrouded there were many things we would never be sure about. He had been a wanderer. For years he had drifted on the roads of central and southern Spain, taking jobs that had a habit of landing him in trouble. He had been both imprisoned and excommunicated at least twice and counted gamblers and criminals among his friends. His family life had been touched by scandal and he had an illegitimate daughter, but he was not otherwise a womaniser. Some said that he was a Jew, though he professed catholicism. Some said that he was gay, though others thought he had loved his wife, at least at the beginning. Everyone agreed that he was poor.

How much did these things matter now? He was dead, after all. Once a life is over the failures fade. The priest spoke the words of the mass quickly and in a low murmur, as if not to disturb the dead man, or some of the sleepier members of the congregation. But every so often a shrill lament disturbed his intonation. The chant seemed to rise from nowhere, as if it were drifting upwards from vents in the aisle or via the same mechanism that pipes muzak into shopping malls. At first I thought it was a recording, then I realised that the sound was being produced by the Barefoot Trinitarian Sisters, hidden from view in barred recesses behind the altar.

The nuns had been *in claustura*, shut up and cut off for years, decades even, from the outside world. Many of them would have taken up their vocations when Spain was a dictatorship and the choices for unmarried women were limited. I wondered if they felt cheated when they saw how women today could go out to work, or raise children on their own. Perhaps the priest sensed their breath on his neck; when called to raise his eyes to God he did so with the exasperation of one who would much rather be in bed. The air and the hush in the chapel were chilly, the congregation huddled into itself. If the nuns really were barefoot under their robes, their feet must have been cold.

The purple drape on the coffin shimmered in the candlelight. The low light and chanting, the priest's gentle sniffing created a peaceful atmosphere. The span of the dead man's life, on the other hand, showed more turbulence than calm. His failure to be recognised as a poet had always rankled with him, his attempts as a playwright were generally dismal. For twenty years he had published nothing, resigned to the fact that he would never make any money out of writing. No one knew for sure what had prompted him to take up the pen again, towards the end of his life, but a spell in prison may have been the motivation. Perhaps he felt, by then, that he had nothing left to lose. He was poor anyway, his life was wretched and all he had ever wanted to do was write.

A thin girl holding some university files arrived late and squeezed on to the end of our row, trying to muscle in on the storage heater to which she stretched out her hands. Her nose, slightly pink, seemed to pay tribute to the priest's.

But what if a life of disappointments were weighed against one, resounding success? Could it be enough to make up for the defeats and hardship? On top of the coffin there was a cushion, head-dented, as if a body had been resting there until moments ago, then moved on, heavenwards perhaps. Behind the coffin a dozen members of the Royal Academy of the Spanish Language were ranged in splendid gilt chairs. They were elderly, creaking when they genuflected. The nuns were also very old, you could tell by the calibre of their trilling. Spain, which used to seem full of children, was now a country that worried about ageing. The birth rate was the lowest in Europe and the United Nations had said that twenty million immigrants would be needed to replace the dwindling stock of workers. Historically frightened of immigrants, Spain quaked at the prospect of another Moorish invasion.

When the time came for communion, the priest rang his little bell to signify the transformation of bread to body. As he approached the cage behind the altar two figures could be seen emerging from its shadows. Two sets of hands poked through the bars to receive the holy wafer. The other nuns – and the singing suggested that there were many more than two – were nowhere to be seen. I watched the old fingers appearing through the bars and could not help thinking again about the corresponding feet, gnarled and calloused. I thought of them pounding down the corridors on that day, in 1936, when extremists had stormed Madrid's convents. The anti-clerical hatred that had been brewing in Spain for decades had erupted in a terrifying violence that saw parish priests crucified and the corpses of nuns wrenched from their coffins. Spain's Republican president, Manuel Azaña, predicted that the blood would 'drown us all'. He was right, because civil war broke out soon afterwards.

The men and women of the congregation came forward to take communion from the priest who placed the wafers directly on to each proferred tongue. Then the communicants returned quietly to their pews, carrying God's blessing and the priest's virus. Some bowed their heads to pray.

A sense of sobriety and regret hung in the air of the chapel, but there were no tears. The mourners had no great grief to battle or assuage. They came to this funeral mass every year, so they knew that the coffin was empty. The man who should have occupied it had been dead for nearly four hundred years. He was now nothing more than a heap of bones, and even the bones were no longer heaped. He had been buried in the convent in 1616, but the skeleton was disturbed and scattered when the building was rebuilt at the end of the seventeenth century. No one knew exactly where he lay now.

He had no descendants; his possessions had been pawned and

lost. The only physical pressence of the dead man was his work; four dusty tomes piled on the coffin contained his life's writing. Taken together they bore witness to his general failure and to his one, extraordinary triumph, because while some of the books were good, and others mediocre, one of them was the most successful novel in the history of publishing, the most translated work after the Bible. Indeed it was widely claimed as the world's first novel. The book was *Don Quixote de la Mancha*.

'We commend the soul of Miguel de Cervantes Saavedra to the Lord,' sniffed the priest. The academicians genuflected. The nuns trilled. The pink-nosed student shivered and moved closer to a source of heat.

Don Quixote is Spain's most famous book, but its most striking effect has often been on readers who were not Spanish. The young Sigmund Freud skipped medical lectures to read it, and noted its influence on his ideas about psychoanalysis. Karl Marx inscribed a copy of it to Engels. Dostoevsky believed that 'a more profound and more powerful work than this one is not to be found. It is the finest and greatest utterance of the human mind.' Virginia Woolf said, 'Everything is there, in solution.'

The novel tells the story of Alonso Quixano, a fifty-year-old country gentleman who goes mad from reading too many chivalric adventures and decides to emulate them, styling himself 'Quixote'. A local labourer, the flatulent, wise-cracking Sancho Panza, agrees to act as squire. There is a supporting cast of academics, nuns, students and priests – and there is an imaginary girlfriend, Dulcinea. What makes *Don Quixote* extraordinary is the humanity of its characters. Previously, 'romances' presented an idealised picture of life. In *Don Quixote* the characters are complex, unpredictable and able to change their minds about things.

Cervantes' own life was full of failures, misunderstandings, bankruptcies and prison sentences. He may have been in gaol when he got the idea for his famous novel. He must often have felt himself to be as beleaguered as Don Quixote.

He was born in 1547 at Alcalá de Henares, a small town close to Madrid which was, at that time, home to one of Europe's most important universities and a great centre of humanist teaching. However, Spain's intellectual life suffered under the regime of Philip II, in the second half of the sixteenth century, and, during Cervantes' lifetime, the country was increasingly cut off from the ideas of the Renaissance.

At the time of his birth, Spain's empire had reached its apogee and was poised for a long and painful descent. Heavily dependent on bank loans secured on the riches flowing from the New World, Spain made no efforts to modernise its economy. 'Everything', Philip II said, 'comes down to one thing: money and more money,' but many of the people who worked hardest for Spain were being forced to leave it.

After years of growing panic about the suspected duplicity of *conversos* – Jews who had converted to Christianity – all unbaptised Jews had been expelled in 1492. Some 300,000 Muslims would be made to go in 1609. In 1600 the political theorist Martín de Cellorigo voiced a concern that would be heard repeatedly over the next four centuries. He said that Spain's fear of progress and a lack of realism in government risked turning it into 'a nation of enchanted people who live outside the natural order', a nation of Quixotes, in other words.

The son of a second-rate surgeon and blood-letter, Cervantes did not attend university, but when his family moved to Madrid, he studied with a follower of Erasmus, who encouraged him to be a writer. In 1569 Cervantes may have wounded someone in a duel – records show that a man of his name was ordered to be arrested and to have his right hand cut off. Such a dramatic sentence would explain his hasty departure to Italy, where he took a job as chamberlain to a young Italian Monsignor. In order to get the position, he had to provide, as proof of his 'purity of blood', a certificate stating that he was not illegitimate and that there were no Muslims, Jews, *conversos* or anyone who had been in trouble with the Inquisition among his ancestors. He would spend the rest of his life producing such documents for one reason or another.

While in Italy Cervantes joined the army and at the Battle of Lepanto he received three harquebus wounds – two in the breast and one that permanently maimed his left hand. If he had gone to Italy to save his right hand, he paid the price with the left, but he always claimed to consider his disability a 'beautiful' reminder of his part in the battle. The injury earned him a distinguished sobriquet by which he is still known in Spain: El Manco de Lepanto – The One-Handed Man of Lepanto.

Cervantes fought again, in Corfu, Navarino and Tunis. In 1575 he was twenty-eight and on his way back to look for work in Spain – he may even have been in sight of the northern coast – when his ship was ambushed by slave-trading pirates. The passengers were taken to Algiers, where Cervantes was held for a ransom that was arbitrarily raised on the several occasions that Spanish representatives were sent to negotiate his release. Over the next five years his family put all their money, including their two daughters' dowries, towards the ransom. Cervantes made several unsuccessful attempts to escape and was threatened with execution, but finally two Trinitarian monks secured his release and returned him to Spain. He never forgot the debt of honour, and chose the Trinitarian convent for his final resting place.

His five years as a hostage must have marked Cervantes, and perhaps his long absence made it more difficult for him to find the sort of work he felt he deserved, in the king's service. Denied a pension, he was finally offered a post requisitioning corn for the Armada. But his seizure of corn belonging to the Church earned his excommunication and his poor accounts landed him in prison. His simultaneous attempts to write went largely unrewarded. At a time when Spain's theatre was dominated by the great Lope de Vega, his plays barely rated a mention. He had limited success with *La Galatea*, a novel written in the popular pastoral genre. He married Catalina de Palacios, a young widow, in 1584, but the union seems not to have been a happy one, and he spent years away from his wife. Poverty, family responsibilities and the burden of his empty marriage may have conspired against his chances. By the time Cervantes wrote *Don Quixote*, in his early fifties, he was a shipwreck.

'It may help a little to be distracted in order to write a masterpiece,' said Jorge Luis Borges of this late flowering creativity. Cervantes wondered how the public would receive his book 'after all these years I have spent sleeping in the silence of oblivion'.

The literary world into which *Don Quixote* was launched in 1605 was competitive and bitchy and there were plenty of writers who wanted the novel to fail. Lope de Vega, once Cervantes' friend, said that a reader would have to be 'stupid' to see any merit in it. After the novel's publication he sent Cervantes this note:

> That trivial Don Quixote of yours now goes
> Through the world from arse to arse, or serves
> As wrapping paper for spices and cheap saffron,
> And finally will end up in dumps and privies.

The letter was sent unstamped, so Cervantes also suffered the indignity of paying for this abuse.

The magnitude of his sudden success must have dazzled the man who was so used to failure. Within a few weeks *Don Quixote* had broken all publishing records. Seven editions, including pirate versions, were produced in the first year. An Englishman travelling in seventeenth-century Spain reported that copies of it could be found 'not only in almost every gentleman's house, but not seldom in inns, in barbers' shops, and in peasants' cottages and boys and girls, ten years old, understand it as well'.

Soon the book was translated into French, German and English. In France, Molière starred in a stage version. Quixote's reputation preceded him in England where the first translation appeared in 1612: five years earlier a character in a play by George Wilkins had declared that he was 'armed and ready to fight a windmill'. By the middle of the century, 'quixote' had become a common noun, used to denigrate Puritans.

William Shakespeare probably read *Don Quixote* and certainly collaborated on a play, since lost, inspired by one of its anecdotes. The knight and his squire soon became popular outside Europe, too, appearing at festivals in South America. Cervantes boasted that the Emperor of China had invited him to be rector of an Academy which would use his book as a text to teach Chinese students Spanish.

Cervantes was soon at work on a second part, but before he could finish it, another sequel was produced by a writer about whom nothing is known other than his name, or pseudonym: Avellaneda. Writing a sequel to someone else's work was not unusual, but Avellaneda's stands out for its personal attacks on the author it plagiarises.

Cervantes hurried out his own sequel in 1615 – with a prologue trouncing his usurper – and this second volume is generally admired as an even greater accomplishment than the first. Yet for some reason, perhaps jealousy, Cervantes was never acclaimed by his contemporaries. A literary companion of the time devoted fourteen pages to Lope de Vega and only half a page to El Manco.

His fame and the success of his novel won Cervantes neither money nor prestige. In June 1605, when a friend was fatally wounded outside the Cervantes family home, he was arrested on suspicion of murder and locked in a cell which both his father and grandfather had briefly inhabited before him. A neighbour testified that he was in the habit of receiving 'scandalous' visits, that he was often involved in shady business deals and visited gambling dens. Cervantes cleared his name, but he never escaped poverty.

His last days were spent in a frenzy of activity. He was struggling to finish a book, *Persiles and Sigismunda*, and this time the deadline was death itself. Diabetes or possibly cirrhosis of the liver were doing him in. On 19 April 1616, he wrote to his patron: 'The foot poised in the stirrup, the pallor of death already on my cheeks, I write to you, illustrious lord, these lines. Yesterday I received the last rites, today I write you this letter; the time-span is brief, the breathlessness increases, hope diminishes, and yet the will to live keeps me upright.'

He died three days later, on 23 April, the same date as Shakespeare (though really a week after him, because Britain and Spain used different calendars at that time). He had ten masses said for his soul and was buried in a rough Franciscan habit, somewhere in the ground beneath the Barefoot Trinitarians' calloused feet. Cervantes did not, however, die alone: he had been careful to make sure that Don Quixote died with him. In an epilogue to Part Two he let the world know that they should never be separated. 'For me alone Don Quixote was born, and I for him; he knew how to act, and I how to write . . . we two are one.'

The coffin was empty, and since it only contained Cervantes' imaginary bones, one might just as well lay Don Quixote's dusty skeleton there, too, accompanied in death, as in life, by a pile of books. His was the presence in the chapel, invisible and melancholic. His was the spirit that had intrigued and perplexed readers for four centuries.

It was only when the mass finished, and we were filing out of the chapel that I saw the rest of the nuns: they were in a choir gallery above the apse, enclosed within bars. There was something girlish about the way they looked down on the congregation, like children trying to spot their parents at a school carol concert. But the enclosure was formidable: reinforced with long spikes, it was a reminder that the chastity of women had been a concern in Spain for many hundreds of years.

~ ~ ~

The morning of the memorial mass, I had returned to the street in the central neighbourhood of Chueca where I had lived as a student, from 1987 to 1988. I was quite nervous about this appointment with the past. As the train glided towards my old stop, a metallic anxiety traced the lining of my stomach. We arrived, there was a familiar sigh of sliding doors and I descended on to old territory.

Things seemed not to have changed much in the intervening years. At the entrance to the metro station, there were still Africans crouched like sprinters over blankets spread with contraband jewellery. Close to the Gran Vía, I found a sweet shop that was memorable for its window, a kaleidoscope of coloured wrappers. Next door there was a shoe shop with the same peculiar neon sign 'Don't shop here, we're expensive'.

Arriving at my old street, I recognised a leather fetish bar and even the owner who was standing chatting at the door in a fantasy outfit that incorporated many zips and chains. There had been a proliferation of gay bars over the years and I heard that the neighbourhood even had a gay travel agency now. When I lived there the street was already a magnet for those in search of drugs or sex, though this transient population lived fairly compatibly alongside the more conventional residents. One spring morning, two homosexuals had staged a mock wedding in a bar at one end of the street, and a reception in one at the other end. After a theatrical ceremony, in which even the phoney priest wept, the wedding party had made its way down the street to the reception, he in top hat and tails, 'she' with tiny stars scattered over both cheeks.

Next to the fetish bar, a bakery flushed the air with a sweet propaganda I identified from long-ago lunchtimes. Opposite that was a wood-fronted bar where we sometimes drank vermouth on weekends. Inside, shelves running high along the walls, were lined with rows of manzanilla bottles, like Spanish ladies, their shoulders mantled in dust. Beneath the shelf, on posters that were curling away from the wall, half a dozen bullfighters struck fading poses. The three brothers who worked behind the bar looked like butchers in their striped aprons and handlebar moustaches and there was a rhythm about their work that was soothing to watch. They served sherry and vermouth from wooden barrels behind the bar, bobbing and dipping around each other in the confined space, but never quite touching, as if a heavy weight were pitted at the bottom of each of their round bellies.

Here, as in many bars, only a rough tally of drinks was kept, it being up to the customers to remember what they had consumed and confess it to the brothers at the end of the evening. Once a friend and I forgot to declare a gherkin we had ordered on a whim. The next time we went to the bar, weeks later, one of the brothers shouted across the crowd at us: 'You still owe us for the pickle!'

That year spent in Madrid was one of the happiest, though least comfortable, of my life. Sitting on the balcony of the first-floor flat I shared with two others was a theatrical experience. At about noon, on an average day, the transvestites would emerge, yawning and rubbing away the remnants of last night's make-up. Carmen, my flatmate, used to shout from our window: 'Reina, you look gorgeous!'

'But I feel like a wreck, darling,' Reina would reply in a baritone that was proving resilient both to hormones and elocution lessons. Reina was the tallest of the transvestites who worked in our street and she was barrel-busted with long, strong legs she was at pains to keep hairless. I think Reina's only project in life was womanhood, and even then she wanted it at its most womanly. She might have been happiest in lambswool and pearls, working as a secretary and meeting friends for chit-chat. Reina's tragedy was that the only way to approximate her feminine ideal was to parody it – to peddle it, in fact.

At dusk, real women arrived for work at the brothel across the road. It was called The Windmill, a hopeful allusion to the Moulin Rouge, perhaps, though this was a much smaller and dingier affair. The women who worked there were middle-aged, most of them were also mothers. When it was raining, one of them wore a transparent, plastic headscarf through which a comforting arrangement of home-made curls could be discerned. I was fascinated to see that every day, when she arrived to do battle at The Windmill, this woman crossed herself before stepping over the threshold. My mental exercise was to try to join her at that moment of transformation: her Jekyll temporarily discarded in a world of supermarkets, square meals and feet up in front of the telly; her Hyde advancing into a smoky night where the vodka shone green beneath neon lights and the corsets were second-hand.

The owner of the brothel lived in a small flat over the business, with her son, Juanito, who had a lazy eye. Sometimes this boy stood on their balcony, dangling a yo-yo into the street and looking mournfully across at us. Juanito must have been very lonely. He wore a strong pair of glasses that grossly magnified the disobedient eye, which seemed to have not only an independent trajectory, but a separate, sinister motivation. A conversation with this boy could be disconcerting, because while his right eye remained childishly attentive, the left one roamed about, appraising his interlocutor with lascivious knowingness. While the eight-year-old gabbled about homework, insects and machine guns, that pale, magnified eye was like a window into an older, cynical soul.

For the year that I lived in Madrid, the sweeping of the brothel-owner's broom in the street outside was a background to my waking and breakfasting. Every morning she washed precisely that part of the street that corresponded to her business. If my flatmate and I happened to be on the balcony, she spoke to us quite naturally, as if we were three friends sitting together in a room. She was always concerned about politics, and especially about Spain's hopes to join the Common Market. She used to complain bitterly about the coming of 'Europe', as if it were a war, or some devastating plague. Once she had finished her sweeping, it was a kind of signing-off to disparage the haphazard array of plants we kept on the balcony. 'Those wretched things will die soon,' she promised. On more than one occasion, she hinted that my flatmate, who was eighteen and hoped to become a model, might be better off working for her in the brothel. She knew how hard it was for young girls to get by in Madrid, and she must have regarded Carmen as ripe fruit ready to drop from our balcony into her arms. As it turned out, she was wrong about that, but right about the plants.

The house was a wreck when we lived in it, and ten years on it had become even more desperate. It had been one of twins at the end of a terrace, but apparently number 34 had been bombed during the Civil War – our street was very close to the telephone headquarters – and 32 never got over the loss. The side of the building that had once joined 32, siamese-like, to its twin, now bulged grievously into the empty lot where some of 34's broken bones still lay.

When I lived there a gaping crack extended from the first floor, our flat, to the fourth. I used to kneel on the bed, put an eye to the crack, and glean a fractured view of the outside world. Over the debris of vanquished 34, rubbish had piled up with a determined eclecticism: there were mattresses and bicycles, one of them hung jauntily about with old bits of underwear. There were large objects like sofas that must have presented quite a challenge to the dumpers. The chaotic pile threatened to reach the level of my bedroom, but in the mean time I could still see over it to the corner bar where the transvestites spent their afternoons. By late afternoon they were made up and ready to take business from the evening's haul of curious or perverted men. Most of them were saving up for sex changes and in preparation they had started taking drugs to make themselves womanly. In the summer they wore bikini tops and tight shorts to show off their burgeoning curves. But for all the hormonal plumpness of their hips, the long legs protruding from their mini-skirts were thin and knobbly as only a man's can be.

The crack in the wall and everything beyond it troubled me. It made the room much colder in winter and suggested that the wall was an unreliable defence against the outside world. Sometimes I lay in bed in the early mornings, listening to the bustle outside, and imagined a miasma penetrating the liquid atmosphere above my bed, carrying the accumulated consciousness of all the people who lived in and around our house.

They were a strange collection of neighbours. At the top of our building lived a tiny, bird-like woman, about whom we knew only that she had been a republican during the Civil War. Someone said that she had been a muse, though no one was sure exactly what that entailed. Once I had got as far as her flight of stairs, on the pretext of offering help with something. But as I lingered on the step an aura of old age embraced me, and I fled.

Very rarely the muse ventured downstairs, to buy tinned food from the local shop. On one of these occasions she came across a young drug addict who habitually injected himself in our communal front hall. Our building was the only one in the street that had no entry phone, and the door was always open, an invitation to those junkies who still cared about privacy. The muse's confinement on the top floor meant that she was neither as used nor as resigned to this dismal scenario as the other residents were. Her explosion of outrage was almost enough to raise our crumbling roof, and the drug addict fled without his fix. It may have been the muse's last rallying cry, because she died not long after. At any rate, it was a *no pasarán* that kept the junkies at bay for more than a week.

Pik and Hans, two Dutch students who loved jazz, were on the third floor. They wore hair gel and black clothes and, like so many young people at that time, they had come to Madrid looking for *marcha*. This was the famous nightlife that had convulsed the city since the death of General Franco, drawing young people from all over Europe. Most nights they found it, in clubs and discos that stayed open until dawn. On the fourth floor was a young man, not more than about twenty-five, who made a living out of impersonating Dracula at children's parties and other events. We used to see him racing up and down the stairs, his trousers grown shiny from too much dry-cleaning. Like his name-sake, he was busiest at night.

The tenants on the second floor gave us the most trouble. They were an extended Chinese family, but it was not their number that bothered us, for they were very quiet, but their habit of hanging salted fish out on the washing line, just above our drying clothes. Explaining the problem with the fish was difficult because whenever we went to visit these neighbours there was no one available who spoke Spanish or English. Several times we climbed the stairs and had smiling exchanges with different members of the family, which they seemed to understand, yet the fish stayed in place. Eventually our point was conveyed with the help of a diagram, and with many more smiles and bows, the family agreed to be more considerate of our washing. The fish were transferred on to the front balcony, where they dripped on to our plants, and probably helped to kill them.

CHAPTER TWO
The Taxi-Driver's Cousin's Friend

Every evening, at about eight o'clock, a certain smell descends on Spain. At the moment when offices close and there is a collective recognition that the serious part of the day has ended, a marriage of hairspray and cologne breezes down the city streets. The aroma seems to be the same, give or take a floral note, everywhere in Spain. For all that they rail against the centre, the Basques smell like Castilians. The southern Andalusians' character may be nothing like the north-eastern Galicians', but they smell the same in the evening. Just as it identifies the end of the working day this smell marks the beginning of a night that can stretch as far as you want to push it – even to the next day's breakfast. In Spain, time is elastic, and mañana always deferrable. Spaniards love to go out, to be in the street and to talk, or rather to shout to one another in a way that makes other countries seem eerily quiet.

A government survey carried out in 1990 found that Spain had only slightly fewer bars than the rest of the European Union put together. Spaniards are the most social Europeans, spending at least two and a half hours with friends, usually in bars, every day. Even after a wedding, rather than drive to a private reception, sometimes the bride and groom will descend, in ruffles and tulle, on the bars and discos of their town. There are housewives who spend their day in a housecoat, then dress with meticulous care for the evening stroll, an institution that has its own name, *el paseo*. Nothing evokes Spain for me as much as the smell that accompanies this ritual.

I noticed it the first time I arrived in Madrid and it was this same scent that gusted in from the street, as we emerged from the Cervantes' memorial service. In some of the congregation it triggered the urge to set off for a glass of wine, while others lingered chatting in the convent's portals. The academicians retired to a small room beside the chapel to drink sherry and eat marzipans, which had been made by the nuns. This was the room usually used for visits and although there were more iron bars here, the nuns were allowed to stand behind them, and to talk to some of their distinguished guests, which included at least one South American celebrity. They were flirtatious, bony hands slipping between the bars to recommend one or other delicacy.

Meanwhile the academicians' wives waited outside coveting the food and wondering how to get some of it.

'Who would become a nun nowadays?' asked one woman with a helmet-shaped perm and an armoured bosom. 'It seems so pointless.'

'My aunt is a nun,' said her friend.

'Everyone has an aunt who's a nun,' said one, 'but do you know anyone with a *niece* who wants to be a nun?' There was some dissentive tutting and people agreed that there were very few such nieces around. Somebody pointed out that the only young nun among the Barefoot Trinitarians was black. Was she African?

'No – they're bringing them in from South America these days,' said the woman with the perm and bosom. 'The Spanish ones are dying off so they have to import replacements.'

They may be dying off but nuns still seem to be everywhere in Spain, so omnipresent that you can never take a bus, or a photograph without finding a nun has slipped into it. They might be filling some government quota designed to infuse life with religion, or at least the memory of it. Like the young men doing military service, nuns in Spain are always on the move. You often see them at railway stations, tortilla sandwiches wrapped up in foil protruding from their handbags.

Spanish children take a particularly close interest in them. 'Hello, little nun!' I heard one announce brightly as she crossed paths with a severe-looking specimen. Once, in Madrid, I crept into a church attached to a closed order where a service for schoolchildren had just ended. The children were fidgeting in the pews. A teacher stood at the front of the church and announced: 'I know you've all been waiting to see the *monjitas* – little nuns. If you make an orderly queue, you can go and say hello to them.' The children excitedly piled into the aisles and small groups of them were allowed to approach the barred recesses behind the altar where the nuns were confined, like an endangered species.

I wanted to meet nuns too. Earlier that day I had stood in the street, hopefully knocking on the Trinitarians' convent door. As is often the way in Spain, I soon had company. An old lady who had been making her way down the street with shopping bags came to a curious halt beside me. 'I've lived here for thirty years and I've never seen any of the *monjitas* come out,' she said. 'But they do keep the place looking nice.' She pointed up at the balconies where pots full of geraniums had just been watered by an invisible hand. Water was still dripping on to the pavement below.

Finally I had been permitted to enter the convent and to stand on one side of an oak door while the invisible Mother Superior stood on the other side, lamenting the lack of novices. 'Life is so much harder now than it was when I was young,' mused a detached voice. 'There are so many distractions for young women. A life of contemplation strikes them as being too difficult. We were lucky to have fewer choices.'

After the Civil War, the victorious General Franco had undone all the anti-clerical reforms of the Republic and announced that Spain's destiny lay within the Catholic faith. Only now were Spaniards beginning to question that destiny. Large numbers of couples were opting for civil weddings, or not to marry at all. The fall in vocations was deemed a national crisis. Church leaders complained about 'galloping secularisation'.

The Mother Superior told me that they almost never went into the street, though they could hear the noise around them. 'There is no need to go outside, we have everything we need here.' She had not seen Spain since it became a democracy. 'I suppose it must have changed enormously.'

'How long have you been here?' I asked.

'Much too long to remember,' she said, with a sigh that seemed to slip under the heavy oak door and dash towards the street.

After we had been watching the men eat marzipan for about ten minutes one of the pushier women said, 'Let's go in, while there's still something left to eat!'

Now that there was a leader poised to storm the reception, a murmur of revolution rose among the others. I was trying to conceal myself in the crowd rushing in when a small man with white hair came to the door.

'There you are,' he said to me. 'Shall we go?'

Don Gregorio was a writer and the Royal Academician charged with monitoring the way in which language was changing in South America. We had met a year previously when he told me, with great enthusiasm and many references to his dictionaries, about words used to describe a ballpoint pen in different parts of the New World. Since then, Don Gregorio told me, he had developed heart trouble and been told to walk for an hour a day. So we took off at a brisk pace to cross Madrid to the north side of

the city centre, where Don Gregorio lived. He was small and
lively, given to interrupting our walk suddenly to emphasise, on
some street corner or other, the importance of what he was
saying.

'Why the interest in Cervantes?' asked Don Gregorio.

'I've recently reread *Don Quixote*. It made so much more sense
to me than when I studied it at university.'

'In years past Cervantes' coffin used to be accompanied by a
guard of honour, six mutilated veterans of war, in deference to
Cervantes' own injury. He lost the use of his left hand at the Battle
of Lepanto. Records show that Cervantes should not have fought
that day because he had a fever, but he insisted on fighting
anyway. He was a very courageous soldier.'

'Why is there no longer a guard of honour?'

'It's sixty years since the Civil War now. There are not as many
mutilados around as there were.'

Close to the convent, we passed through Calle Huertas, the
street where Cervantes had lived out his last days. 'Perhaps a time
will come when I can take up this broken thread and say what is
left to say, and what needs to be said', he wrote, days before he
died.

'For all that he sought patronage, Cervantes was never
fashionable with the court,' said Don Gregorio.

In 1615, one of the censors of *Don Quixote* Part Two recorded
a meeting with some French courtiers who were curious about
Cervantes. 'They questioned me closely about his age, his
profession, his quality and quantity. I found myself forced to tell
them that he was old, a soldier, a gentleman, and poor. To which
one responded in these very words: "Then Spain does not make
such a man rich and support him from the public treasury?"
Another Frenchman retorted with this witty remark: "If poverty
will force him to write, then may it please God that he never have
wealth, so that, though he is poor, he may make the whole world
rich with his works."'

We rode a wave of cologne and hairspray down towards the Puerta del Sol, the heart of Madrid, even of Spain. Literally called 'The Gateway of the Sun', this large and bustling square marks the 'zero point' from which Spain's huge road network radiates. It is Spain's hub in other ways too. Revolutions have started here. In 1912, the liberal Prime Minister José Canalejas was assassinated in the square. In 1931, the Second Republic was proclaimed from the balcony of the Ministry of the Interior, on the square's southern side.

In October 1936, two months after the outbreak of the Civil War, the Nationalist General Mola vowed that within the month he would take Madrid, entering the Puerta del Sol on a white horse. The General joked that he would have a coffee there with the correspondent of London's *Daily Express*. Republicans responded to the taunt by keeping a table permanently ready for him, though it was three more years before Madrid finally fell to the Nationalists. 'His coffee's getting cold,' jeered Madrid's Republicans.

In 1987 a gathering of lesbians staged a demonstration in the square, in protest at the arrest of two women for kissing in public. Although the threat of arrest has lifted, they still come here every year for a nostalgic kiss-in.

Don Gregorio said he had read *Don Quixote* four times. 'The first time I was twelve, I enjoyed the humour of it. Then I read it in my twenties. I was interested then in the philosophical ideas contained in the book and I filled my copy with pretentious notes and underlinings. When I read it in my forties I was a teacher, preparing the text for my students.'

He had read it for the fourth time only a year ago, Don Gregorio said, and he detained me on a street corner by a shop specialising in fans. 'My left eye has always been rather lazy, so I used to read with my right eye, then, last year, I had a thrombosis and went blind in my right eye. So at seventy I had to set about

Don Quixote again, to educate the left eye, which had never read it before.'

'Which eye enjoyed it more?'

'I liked it best the last time I read it, but that may have more to do with age than eyes. It gets better, you know, the more you read it.'

In the centre of the Puerta del Sol four Spanish teenagers were grinding out a pop song in effortless English. As they jumped and pointed at the sky it became apparent that they were evangelists, though this may have been lost on the crowd who had gathered around them, as though sharing in the effort, because it was so difficult to make out what their words were. English pop was a way to get the attention of young people in any country, but what was the point of getting it, if the message could not then be communicated? Their chorus was: 'The only way is God!'

'Terrible', murmured Don Gregorio, from the safety of our street corner. 'Spain, and I, have changed so much. You say you are going to make a journey around central Spain?'

'I want to see how different things are since I lived here ten years ago.

'Everything is different,' said Don Gregorio. Yet as we walked through the streets of Madrid, I was surprised how much had stayed the same. Graffiti on the monastery walls still promised anarchy and was written in the same thin black scrawl I recognised from my student days; perhaps it was even written in the same hand. There were still drug addicts lolling on door steps, though friends told me that many of the old loiterers had been displaced in an effort to smarten up the city centre.

We walked up the Calle Preciados, a pedestrianised street of smart department stores, to arrive at the Gran Vía, Madrid's great thoroughfare. Among the cologne-drenched crowds coming the other way was a man carrying a billboard about the end of the world. Some things are the same wherever you go. The bars of the Gran Vía were packed with people shouting at one another. A beggar attached himself to our jackets and was carried along with us through the crowd for a few blocks before detaching himself with a disgusted comment about the calibre of charity these days.

'Are Spaniards quixotic by nature?' I asked Don Gregorio.

'Very much so, unfortunately.'

'In what way?'

'They're stubborn like him. It's something to do with the determination to make the world fit your ideal. Spaniards don't adapt themselves to the world, they try to force reality into their own mould.' Don Gregorio stopped me on a street corner, and got into his stride. 'The Civil War is the most extreme example of that. There was no absolute truth, no one group was right, yet we tore one another apart. There were ten of us in my family and I had a brother on each side. Those two didn't speak to one another for twenty years after the war. It took my father's funeral to reunite them. It's terrible that it should take a dead body to reconcile two brothers, but these schisms were so common in Spain that it is quite rare to find a family where something similar did not happen.'

We descended the Gran Vía past the cinemas with gigantic painted boards advertising the latest adventures from Hollywood. 'Quixotic types abound in Spanish history,' said Don Gregorio. 'Look at the conquistadores: South America was the stuff of fiction to them. They even took the names "Patagonia" and "California" from chivalric novels. But if they had been realistic about the venture they could never have achieved so much. It was their quixotism that drove their success.'

For Cervantes the New World was 'the refuge and shelter of all Spaniards who have lost hope'. In 1590, broke and desperate, he petitioned the Council of the Indies for a position there. He had done his research and knew that there were posts vacant in Guatemala, Cartagena and La Paz, any of which he would accept as 'a capable and competent man, deserving of Your Majesty's favour'. He made reference to his prestigious, though distant war record, and mixed in some of his brother's record for good measure.

For whatever reason, the king could not be bothered with this middle-aged no-hoper. 'Let him find something here,' was a bureacrat's scornful reply, scrawled in the margin of the petition. Don Gregorio thought that Cervantes was refused a position because he had Jewish blood. 'Otherwise he would have triumphed in South America, I'm sure.'

And yet Cervantes did 'find something here' because five years later, the first part of *Don Quixote* was published and the world's literature was changed for ever.

'Cervantes himself was not quixotic,' said Don Gregorio. 'Rather than holding absolute beliefs, he was evidently a man of great doubts. I identify with him to a certain extent,' he said, as we reached the block of flats where he lived. As he fumbled for his key he said, 'I'm not at all quixotic – but my wife is.'

∼∼∼

I was twenty when I first arrived in Madrid in 1987. My university studies demanded that I spend a year in Spain and I had chosen the capital, where I knew no one. The months ahead, virtually free of obligations, sparkled with romantic potential: language students often devoted the 'year abroad' to cavorting in olive groves, then returned home to prepare for careers in accountancy and banking. My aims were more specific. I had read something that George Orwell wrote about the Spanish Civil War. 'No one who was in Spain during the months when people still believed in the revolution will ever forget that strange and moving experience,' he said, 'it has left something behind that no dictatorship, not even Franco's will be able to efface.' I wanted to sample the spirit of revolution, if it was still to be found in Spain.

Although I had only ever visited the Spanish capital briefly, my studies suggested that idealists were in ample supply there. I left

London on a cold autumn morning, and on arrival at Barajas airport, I picked up a map for tourists. A tiny pensive face sucking on a quill identified the area just north-east of the Puerta del Sol where writers and poets lived. This was easy: all I had to do was ask a taxi-driver to take me to Santa Bárbara. It was the middle of September, but still very hot. A light sweat played on the taxi-driver's forehead which I imagined might rise and fall as the heat grew and ebbed. He made no attempt to interrupt the cycle with one of his fat, speckled hands. As we travelled down the motorway, he said, 'The only word of English I know is "pudding"!' The mere sound of the word made the taxi-driver laugh heartily.

He hooted his laughter into the rear-view mirror, obliging me to meet his eye there and laugh too. His stomach – pudding-like, in fact – heaved and his right hand came up to his eye to relieve it of a tear provoked by his mirth. 'Pudding,' he muttered two or three times, shaking his head with amazement.

As we neared the centre of town, the noise and heat swelled, and the backseat of the taxi began to release a warm smell of plastic. We crawled past the gaudy cinemas of the Gran Vía, and I became aware of the restless crowds pushing their way up and down the pavements on either side.

While we were sitting in the traffic, the taxi-driver scratched a finger across his belly. 'I don't think there are any boarding houses in the area you mentioned,' he said. 'But my cousin knows someone who's got a little place.'

My plan, so easily put into action, had been thwarted just as swiftly, and I had nothing in reserve. I did not know anybody in Madrid or have the addresses of any hotels. The only solution seemed to be to put my fate in the hands of the taxi-driver, as Don Quixote leaves his to the whims of his horse, Rocinante. We sped away from the centre again, northwards, to an area I later discovered was called Cuatro Caminos. Finally we drew up outside a boarding house that was next to a flyover under which a family of gypsies was selling contraceptive pills, in incomplete sets. Still, it seemed like a respectable enough place from the outside; I waited in the taxi while my driver ran up the stairs to see if it was suitable.

He returned a few minutes later puffing and sweating. 'There's no one there at the moment, but it looks clean,' he said, and this was heartening news. As the taxi-driver unloaded my luggage, he warned me not to go anywhere by myself in Madrid. He could tell stories, he said, of people who had been beaten up, raped or murdered even in quite respectable parts of the city centre. He would never allow his own daughter to spend a night alone in the capital, he said, but then he supposed that Protestants must be very different. Was it true that they were heretics? He embraced me before he sped off, leaving with me my suitcases and a conviction that I would be dead by nightfall.

A sign on the *pensión* door upstairs said 'back in five minutes', but it was about half an hour before I heard footsteps and looked down through the banisters to see a black-haired man approaching, perhaps my taxi-driver's cousin's friend. He wore a pair of dark trousers that very slightly sparkled and some brown scuffed loafers which he wiped wearily across each stone step as he ascended. When he sensed my presence, the man glanced up, offering a face that looked like a soft, pickled fruit, with small dark pits for eyes. 'Do you want a room?' he asked. Sitting there with two suitcases, I felt it was too late to say that I had changed my mind.

I should have said 'no'. For all that it had looked clean from the outside, inside, the boarding house was so foul it was literary. The brown walls of its dimly lit corridor sweated rivulets of grimy water; an old patterned carpet recoiled from the dirty skirting boards and these bore the traces of rubber-soled shoes, suggesting a scuffle. At the corridor's end, the bathroom door was open to reveal a bucket filled with used lavatory paper – a symbol of poor plumbing with which I was to become uncomfortably familiar during that year.

The manager was chewing gum, not champing it, but nursing it between his lips, as though it were a small, succulent piece of flesh. When he pinned open my passport to copy the details into a register, I noticed that his fingernails were curled protectively over encrusted dirt.

Once I had paid for the night ahead, I retired to my room, locked the door, and arranged myself on the bed in such a way that not even an inch of skin was making contact with the counterpane. From next door came the noise of put-upon bedsprings. I could hear muffled squealing and the odd grunt.

I shifted on the bed, drawing a rusty complaint from my own bed's springs, and switched on the bedside lamp. It was still early afternoon, but I had no intention of venturing into the street, nor even of raising the blind. It was very hot, but I did not want to open the window; I had no desire to see what might be outside.

I would not unpack my suitcases, because I was determined not to stay in the boarding house any longer than the night that was already paid for, indeed I had every intention of returning to London the next morning. All I had to do was to see out the day – and the night – and that would be hard enough because I felt too frightened to leave the room. There were hours to fill before I could go back to the airport. Without unpacking my bags, all I had to hand was the copy of *Don Quixote* I meant to read during my year abroad. I opened it at the first chapter.

> In a certain village in La Mancha, which I do not wish to name, there lived not long ago a gentleman – one of those who have always a lance in the rack, an ancient shield, a lean hack and a greyhound for coursing. His habitual diet consisted of a stew, more beef than mutton, of hash most nights, boiled bones on Saturdays, lentils on Fridays, and a young pigeon as a Sunday treat; and on this he spent three-quarters of his income. The rest of it went on a fine cloth doublet, velvet breeches and slippers for holidays, and a

homespun suit of the best in which he decked himself on weekdays. His household consisted of a housekeeper of rather more than forty, a niece not yet twenty, and a lad for the field and market, who saddled his horse and wielded the pruning hook.

I read how Don Quixote sets out on his first expedition from home on a day so hot that, the narrator notes, it would have been enough to turn his brain, if he had had any. Some miles from his village he arrives at a simple inn and thinks he sees a castle. Imagining the innkeeper to be a lord, and a couple of local prostitutes to be damsels, he decides that this is the perfect spot for his initiation into the world of chivalry. The innkeeper, who is also a fan of chivalric literature, realises that Don Quixote is mad, and tips off everyone else at the inn so that they can all have some fun at his expense. The innkeeper agrees to knight him, pretending to read from a courtly manual, while the prostitutes, stifling giggles, stand honour. A trough for feeding pigs serves as the spot for Don Quixote to stand vigil over his arms, as ritual demands. Though later he will fight windmills and imagine himself pursued by giants and enchanters, this is Quixote's first venture into lunacy, and the first time we see how others go along with his fantasies in order to mock him.

I read for a little while, but it was hard to concentrate. Alone in a foreign and friendless city, I knew now that the taxi-driver had made a terrible mistake about the suitability of these lodgings. Either he, his cousin or his cousin's friend was misinformed, or perhaps all of them knew what I did not, and this was some sort of fun-making at my expense. It was hard to believe that the taxi-driver, who had been so friendly, would let me down – but then it was also true that he had practically called me a heretic.

I lay listening to the mounting cries next door and realised that I had fathomed a boarding house out of a brothel. So it was that I spent my first night away from home not with writers and idealists, but like Don Quixote, in the company of prostitutes.

CHAPTER THREE
Don Quixote's Delusions

Don Quixote wants to be a hero, but the world in which he sets out to prove his heroism does not exist, so he invents it, either deliberately or as a consequence of his illness. The fascination of Cervantes' book lies in this grey area: the extent to which Quixote is the victim or the artist of his delusions.

Where there are windmills, Quixote sees giants; he addresses prostitutes as though they were princesses and attacks a puppet show because he believes it to be showing a genuine scene of pillage. Behaviour that is so absurdly wrong for its context might be described as 'quixotic', but we have softened the adjective with overuse and wrongly attach it to those who are merely eccentric or absent-minded. The writer Vladimir Nabokov complained that people used 'quixotic' to mean anything they wanted, but especially 'admirably idealistic', when it should mean 'something like hallucinated' or 'self-hypnotised'. This was not Nabokov's only complaint about the misinterpretation of Cervantes' work. He regarded the novel as having been misunderstood for centuries.

Nabokov himself had been one of the worst offenders. For

years he believed *Don Quixote* to be a 'cruel and crude old book', a fraud among the classics. He refused to teach *Don Quixote* on his literature course at Cornell University, but Harvard insisted he include it in the series of lectures he was to give there in the 1950s. When he came to reread the novel, Nabokov discovered a text that had almost nothing to do with its reputation. Years of misreading, and especially misteaching by 'prissy professors' had gentrified it into a comic fable when really, he decided, it was a much greater book, 'a kind of treatise about how meaning gets into things and lives'.

Nabokov was won over by *Don Quixote* – he even published a series of lectures on the book – but he could not warm to its author or forgive Cervantes for the cruel treatment meted out to his protagonist. As for readers who dared to chortle at the jokes, he compared them to those bystanders at the cross who laughed when Christ was offered vinegar to drink instead of water.

Don Quixote is a great book, Nabokov seemed to conclude, because of a conspiracy between its hero and its readers, which bypasses the author and even sabotages his original plan. 'Cervantes' old man who had read himself into insanity and his smelly squire were created to be the butt of mockery . . . but quite early readers and critics began to sidestep this Spanish fun and to interpret the story as another kind of satire: one in which an essentially sane, humane soul in a crass and unromantic world can only appear as insane.' By the end of the novel, says Nabokov, 'we do not laugh at Don Quixote any longer. His blazon is pity, his banner is beauty. He stands for everything that is gentle, forlorn, pure, unselfish and gallant.'

For a writer to create so sympathetic a character that he brings antipathy on his own head must be rare, but Nabokov is far from being the only reader to have taken so strongly against Cervantes. Miguel de Unamuno, the Spanish philosopher, devoted a book to his love of Quixote and hatred of Cervantes. The former, for him, is a real man, and the latter a shadowy fiction.

Other readers, while less violently opposed to Cervantes, seem also to believe in the superior genius of his creation. Thomas Mann described the process of the author being taken over by his creature as 'perhaps the most fascinating thing in the whole novel, it is a novel in itself'. Dostoevsky thought that only a twentieth century mind could *knowingly* create such a work. A Spanish writer, Carlos Coello, agreed that Cervantes could not have known what he was doing when he created Quixote, but thought that his merit was no smaller for that. 'The sun cannot see itself,' he wrote in 1878, 'but we all see because the sun shines.'

$$\sim\!\!\sim\!\!\sim$$

The premise of Cervantes' novel is straightforward: a middle-aged gentleman has gone mad from reading too many romantic novels of chivalry. The truth is more complicated than that. Quixote's desire to escape reality may have preceded his passion for books – he may use them as a refuge from reality. Quixote is liable to make fogeyish pronouncements about 'this hateful age of ours'. He believes the invention of modern warfare – with powder and lead – to be 'detestable' and dismisses a student's prejudice against knight errantry as a matter of fashion.

But it also seems that Quixote does not understand reality – he is unsure how to interpret the evidence of his eyes. The uncertainty must be contagious, because his creator suffers from it too. Cervantes claims not to know what his hero's real name was before he changed it to sound more knightly, though possible candidates are Quixada or Quesada. Other details of Quixote's life also elude Cervantes, but he does know, for example, what the knight ate and wore every day. He knows, too, where Quixote lived, but in the first line of the novel he says he would rather not divulge that information. So it is that the circumstances of Quixote's life are subject to confusion, conjecture and secrecy. In this sense alone, *Don Quixote* is unprecedented. Before its publication, authors were sure of their creations who, more importantly, were sure of themselves. *Don Quixote* is the story of one confused middle-aged man, written by another.

Up until his crucial mid-life, Don Quixote seems to have led a relatively untroubled existence. Cervantes tells us that he is verging on fifty and 'of tough constitution, lean-bodied, thin-faced, a great early riser and a lover of hunting'. We do not know if he has always been a reader, or if books are a new passion with him. In whichever case, they have had a devastating effect – Cervantes' novel finds him at the point where his mind has started to disintegrate: literature has taken over his life to the extent that he has abandoned hunting and started to sell off his land in order to buy more and more books.

It is not as if Quixote were devoting his time to improving literature, either. He is pompous in his tastes: although classics such as Amadís of Gaul and Palmerín of England are among his favourites, he also loves the high-falutin style adopted by some writers to mask meagre content. Cervantes gives us an example from Feliciano de Silva, a genuine source: 'The reason for the unreason with which you treat my reason, so weakens my reason that with reason I complain of your beauty.' Passages of this sort 'drove the poor knight out of his wits; and he passed sleepless nights trying to understand them and disentangle their meaning, though Aristotle himself would never have unravelled or understood them, even if he had been resurrected for that sole purpose.'

Any keen reader hopes to be transported by a good book but what if you could be permanently altered by a passion for reading? Quixote's mania is such that, according to his niece, he has long been able to achieve hallucinatory transportations, fuelled by dangerously extended reading sessions. 'He will fling the book down, draw his sword and go slashing the walls; and when he is exhausted he will say that he has killed four giants as tall as towers, and that the sweat that is pouring from him out of exhaustion is blood from the wounds he had got in battle.'

33

The example of Don Quixote's book-fuelled madness inspired Gustave Flaubert to write *Madame Bovary*. Flaubert, who suffered from hallucinations brought on by epilepsy, described *Don Quixote* as a book he had 'known' long before he read it. 'What dwarfs all other books are by comparison,' he wrote in a letter to his mistress Fanny Smith. 'God, how small one feels! How small!'

Perhaps Quixote's problems are not all down to books but some deeper-rooted malady. He has no family to speak of, living at home with a housekeeper and a niece. Edmund Gayton, writing in 1654, thought the niece was probably frigid. 'A London girl would have been more compassionate.'

Quixote could be suffering from a loss of status. The sixteenth century was an uncertain time for a Spanish gentleman. Up until then, society had been divided between commoners, who worked and paid taxes, and nobles, who were exempt from tax, but served the king in war. As a low-ranking noble or 'hidalgo', Don Quixote might have had a role accompanying a superior into battle, carrying his shield and weapon, but with the new professionalism of the army, such a service was no longer required. Spain was evolving from a feudal state into a capitalist one. An influx of gold and precious metals from the New World was driving up prices and many small landowners could not keep up. Hidalgos were caught in a double bind: they were poor, but it was socially unacceptable for them to work. Though some moved to the cities and took jobs as staff to the aristocracy, many were torn between hunger and the need to keep up appearances.

Is Quixote a loser? Nabokov made a conscientious study of all his battles and skirmishes and found that, although he lost twenty, he also won twenty, hardly a shameful tally. Is he a victim of the modern world? Europe was beginning to be intrigued by the way experience can damage the mind. In the same year that *Don Quixote* was published, Shakespeare produced another study of madness in King Lear.

Cervantes is known to have read *Un Examen de Ingenios*, a ground-breaking and hugely influential work of psychology by the Spanish surgeon Juan Huarte, which was published in 1575 and banned by the Inquisition eight years later, after pressure from envious academics. Huarte believed that the four bodily humours, melancholy, blood, choler and phlegm occurred in different proportions in each person. A perfect balance of the four made for a mediocre personality, but an imbalance, though potentially dangerous, could be turned into an exceptional quality, an *ingenio*, in a properly guided person. Food, drink, climate, astrology, domestic life and education also had a part to play in predisposing a person to a particular path in life. The full title of Cervantes' novel is *Don Quixote, Ingenious Knight of La Mancha*. He is, in Huarte's sense, unbalanced; the imbalance could either be his downfall or the key to his genius.

Our modern age might focus on Quixote's sex life, the lack of a girlfriend. More than one academic study has examined the possibility of his homosexuality. Another argues that he suffers from a schizo-affected disorder. In *Madness and Lust*, Professor Carroll B. Johnson of the University of California makes a 200-page case for the quixotic effects of the male menopause. 'The oedipal conflict that Don Quixote re-experiences is one which was not resolved, at least in the usual way, in adolescence.' Quixote on a chat show might be encouraged to confront the truth of his non-relationship with Dulcinea. How can he really love a woman he has barely – if ever – met?

Over the centuries many illustrators have depicted Don Quixote and Sancho Panza. The image that survives, especially in Spain, is of a funny thin man and a hearty fat one. Picasso, Cruikshank and Hogarth all made portraits of him, but Gustave Doré's illustrations show, more than any others, a man painfully enslaved to books. In the frontispiece he created for the 1863 edition, Quixote sits surrounded by them, with the fabulous creatures of chivalric mythology looming threateningly over his shoulders. Another print shows him riding across the empty flatlands of La Mancha, the sky above him stuffed with monsters. These images are frightening – if reading is his drug, it does not look like an enjoyable fix. Cervantes makes this much clear: Quixote has lost his reason to books; because of them, he can no longer lead a normal life. As Nabokov pointed out so forcefully, there is nothing funny about that.

~ ~ ~

Of all the world's famous literary figures, Don Quixote is perhaps the one we hold most clearly in our mind's eye. Anyone can imagine a picture of its hero: tall, emaciated and dressed in creaky second-hand armour. We most commonly envisage him in full attack on the windmills he imagines are giants, his lance raised, or perhaps surrounded by the books of chivalric romance that are supposed to have turned his brain to porridge.

Beside him, Sancho Panza, the squire he chooses to accompany him on his adventures, is short and practically spherical. Their two mounts mirror them physically: Don Quixote's horse, Rocinante, is a skinny old nag, as unlucky in love as his master and so mal-coordinated that the narrator tells us he has only once in his life broken into a gallop. Sancho trots behind him on a short, fat donkey. Dulcinea, the novel's love interest, is harder to picture because, after all, she is a figment of Don Quixote's imagination. He believes an aching heart to be a prerequisite for any knight errant, so he simply takes the idealised characteristics of the mythical princesses he has read about and fixes them on to a peasant girl, Aldonza, who lives in the neighbouring village of El Toboso and about whom Don Quixote is vague. Initially it seems that he may have seen her up to four times in the past twelve years. Later it emerges that he may never have seen her at all.

Cervantes provides a wealth of information about the appearance of his hero. We know that he is tall and lanky with a brown bristly mole in the middle of his back and a hairy chest which Sancho assures him is a sign of strength. He has a crooked nose, deep-sunken eyes, a bushy moustache and greying hair. His skin is described as very dry, symptomatic of an imbalance in the humours. His face is so gaunt that his cheeks, in the author's words, appear 'to be kissing one another inside his mouth'. Even before our hero's adventures take their toll, his expression is so beleaguered that Sancho dubs him 'The Knight of the Sad Countenance', a title which Don Quixote likes very much.

By the end of Part One, Quixote will have lost several of his few remaining teeth and half of one of his ears, he will have been clobbered on the head, vomited over and suspended by one arm from an upstairs window for an entire night. In the ultimate humiliation he will be returned to his village locked in an animal's cage. We can assume that, Tom and Jerry style, he recovers from the numerous physical injuries, grows back the ear and perhaps the teeth, but the humiliation sticks, and that is partly what makes *Don Quixote* such a powerful book.

His armour is mouldy, his tights have ladders in them which are stitched in the wrong colour. His legs are long, thin and dirty. He suffers from a complaint of the kidneys which makes sleeping outside on the ground uncomfortable, and yet this is what he has resolved to do, to show that he is as much a knight errant as those heroes of romances whom he aspires to imitate. Occasionally he is presented wearing nothing but his shirt which, Cervantes meanly points out, is not long enough to cover his nether regions. Sancho sometimes has to avert Rocinante's gaze, to prevent the horse being scandalised by exposure to his master's private parts.

For many readers, it is in the second part of *Don Quixote* that Cervantes attains the greatest insight into his characters' minds. By sheer effort of will, his put-upon knight seems to climb out of the domain of fiction and make himself real. No character has done as much as Quixote to insist on his own humanity.

Lines have been drawn from *Don Quixote* to Dickens,

Stendhal, Gogol and Joyce. Swift was a great admirer. Henry Fielding compared Cervantes to Homer, Virgil and Milton and thought he might be better than all these three. Borges praised his clarity of prose. References to Quixote slip into Proust, Orwell and into the diaries and notebooks of great writers. Just as the novel's unprecedented psychological realism left its mark on the great writers of the nineteenth century, so its tricks and devices turn up in post-modern novels of the twentieth century. Don Quixote and Sancho, for instance, are made aware of the fact that they are characters in a novel by Cervantes. In a twist worthy of Borges, they meet a fictional character from Avellaneda's rival sequel.

Much more than a man who goes bonkers reading books about knights, Don Quixote has real psychological depth. He is kind, intelligent and thoughtful, but also vain, pompous and misguided. He suffers with his bowels, he gets aches and pains from sleeping in the fields. His motives are decidedly mixed. Unlike the fictional heroes who came before him, Quixote has profound doubts about what he is doing. He is the first modern hero, the first hero built to a human scale, rather than an idealised one. And since the human measure is so much more complex, so much more affecting, it is far greater.

A reading of the first seven chapters of *Don Quixote* suggests that Cervantes' original aim was merely to write a skit on chivalric novels. Somehow, though, he was ambushed by his own creation – Don Quixote came to life in his hands. The transition comes at the end of the seventh chapter. Quixote, not yet accompanied by Sancho, has set off on his first expedition and quickly comes a cropper while trying to engage some merchants from Toledo in battle. Lying on the ground, immobilised by his heavy armour, he whiles away the time by recalling favourite passages from chivalric literature. A neighbour from his village recognises him and asks him why he is behaving so strangely.

Quixote rambles incoherently about his knightly duties. The neighbour gently reminds him who he is.

Although Don Quixote allows himself to be led home, his response to this is far from submissive. '*I know who I am*,' he insists, and with these five words, the scale and scope of Cervantes' novel suddenly change. The question from now on will be, does he really know who he is? Can anyone have such self-assurance?

~ ~ ~

I survived my first night in Spain, at the boarding-house brothel, though for ever afterwards I would remember it as a dreadful passage through darkness punctuated by stifled laughter, cries and lurching noises in the corridor. Some of the nocturnal activity centred on the bathroom next to my bedroom and at one point, just before dawn, it seemed to me that there were several people cavorting there. Fearful of bed-bugs, or larger assailants, I slept fully clothed, on top of the counterpane.

At least the experience gave me courage: by morning I had decided not to go home after all, though I urgently needed somewhere else to stay. I found the solution in a local newsagent, where there was an advertisement for lodgings offered by a 'respectable lady', a few streets away. Señora Jiménez had just one bedroom which she rented out to supplement her pension, removing herself to a camp bed in the sitting-room on those nights when she had what she liked to call 'guests'. She was appalled to hear that I had spent a night in the 'bad reputation' boarding house especially since, as a Protestant, I was more liable to be corrupted. She may have thought that it was her mission to protect me and, if so, I was happy to be taken under her wing. Some evenings we sat together watching television. When I went to bed, Señora Jiménez instructed me to dream of angels. There was comfort for both of us in the ritual.

39

In the sitting-room there was a copy of Picasso's line drawing of Don Quixote and Sancho Panza. The bedroom was a shrine of sorts. Over the bed hung a photograph of the Pope, adorned with plastic flowers, and scattered around the room there were miniature religious statues, rosaries and even a little bottle containing the miracle-working tears of one of the lesser-known saints. When I turned out the light, a luminous plastic virgin lit up the night. It startled me to wake and see it there, a green phallus floating in the dark. Once I tried to subvert its disconcerting presence by using it to light my way to the bathroom, but there was a contagious fear of blasphemy in Señora Jiménez's flat, and I never did so again.

It was 1987, Franco had been dead for twelve years and, even though there had been an attempted coup in 1981, its powerful rejection meant that few people now doubted the strength of the democracy. The Socialist president, Felipe González, was charismatic and popular with the young. The economy was booming.

One of my Spanish teachers had provided a metaphor for how quickly things had changed. After the attempted coup, she said, she and her husband kept a packed suitcase under the bed, ready to make a run for the Pyrenees as her Republican parents had once done, nearly fifty years before. Three years later she unpacked the suitcase and found that the newspapers lining the bottom described a world she barely recognised.

Like any country discovering democracy after a long dictatorship, Spain seemed to make swipes at liberty, indiscriminately lifting restrictions that smacked of the old regime. Public consumption of narcotics which, thanks to some kink in the law, had always been legal, was now openly tolerated. Divorce was legalised alongside regional languages and contraceptives.

In the streets where it had recently been forbidden to kiss, pornography magazines now hung like democratic tinsel on newsstands. They had curiously coy titles like *Fantastic Breasts from*

Around the World!, as if dictatorship had come down to this: a deprivation of foreign breasts.

In a way, the opposite was true. During the last two decades of Franco's rule, the flood of foreign tourists from northern Europe had bolstered the economy and turned tourism into the country's major industry. Between 1959 and 1973, the number of tourists leaped from 3 million to 34 million, doubling the native population for a few weeks every year. The presence of so many outsiders made Spain's isolation from foreign ideas increasingly untenable. The visiting women's determination to be topless exhausted the police, whose job it was to enforce decency on the beach, and drove some of the local men to distraction. In 1971, 90 per cent of all cases of non-chronic mental illness in rural parts of Málaga were among teenage men who had been working in the coastal resorts.

It was, in no small part, exposure to foreign ideas (and breasts) that made Spaniards want a different way of life. By the time of Franco's death, the desire for change was unstoppable. When Luis Carrero Blanco, Franco's appointed successor, was assassinated by the Basque separatists ETA, in 1973, it was clear that authoritarianism had no future in Spain. The transition to democracy was achieved with remarkable ease thanks to the determination of all the parties involved. Not least of these was Juan Carlos de Borbón, who had become king on Franco's death, Spain's first monarch for more than forty years.

Spaniards, who are mostly suspicious of monarchy, had particular reasons to distrust the young man who had been groomed for the throne by Franco. They had no idea of the prince's secret role in forging Spain's new democracy. Juan Carlos had spent the last years of the dictatorship meeting thinkers and politicians of all persuasions to hear their ideas on how Spain's future should be shaped. Some of them had to be smuggled into his residence, in the backs of cars, or disguised with crash helmets. Once he had become king, Juan Carlos wasted no time appointing a prime minister capable of overseeing a swift transition. Six years later, it was the king's determined stand that wrong-footed an attempted military coup. His role in bringing about democracy earned Juan Carlos the respect even of staunch anti-monarchists. Polls have shown that two-thirds of Spaniards do not believe democracy would be possible without him.

While staying with Señora Jiménez, I spent a fortnight on unsuccessful flat-hunting; students were not popular tenants in Madrid, much less so if they were foreign. One prospective landlady who seemed amenable at first demurred on a second phone call. On consideration, she said, she thought that there might not be enough light in the room for me to do my *reading* by. The emphasis she put on this made it sound like a rare and complex activity, as if I were a medieval student needing to pore over illuminated scripts by candlelight.

Then one afternoon I spotted an advertisement on a university pin-board. The room offered was in a flat close to the literary area I had favoured in the first place; in fact when I knocked at the front door it was opened by a short, bearded man who looked promisingly like the tiny *literato* on my tourist map. Yet it was soon apparent that Alvaro, as he introduced himself, was not a man to let his face be easily transformed by wonder or profound thoughts. He shifted expressions only grudgingly, like a learner-driver using gears. Physically, everything about him was mean. His hair clung to his face in tight curls, his glasses had pinched a red indentation on to his nose and an old sweater was stretched to the limit across his childishly plump chest.

Alvaro introduced himself as a post-graduate student of Geology, and I told him that I was a student of Spanish language and literature, and that I would be staying in Madrid for the academic year. For a moment he stood in the doorway squinting at me, as if denying me even the magnanimity of fully opened eyes. Then he led me down the corridor to a main room, his short, corduroy-clad legs wheezing as they rubbed against one another.

There, sitting on a sofa that looked too weary itself to offer repose, was a bored-looking, very beautiful girl of about eighteen.

'This is Carmen,' said Alvaro. 'She's moving into the boxroom. She wants to be a model.' He grinned in a way that suggested he found her ambition both ridiculous and exciting. Carmen, ignoring Alvaro's remark and my polite show of interest in it, admired her manicured fingernails and their involvement in her minutely-plaited hair. The only other piece of furniture in the room was a wooden table, but there were large balcony windows open on to the street, incorporating this public area as a part of the flat.

'Since I was here first, I'm taking the two adjoining rooms to the left of the sitting-room,' said Alvaro. His speech was slow, almost effortful, like a toad jumping between lily pads. Every few words he paused, as though to consolidate his balance before taking another linguistic leap.

'The room on the right is the one that's available.'

With a pudgy finger, Alvaro pushed open the door on to a room that could be mine for about £90 a month. There was a small bed, a huge wardrobe and balcony windows that matched those in the main room. I agreed to take it and Alvaro said I could sign the lease that afternoon when the landlady was coming to collect rent. That gave me enough time to pick up my bags and go to the bank.

When I arrived back at the flat, the landlady was already there bending over the lease that was to be signed by the three of us. She was tall, with dyed black hair and a look of having made money out of people. She owned all the flats in the building, but her tenants paid her at different rates because, under Spanish law, it was difficult to put the rent up once a tenant was installed. We would be paying at least five times as much as the old lady living next door, even though we were students. The landlady's facial expressions were at the mercy of her tongue, a large, rough-edged piece of pink that craved exposure. As she pored over the contract it was alternately wedged between her teeth, mimicking concentration, or dabbing saliva on to the finger that turned the pages.

The first thing she said to me was: 'You're decent, I hope, are you? This is a decent house.' She looked at me and curled the spongey tip of her tongue around a yellow canine.

'I think so,' I said, and it occurred to me then that the house might not be decent, for her to have to say that it was.

'She's English,' explained Alvaro. The landlady continued to flick through the contract. Alvaro filled the silence with an aimless hum.

'Well she can't help that,' said the landlady finally, indicating where I should sign my name. 'I just hope she's not one of these *jooligans.*'

She bundled our rent money into her handbag then used the pen to point at us, singling each of us out for a dose of opprobrium. 'I don't want any trouble from you people. And you, young lady' – she wagged the pen at me – 'on your best behaviour here. Never mind what they get up to in England.'

Then she strode towards the door, making wet clucking noises, which Alvaro, following behind, accompanied with his corduroy swish. I heard her reprimand him for taking a foreign student with no references. Alvaro mumbled apologies.

'Welcome in Spain,' said Carmen, in a flawed English that was nevertheless loaded with irony.

I laughed and joined her on the balcony, where she was leaning over the railing, smoking. She looked even taller and slighter than she had on the sofa, and I saw that the sleek, black plaits were synthetic extensions attached to her own, much shorter hair.

We were leaning together on the balcony in what felt like a companionable sort of way, until I followed Carmen's downward gaze and saw that on the street below us, a young man was sitting in a doorway. Apparently oblivious to passers-by, the man had rolled up one of his trouser legs and was looking for a vein into which to inject drugs – heroin. He searched about his skin with

44

some annoyance, like a late-running commuter groping under the bed for a stray shoe. Carmen took in the scene quite casually as she smoked, but I was very shocked. Even though I had arrived from Edinburgh, a city with a bad drugs problem, I had never before seen a junkie getting a fix.

'Is this neighbourhood as rough as people say it is?' I asked, trying to sound nonchalant.

My question hung in the air, and Carmen drew deeply on her cigarette as she considered it. She took so long to answer that it occurred to me that she might not bother to say anything at all. As I waited, I noticed a tiny gold heart glittering in the soft indentation at the base of her throat. Finally, with a flick of her cigarette, she turned her eyes on me for the first time since we had been introduced. They were framed in blue-black mascara and, although they were not hostile, they made no offer of friendship.

'People have died on this street,' was all she said.

CHAPTER FOUR

Transvestites, Anarchists and a Peruvian Poet

If a fear of junkies initially confined me to the flat, an encounter with cockroaches drove me out of it, after a few days, in search of some deadly spray or poison. The flat had not been inhabited for some months, and in that time a sticky residue had crept over all its surfaces. There was a musty smell about the place that was hard to define. I associated it with petty crime, because Alvaro had learned from the landlady that the last occupants had a business selling pirated designer clothes. The odour was tenacious, and we could not conquer it with cleaning sprays, but over the months it grew fainter or perhaps we simply got used to it: it became our smell.

The designer-pirates had left enormous wardrobes in each of the bedrooms, where their clients had come to try on imitation Chanel or Versace. We counted up to 250 coat-hangers. Carmen's wardrobe occupied almost all her room, leaving her only enough floor-space for a mattress. Once I had put away my clothes and books, my wardrobe still had enough space to sit or stand in.

We spoke to the landlady about the possibility of removing the wardrobes and replacing them with something smaller, but she thought this was a troublesome request. The comfort of her tenants was probably not a paramount concern. In the main room, a light switch hung out of the wall on a fraying wire. Once I saw Carmen get a shock from it, but even this seemed not to surprise her, she was so coolly in control. The bathroom had a large old bath with clawed feet and an unreliable shower attachment. Its plughole was forever clogging up, a problem that allowed Alvaro to make manly with a plunger. The front door had a spy-hole and a surfeit of bolts, as if previous tenants had felt the need for extra protection, from junkies, or the police. Our hot water and oven ran off a gas canister that we bought every few weeks from a truck that carried the bright orange *bombillas* throughout the neighbourhood.

In the kitchen, a back window gazed fixedly at the back window of the old lady whose rent was a fifth of ours. A washing line strung between these two windows worked on a pulley, so that as you pulled more of the unoccupied line towards you, the garments you had already hung up travelled towards the neighbour's window, prompting hers to set off in our direction. If there was enough washing, a complete swap might take place: Carmen's lacy G-string knickers could end up fluttering at the window of our octogenarian neighbour while her widow's black skirts flapped with foreboding outside ours. It was a perfect exchange of old and new Spain. Above it all hung an international contribution: the Chinese family's fish.

After a frosty start, Carmen and I brokered our friendship in the female way, by cleaning together. Later we would cement it by dieting together. We sought out the health-food shops that were growing in number in Madrid, and bought heavy breads and vitamin supplements. We ate sautéd spinach and drank cucumber juice, which was revolting. Once we tried to drink the spinach and sauté the cucumber, which was worse. Later, and very briefly, we took up jogging.

Carmen was of mixed race, which was so unusual in Spain that we could go nowhere without someone commenting on her striking looks. She was the Spaniard and I the outsider, but it felt the other way around because people – mostly admiring men – were always asking her where she was from. When she said 'a little village near Segovia', they refused to believe her. As we cleaned, in those early days, Carmen told me about the place where she had grown up, fatherless, the only black girl in a group of very conventional white ones. 'I realised young that I would never fit in.' It was part of the reason she had come to live in Madrid, much against the wishes of her mother.

Alvaro was more than willing to play the part of enemy to our alliance. He forbore to do any housework at all, reckoning that he lacked some vital component that might have made it possible for him to wield a broom or sponge. The precision with which he exercised his avarice was something to see. For instance, his food was kept in containers which were marked and monitored with a black felt-tip pen. This meant that he could at any time insist, and prove, that there should be a certain number of biscuits in his tin, or yoghurts on his shelf in the fridge. Alvaro was never short of food, much of it provided by his mother, to whom he retreated every weekend. Carmen and I, who made no attempt to keep stocked up, and had no one to provide for us, were tantalised by his twice-daily three-course meals.

The wooden table in the sitting-room was round, with a hole in the base into which a heater could be fitted. In years past this would have been a brasier containing hot coals. Nowadays *braseros* were usually fitted with electric heaters. Over the table went a heavy cloth with skirts to the floor. Anyone sitting at the table had only to pull the cloth up and over their legs to be intimately warmed by the hidden heater.

Although they were notorious for starting fires, *braseros* were a godsend on cold days in Madrid and since our flat had no other form of heating, the three of us usually gathered around the table in the evenings. While Alvaro pored over the newspapers or one of his complicated jigsaw puzzles, I helped Carmen with her English homework. She was still trying to pass the exams that would release her from school and equip her to do the secretarial course her mother had in mind for her, though Carmen had other, more glamorous plans. Sometimes she talked about her modelling ambitions and the fashion world, within which she was beginning to make contacts. She was going to have photographs taken for a portfolio, then would start approaching agencies. One evening, Carmen explained how computers were used nowadays to enhance the look of a model – for instance to make her taller or slimmer. 'Most people have one eye bigger than the other. Computers can even things out.'

'That's a con!' Alvaro cried excitedly, his voice growing loud with marvel. 'It's not real!' His short fingers tugged excitedly at his wiry chin, as if he might manipulate his own features into something fashionable.

'It is real,' said Carmen, with irritation. 'It's just a bit better.'

Alvaro was a fascinatingly lacklustre character, usually to be found in his study, spinning out a degree course in geology that had already lasted eight years. His plan was to be too old, by the end of his studies, to undertake military service. This evasion was a complicated procedure that had come to involve as much commitment as the course itself. It required the judicious failing of certain exams, enough to keep Alvaro's studies indefinitely prolonged, but not so many that he would be thrown out of university altogether.

Many of Alvaro's friends were playing the same game. A cohort of them came regularly to our flat to eat biscuits which were baked by Alvaro's mother, and sometimes brought to him by an aunt. There was something reassuring about Alvaro's friends and the lazy arrangement of their short, corduroy-clad thighs on our sofa, snug against one another like fat sheep in a pen. Their strategies for avoiding military service, without the stigma of resorting to conscientious objection, were ingenious. One man was trying to eat himself into unsuitability – his girlfriend proudly revealed that he had already gained twenty kilos, and had difficulty getting out of the bath. Another hoped to pull strings through an uncle who was in the police force. In return, he promised to use his legal expertise to help the uncle with a land dispute. The cohort swapped stories of friends who had invented ruses to avoid *la mili* and were now free of the worry of it for life. Then everyone would sigh and dip their hands back into the tin for one of Alvaro's chocolate biscuits, heavy with butter and mother-love.

Carmen also had an aunt in the city who had been instructed to keep an eye on her. However, while Alvaro's aunt kept her visits to a minimum, preferring to express her duty of care through baking, Carmen's aunt was much more worried about her charge. She and Carmen's mother had gruesome ideas about what could happen to a young girl in Madrid. They terrified themselves with fantasies of abduction and forced prostitution in some foreign flesh-pot. The aunt's policy was to arrive unannounced, in the hope of catching her niece embroiled in scandal. Once, when Carmen was slow to open the door, we heard her cry from the other side 'For God's sake! What's going on in there?'

In fact, Carmen's aunt had some cause to be worried. Her niece was gregarious and generous with our hospitality. 'Come on up!' she used to shout down to the peculiar characters who frequented our neighbourhood. Transvestites, dancers and jazz musicians were often to be found around our sitting-room table. She was protectively fond of Mohammed, one of the Morroccan hashish-sellers, and sometimes I would return from university lectures to find him curled up asleep on the sofa, Alvaro's empty biscuit tin beside him.

Alvaro's weekend visits to his mother not only left his biscuits unprotected but the whole apartment at the mercy of our carnivalesque friends. Almost every weekend, it seemed, there would be a calamity in the house, usually befalling something of

Alvaro's: someone would be sick in his room, or break a mug of his. Once a cat urinated on his counterpane. We would race about with buckets and sponges in the hours before his return, trying to repair the damage. It was impossible to protect Alvaro's food from our ravenous visitors, so Carmen and I were forever striving to replace it with the right brands and in the exact quantity. The transvestites were alone in respecting his biscuits because they were always on diets.

When Alvaro was in Madrid, everything was very different. A sense of calm prevailed. If any of the transvestites and dealers whistled under our balcony we mouthed warnings at them not to come up. It was a relief, in a way, to have a break from the carnival. Sometimes there was a visit from Alvaro's girlfriend, an anxious young woman who wore thick-lensed glasses. They had been courting, in the Spanish style, for about ten years and seemed resigned to the fact that one day they would marry. In the mean time, she slept in a sleeping bag on the sofa, oblivious to Mohammed, Reina and the other curious characters who preceded her there and whom we kept at bay whenever Alvaro was at home.

Carmen had a boyfriend too, called Miguel. He was a security guard who worked at night in a bank, so often she saw him at breakfast, when his work was finished. Miguel was a handsome, but shy and lumbering man. He was awkward partly because he tried so hard not to be, overly conscious of his body and the need to be tidy with it. He trod softly, as if fearful that he might trample a tiny, fragile object, underfoot. This was a justified concern in Carmen's undersized room, its floor a galaxy of pots, bits of jewellery and the beads she sometimes threaded into her hair.

Miguel wore a pair of leather trousers and a leather jacket that accompanied all his movements, even the rearrangement of his limbs as he sat on our sofa, with a gentle creaking. He carried things, set them down on the table, set himself down on our rickety chairs, with almost pantomimic care, creaking all the while. Once I caught him hovering on one foot, waiting to be helpful with something in the kitchen, and it occurred to me that he looked as funny and as tragic as a dancing bear.

It was not just our flat, with its lingering smell, that emanated a faint criminality – an air of illicit enterprise hung over the whole neighbourhood. Close by, there was a squat inhabited by illegal immigrants and a Cuban bar down the road was said to be a meeting place for international drug-dealers. Once, while having a drink there, we had noticed men in suits and hats disappearing through a door at the back of the room.

Further down the street a friend of mine from university, Tom, was lodging with a poet called Rufus who kept three falsified passports under a rug in the sitting-room. In another respect too Rufus's personality was split three ways. Tom told me that he had a wife, who still lived in Peru, and two girlfriends in Madrid. None of these women knew about the other two, which meant that Rufus led a life of tangled triplicity. If a particularly fashionable film was showing, Rufus might have to see it twice, even three times if his wife was staying. Tom had to think on his feet, because it was his job to answer the telephone and supply plausible alibis. Rufus could be in his bedroom with one of the women and Tom would have to invent a poetry reading or a business meeting to save the feelings of the other two.

Rufus's flat was just what you would expect of a three-timing poet. On the white-washed walls simple indigenous weavings hung alongside French posters advertising long-expired exhibitions. There was a pleasingly higgledy-piggledy view across Madrid's red rooftops. Ethnic rugs concealed the doorways of the two bedrooms; the bathroom and kitchen were combined, so that one person might shower and the other cook quite companionably. At the back of the kitchen was a lavatory that was covered in slogans and poems. 'Rufus's last flatmate was an anarchist,' Tom said. His room, which had been the anarchist's, had also been covered in poems. Above the bed were some lines by Pablo Neruda: 'They can cut all the flowers, but they cannot detain the spring.'

In the sitting-room two uncomfortable chairs faced a sofa, entirely defeated by age, across the rug that hid the passports. Behind the sofa was a book-lined wall, on which *The Encyclopaedia of Sex* occupied an entire shelf. It would require little effort, should Rufus find himself unsure how to proceed in some sexual manoeuvre with one of his three women, to reach the relevant tome from the sofa.

What could such a man look like? I asked Tom and he said, 'Imagine God as a Peruvian.'

A Peruvian poet who looks like God, I thought, must be large, craggy and solemn, something like an Andean peak. In fact, the first time I met Rufus, he fairly blew into the room, like tumbleweed on a desert wind, trailing scarves and exotic perfumes. Though generously bearded, Rufus was not otherwise like God at all. A small dapper man, he dressed carefully in varying tones of yellow and brown; the silk scarf he wore over his raincoat was tassled and, if he had not already looked thoroughly unmanly, the ivory-handled cane he carried threatened to emasculate him once and for all. For all that, Rufus exuded a sexual confidence that thrummed in the air and alerted the senses to danger. If I found myself beside him on the sofa, I fought to resist its gravitational pull – it was a battle to stay upright.

Rufus's conversation was always of passion, and of sweat, which he thought should accompany any truly successful sexual encounter. He insisted on talking about positions and strategies for love-making in a way that caused his pupils to dilate and his beard to quiver. I was often shocked by the things Rufus said, but an English education in reserve prevented me from laughing at him, which would have been the best response. The first time Rufus met Carmen he told her, 'I would like to make love to you until we both catch fire and die asphyxiated by the flames.'

Carmen, fiddling with her plaits, looked quite upset by the idea.

One afternoon I was at Tom's flat when Rufus arrived home with customary panache and sat down beside me on the sofa. A broken spring gasped somewhere underneath us. He had left the door open and there were footsteps on the stairs. As they rang closer I realised that Rufus was waiting for someone to join him. Presently a young man came through the front door. He was holding a sheaf of papers, some of which he handed to Rufus. 'There are your photocopies. We'll probably have another meeting next month.'

'Thanks,' said Rufus. He perused the papers quite seriously for a moment, then he remembered that I was beside him on the sofa and introduced us. He described this newly arrived friend as 'an extremely important man. He's the European representative of the Peruvian Young Communists. Tomorrow he's going to be on television. Later he will probably save the world. He's the kind of person your Lord Byron would have written a poem about.'

At first glance the man seemed an unlikely candidate for world-saving: physically he was no superman. He looked about twenty-five and, from his colouring and high cheekbones, he was at least partly South American Indian. He was of average height, and thin. His faded jeans hung limply from legs that could not have been particularly muscular. His black straight hair appeared often to have been swept off his forehead by anxious hands, and he had the look of someone who works late at night. But there was something about him that was extraordinary. Maybe it was the way his smile intrigued and won over his face by parts, or his eyes, which offered a seducitve complicity. Whatever it was caused my own insides to heave and twang like the sofa's. He was without any doubt the most attractive man I had ever seen in my life.

CHAPTER FIVE

Double Lives and Double Cheeseburgers

Some time after Cervantes' memorial service I found myself in
Salamanca, sitting in front of a cluttered desk on which was
positioned a thoughtful bust of El Manco de Lepanto himself.
Behind the desk sat Antonio, a private detective, vigorously
chewing gum. Cervantes, Antonio had just told me, was his
inspiration. 'When I am feeling depressed I look at him and I feel
uplifted. *Don Quixote* is our greatest book. It's a book about us.
All Spaniards have something quixotic in us.'

He grinned and held the bust up beside his face, as though
inviting me to take a photograph, or draw some parallel. I was not
bold enough to do either, but Antonio might have done, had he
been on my side of the desk. He was, he had told me, an
accomplished face-reader. 'I can tell all kinds of things from a
person's face, things that person thinks are concealed. From your
face, for instance, I can make certain deductions.'

'What sort of deductions?'

'You have problems,' said Antonio. 'I worry about your future,
but I think you may triumph.' He sounded unsure about this. 'At
least, I *hope* you will triumph.'

Salamanca was the first stop on my tour of Castilian cities. It occupied a special place in my affections because I had spent six months there in the mid-1980s, teaching English and practising my Spanish before university. Salamanca is often described by Spaniards as their 'Oxford', for the beauty of its architecture, the purity of its language, and its antiquity as a seat of learning. Its Baroque Plaza Mayor is the most elegant in Spain. The fifteenth-century buildings of the old city are made of sandstone, a perfect foil to the strange, almost blindingly pure light that floods Castilian towns. The university walls are daubed with enigmatic *vítores*, inscriptions, traditionally made in bull's blood, on the graduation of a student.

For four centuries, from the start of the thirteenth, Salamanca's was one of the most important universities in the world. Some of the greatest ideas, especially on the development of international law, emanated from its lecture theatres. Columbus consulted academics here about his expedition to the New World. However, the Church's fear of intellectuals did for the university in the seventeenth and eighteenth centuries when books were banned as a threat to the Catholic faith and Maths and Medicine were removed from the curriculum. In the eighteenth century academics here were discussing what language angels spoke and whether the sky was made of metal or some wine-like fluid.

Although the reputation of the university was now diminished, Salamanca's beauty and the memory of its importance combined to make it the main destination for foreign students of Spanish. The autumn after we left school, a friend and I travelled by ferry and train from Portsmouth to Salamanca. We rented a room in a *pensión* close to the Plaza Mayor for which we paid 300 pesetas each, about £1.50 a night. If we wanted hot water we paid a few pesetas more, but we preferred to make the false economy, and shivered in the shower. The landlady was small and fat with a high-pitched voice. In my memory I have transposed her with

Maritornes, an Asturian maid at the second inn Don Quixote stays in. Cervantes' unforgettable portrait has Maritornes as 'broad-faced, flat-nosed, and with a head that seemed to have no back to it'. In spite of this forbidding appearance, Don Quixote comes close to having his only sexual encounter with Maritornes when he takes her for a princess who has come to make love to him (actually she is on her way to a farrier sleeping in the same room, but trips over Don Quixote en route).

My friend and I took a course at one of the many language schools in Salamanca. In the mornings we learned how to use the subjunctive and in the evenings we roamed the town in packs of foreign students, devouring tapas and cheap wine. Once a polite Finn with neat hair came to visit us at the *pensión*. Lars was much the quietest student on our course, but the excitement of being alone with two girls in a bedroom transformed him. He started romping around the room, giggling and proposing three-in-a-bed, misusing the subjunctive as he did so. It took the two of us a good fifteen minutes to subdue Lars, because once he had stuck his heels in he was as strong and tricky as a bull. Finally we hauled him from the room by his ears and quickly shut the door on him.

Then as now, Salamanca seemed to encapsulate the values of bourgeois, conservative Spain. At the start of the Civil War, it easily fell to the Nationalists. Franco established his headquarters in the city in 1936 and it was in Salamanca that his fellow generals named him 'Generalísimo', according him greater powers than had been enjoyed by any Spanish leader since Philip II.

In the early evenings, the colonnades of the Plaza Mayor filled with that familiar smell of cologne and hairspray as the burghers of Salamanca come out to *pasear*. Sometimes they were entertained by the Tuna, a group of strolling minstrels drawn from university musical societies. Members of the Tuna still wear the costume of a medieval student: to their capes are attached flowing ribbons, love tokens from their admirers. Salamanca's shop windows displayed leather bags, beautiful lingerie and perfumes, all of them quite expensive. There was a sense of continuity, of comfort, wealth and values that are as solid and confident as the architecture. This, at least, was my impression, but once I had spoken to Antonio, the private detective, I realised that things were not what they seemed.

Antonio lived on the second floor of an old building very close to the Plaza Mayor. If a promising air of intrigue lurked in the stairwell, it disappeared when he welcomed me at the front door. No frosted glass here, no pall of smoke or pouting moll. Rather, Antonio's front hall presented a scene of exaggerated domesticity; a baby lying in a cot proved on closer inspection to be a life-size infant Jesus, ruddy-faced, with halo attached. More gaudy religious imagery lined the corridor to Antonio's office – but here was one area of the house my host had managed to wrest from what I took to be his wife's domesticating influence. It was as one might imagine a private detective's office to be. Computers and faxes were at work, tracking the wherabouts of missing teenagers and reporting on the shenanigans of errant husbands. Papers lay around, and from his position on the desk, Cervantes kept an eye on all of it.

Much of his work, the detective explained to me, was spent proving that employees who claimed sick leave from one boss, were fit and well, and probably moonlighting for another. However the change in Spanish society had also altered the nature of his business. These days he was often to be found on the trail of cheating men and women.

'Spanish society's woken up since Franco,' said the detective. 'People put up with less. If a man is cheating, his wife is no longer so prepared to turn a blind eye.'

In the past, Antonio said, there had been a sort of bargain between men and women. So long as their husbands kept bringing the salary home, wives would not ask to know about anything else. The typical worker left home at eight and got home exhausted twelve hours later – there was no time for philandering. Nowadays there was more leisure time and everyone, even philanderers, had higher expectations.

'In Spain, these days, you can get legally separated for all sorts of reasons,' said Antonio. 'Twenty years ago only the high class got divorced, a worker would never even think of it, but now both sexes work and everyone is more aware of their rights. Women want men to help out around the house and modern people share the work but, you know, Spanish men are still *machistas*.'

Part of the trouble, Antonio said, was the speed with which Spanish society had changed. The transformation was giddying. 'In Franco's time we thought of ourselves as fifty years behind countries like France and Britain. Everything was banned or censored. If you went to see a film, just as the couple was about to kiss, a hand would come over the projector, blocking the scene. In Paris there were queues of Spaniards outside the porn cinemas. Nowadays you can watch porn on the television on a Saturday night, *tranquilamente*. There's an incredible freedom – you can do whatever you want, but all that makes marriage less tenable.' The detective chewed thoughtfully on his gum. 'There are people getting married and divorced in the same year now. Another thing – people don't care what their neighbours think any more. In one respect that's good. We've made giant steps forward, but the family is breaking up as a result.'

I said that people in Spain seemed to live very well. Spain ranked fairly far down the international economic league table, but when factors such as health care and education were taken into account, its standard of living was among the best in the world. Life expectancy was the highest in the European Union.

'People do live well,' he agreed. 'They have much more money. You couldn't imagine the amount of prostitution there is nowadays in Salamanca.' Antonio dropped his voice to a stagey whisper. 'There are *married* women who get used to a certain style of life – she wants a fur coat, she's ambitious, and before you know it she's selling herself.'

'Is that really true?' This idea of middle-aged wives selling their bodies in order to buy fur coats sounded vaguely familiar, like a fantasy one might see described in the pages of *Penthouse*.

'I'm telling you – all over Spain, there are women who seem to be leading perfectly normal lives . . .' The detective leaned across his desk, taking Cervantes and me into his confidence. 'They're making *hundreds of thousands of millions* of pesetas on the quiet.' He leaned back again, and chewed quickly on the gum, pleased to have made this revelation. 'The trouble is that money is at the root of everything now. This consumer society is doing our heads in.'

'What's the solution?'

'There isn't one. Now that we've joined the rest of the western world, we have to take the good with the bad. Put it this way: there's a train leaving for the future, you don't know where it's going, but you have to get on it. Who knows? Maybe it will crash. Even so, Spain doesn't have any choice but to catch that train.'

'How do you go about your work?' I asked the detective as he ushered me back past the baby Jesus to the front door. 'Doesn't everyone in Salamanca know you by now?'

'I have ways of concealing myself, obviously', he said and an image came to mind of Antonio dodging behind the columns of the Plaza Mayor. 'I could follow you from the moment you leave home until you get back at night and find out everything you've done and where you've been, and you wouldn't know. If you're leading a double life, I guarantee I'll find it out.'

This last comment of Antonio's was disconcerting, not least because I was leading a double life. I was pregnant, and pregnancy had led me into surprising, furtive patterns of behaviour. In the siesta hours after lunch I had taken to watching gossip programmes about Spanish celebrities and even trivial items about their marriages or separations reduced me to tears. More alarmingly, in spite of a firm opposition to fast-food chains, I had developed a craving for double cheeseburgers.

Fast-food chains first appeared in Spain in the 1980s and have since become the hang-out of teenagers who dismiss bars and pubs as old-fashioned. Alcohol has not, until recently, been much of a draw for the young; Coca-Cola, with its promise of an American lifestyle, has more appeal. Spanish teenagers tend to be neater than their counterparts in northern Europe and a survey has shown them to be the latest in the world (after the Taiwanese) to lose their virginity. But things are changing. In recent years there have been dramatic rises in adolescent drinking and crime.

Salamanca's teenagers seemed tame enough, but I felt acutely self-conscious sitting among them in the burger bars. First there was the embarrassment of placing an order. Since many items were offered with their English names, you had to guess how much Spanish inflection to add.

I tried murmuring, 'un doble-chizboorger', and was rewarded some time later with a small, sweaty package on a tray. To shield myself from the watchful teenagers, I read Miguel de Unamuno's *The Life of Don Quixote and Sancho* as I ate.

One of Spain's best-known philosophers, Unamuno was made rector of Salamanca University in 1900, a title he still held on his death in 1936, although there had been years of demotion, and even exile, in the interim. His house is now a museum. On its façade a *vítor* proclaims 'Truth before Peace' – a fitting epitaph because Don Miguel was agonised by his search for the truth of many things: Spain's failure, God's existence, man's purpose. A passionately religious boy – he entertained hopes of sainthood – then a normally atheistic youth, Unamuno was propelled back to faith by the terrible illness and death of one of his children. However, the gap between his desire to believe and belief itself proved to be a torment. Unamuno could admire faith as 'a miracle of collective humility' but found it agonisingly difficult to sustain it in the knowledge of life's pointlessness. His diaries are so full of references to 'Death' or '*Muerte*' that he ended up abbreviating the dreadful word to 'M'. Every day Unamuno meant to talk to his priest about his anguish, but he always found a reason not to go. 'A year from now,' one diary entry reads, 'either I will be a catholic or I will be a madman.' He salved the daily torment with an unusual hobby: origami.

Unamuno was one of a group of writers known as the 'Generation of 98', named for the year in which Spain lost its last great colony, Cuba. This devastating blow – it became known simply as 'El Desastre' – had Spaniards of all backgrounds inspecting their souls to see what was wrong with the national character. The nineteenth century had been wasted on coups and conflicts between progressives and reactionaries, both groups so headstrong and so incompatible that people spoke of there being 'two Spains'. Progressives saw Spain as an antiquated, corrupt country, resting on the laurels of a vanished empire and falling behind the modern world because of its failure to reform industry. Half of all Spaniards were illiterate, only a minority had the right to vote, the influence of the Church pervaded all areas of life and a sense of apathy enveloped the nation.

'We watch the days and the years go by', wrote Unamuno, 'comfortably vegetating with no pulse and no stimulation, mired in a world of trivial domestic problems.'

The key to Spain's recovery, thought the liberals, was 'regeneration' through education. The middle classes, traditionally snobbish and lazy, must learn to think of themselves as a working, productive group. Students would be encouraged to study abroad, to open their minds to ideas from Europe. The first government to be formed after the 'Desastre' promised a 'revolution from above'.

The Generation of 98 set out to explain Spain's failure by seeking the essence of the nation in its greatest books. Of these, *Don Quixote* – written at the very moment when Spain's decline began – was certainly the greatest, but it also stood for all that was wrong with the country. Unamuno pointed to the scene, early in the book, when Quixote is knocked off his horse and lies on the ground, helpless. He saw in it a picture of Spain itself, wallowing in failure. 'Do we not take pleasure in our defeat and feel a certain pride, like convalescents, in the illness we have suffered?' Spain, like Quixote, had deluded itself, pretending to be a world power when it was barely capable of tilting at windmills. The fact that its last defeat was at the hands of a new country, the United States, seemed all too symbolic.

Among the other writers of the group were Azorín who saw in Don Quixote, 'our mirror and symbol' and Ramiro de Maeztu, who also believed self-delusion to be at the heart of Spain's problems. He believed that Spaniards could usefully study *Don Quixote* to develop a 'quixoticism of spirit' which might help them 'regenerate and raise up the battered, decadent and dying Spain in which they have to live'. Don Quixote could be allowed to live, but he would need rehabilitation. Only then could he – for which, read Spain – be sent out into the world, robust, lucid and with new, efficient weaponry.

The philosopher José Ortega y Gasset noted that foreigners had always been more interested in Don Quixote because 'for them Quixote is a divine curiosity, whereas for us he represents the problems of our destiny . . . he is like the guardian of the Spanish secret, of the errors of Spanish culture.' Hatred and rancour had dulled Spaniards' spirits and they could no longer appreciate their surroundings. He proposed 'a new way of looking', a negation of 'decrepit Spain'.

Unamuno's feelings about the novel were characteristically mixed. In an essay entitled 'Death to Quixote!', he condemned the knight as an arrogant egotist. Comparing Don Quixote with Robinson Crusoe – and implicitly Spain with Britain – Unamuno wrote that 'Robinson Crusoe has always seemed to me to be greater, and more Christian than Don Quixote, making a world of his desert island with industry, patience and science rather than trying to reform a whole society with slashes and blows.'

Only a few years later, however, Unamuno's ideas had changed radically. Now he was all for Quixote. As God had been invented to save mankind, he said, Don Quixote had been invented to save Spain. Cervantes' novel was therefore Spain's Bible. Unamuno's *The Life of Don Quixote and Sancho* was full of evangelist ravings about the destiny of Spain. Far from invoking the death of Don Quixote, now he wanted Spaniards to become quixotic en masse, for Quixotry to be their religion with the hapless don as its prophet. The only way to rebel, he argued, against the stultifying, 'reasoned' life promoted by priests, barbers and canons is to emulate the mad knight. 'Once a hallucination becomes collective, popular and social, it ceases to be a hallucination and becomes reality . . . we must bring to the people of Spain some sort of madness.'

Unamuno went dangerously further. The 'new madness' he wanted for Spain would be a civil war, because only war could regenerate the country, saving it from the quagmire into which it had descended. 'The only human and civilising wars are civil wars,' he wrote in his journal. 'The result of a civil war tends to be the forging and galvanising of the historic race, the human race.' The war he wanted would be of Cain and Abel, 'not even a war between brothers, but one of twins'. The two Spains must fight.

Years later, Unamuno had changed his mind again. You can still see the lecture theatre at Salamanca where, in 1934, he spoke of his visions of blood, his fear of national dissolution. 'Save us from that, my children,' he begged his students, 'Save us for the sake of Spain.' But by then it was too late.

∾ ∾ ∾

At the Faculty of Philosophy in Salamanca I met Ana, a student who casually demolished Unamuno. His ideas were not very good, she told me. His philosophy was mediocre. Ana reminded me of Sansón Carrasco, the clever student from Salamanca University who sets out to defeat Don Quixote in Part Two and finally gets the better of him at the end of the book.

'I feel my life has been marked by the changes in Spain,' said Ana who was tall, fair and serious looking. 'I was born in 1975, the year Franco died. My parents were among the very first to divorce, the first to use contraception, to go against the Church. Now I find myself fighting for some of the same beliefs they fought for more than twenty years ago.'

Spain's new, right-wing government, elected in 1996, had announced that religion would once more become a compulsory subject at school, that there would be grants for religious schools. Ana was horrified to think that the influence of the Church could rise again in Spain.

We spent a Friday night out, starting at a jazz concert outside Franco's old headquarters and ending, some time in the early morning, in a smokey underground bar. Midnight found us cutting a swathe through a Plaza Mayor that was still full of strollers. Antonio may have been lurking there behind one of the columns, on the trail of some adulterer.

'People in Spain don't think enough, they don't ask themselves about the reason for things, they don't analyse,' said Ana. 'They opt for the easy route. They would rather think about what to do at the weekend or football than about death.'

I suggested that it might be better to think about football than death, but Ana said that Spaniards were too shallow. 'I hate generalisations, and it's a cliché to say that Spaniards work less and are more superficial, but it's also true to a certain extent. The climate lends itself to an outside life, with lots of acquaintances, rather than close friends. Spaniards are good at social life, but the flip side of that is their relationships are not so profound. They see life in less tragic terms than northern Europeans. In the north there is more melancholy, more people living with a terrible sense of anguish. I spent a year studying in Germany and during that time several students threw themselves off the Faculty of Philosophy.'

For decades, thousands of young Northern Europeans had been drawn to Spain in search of a more lively, relaxed lifestyle. Ana was an example of an opposite, but growing phenomenon. She wanted *less* fun. She thought of herself as a northern European at heart, or at the very least, a Basque. Her ambition was to study for a doctorate in Germany.

In the mean time, Ana was trying to decide whether or not she wanted to ally herself with a group of local anarchists. The previous weekend she had been out with them in the early morning painting bicycle lanes on the roads, as a protest about the failure of the local authority to provide them. Next weekend they had invited her to a debate on the feasibility of establishing a People's University in a town outside Salamanca. This was the sort of endeavour that had been characteristic of anarchist activity before the Civil War. The Spanish left wing put a huge emphasis on culture and education. The Republican government of the 1930s had sent travelling bands of actors, teachers and artists – including the poet Federico Garcia Lorca – into remote areas, to promote culture, education and civic responsibility. At the outset of the war, when anarchists were attacking churches, the Nationalists went for their cultural institutes.

Ana was in favour of the People's University, but she had her doubts about the anarchists. 'I've been to these things before. Everyone sets off with good intentions, but then they all sit around talking about it and nothing gets done. Finally the whole thing degenerates into a party. It's not that I'm against parties, but I believe in taking action rather than talking.'

∽ ∽ ∽

The private detective had told me that he had connections everywhere in Salamanca, all I had to do was ask and he could organise any kind of meeting. I told him that I would very much like to meet some nuns.

'Nothing could be easier,' said Antonio, 'My aunt is a Mother Superior. I can take you to meet her on Sunday.'

On the Sunday morning I sat in church, studying the murmuring men and women. How many unfaithful were there among the faithful? They looked respectable enough, but if Antonio was right, many of the men were philanderers and a significant number of their wives were part-time prostitutes. It so happened that this Sunday was also *el día de los contemplativos,* an annual tribute to the thousands of Spanish nuns and monks who lived in closed orders – they account for two-thirds of the world's cloistered men and women. On television in the morning, small children were ushered into the presence of some nuns. Usually, the nuns explained to the children, they kept very quiet, having no contact with the outside world, but they were making an exception on this special day. Their laughter and jokes made the exception look like hard work. One of the nuns appealed to viewers to remember the Church when filling in their income tax forms. In an effort to distance the church from the state, the Socialist government elected in 1982 had introduced legislation inviting tax-payers to tick a box if they wanted some of their taxes to go to the church. Otherwise the money could be delivered to secular charities.

At eleven o'clock, Antonio came to collect me from the *pensión* where I was staying. I found him staking out a corner of the lobby: his hair was slicked back, he wore dark glasses and he was chewing gum on one side of his mouth. He looked exactly as private detectives look in films and smelled strongly of cologne. We set off briskly down the street, rounded two corners and arrived five minutes later at the convent. As it turned out, it was a building directly behind my hotel.

'You can't throw a stone in this town without hitting a convent,' Antonio said. He strode into the front hall with all the swagger of a Chicago cop busting a brothel, rapped on the familiar oak door that had so often stood between me and various nuns and, when there was not a response immediately forthcoming, rapped again and shouted: 'Aunty?'

Presently a revolving door set into the wall creaked into action and an enormous, Wonderland-style key appeared on a tray. Behind us there was another heavy oak door into which the key fitted and we let ourselves into a small room.

A few minutes later four nuns appeared and sat down on the other side of a grille. Unused as I was to seeing nuns at such close quarters, I found their entrance rather dramatic. One of them stood up and, smiling, unlocked the grille and swung it open.

'Since the Second Vatican Council, we no longer have to sit behind bars,' she said, though we were still effectively sitting in different rooms – the nuns in the cloister, the detective and I in the venal outside. 'Before the reforms, we were not allowed to visit our relatives, even if they were sick.'

'We had no access to the media,' said one of the others.

Three of the nuns, including Antonio's aunt, the Mother Superior, were old. The other two were in their early twenties and Mexican. All over Spain now, convents were looking to South America to provide the lifeblood they needed to survive.

'The contemplative nun is like the heart giving life to a body. People who walk down this street and see all the bars, then a convent, can think of us inside, praying for them,' said Antonio's aunt.

'That's a nice image,' said the chewing detective. When he opened his mouth, there was a flash of gold at the back of it. 'There are thirty thousand students in Salamanca, so it's quite a lively place, especially at the weekend.'

One of the Mexicans, Sister Carolina said, 'But we don't hear much noise, except the football when Real Madrid scores.'

'Don't you feel envious of people going about in the outside world?' I asked. 'Do you never have doubts that you have made the right decision?'

'Of course there are times of dreadful doubt,' said Sister Carolina, 'but the storm always passes; you talk about your anxieties to someone and things quieten down again.'

'That's wise,' said the detective. 'It's always best to let twenty-four hours pass before you make a big decision about anything.' I could imagine him giving the same advice to the hysterical women who came to see him about their husbands.

'It's necessary to have difficult times,' said Sister Carolina. 'They help you find the right path. As one doubt ends, another is born – until you die. There will always be cloudy days, but you have to wait for the sun.'

'Life is one long struggle,' agreed Antonio. The nuns and the detective nodded together, all pleased by their aphorisms.

'I've always wondered,' said the Mother Superior, 'what it is you Protestants believe that is different?'

'There are a few things,' I said. 'For instance, Protestants don't believe that the communion wafer actually becomes the body of Christ during communion.'

The nuns looked puzzled, as if they were unsure how much belief to attach to the mystery of transubstantiation.

'Does anybody really believe that?' asked the detective.

Then the other young Mexican said, 'Sometimes I think I would love to go to the mountains, and see snow, or one of those beautiful gardens full of flowers. Then I think, how marvellous that I want those things, but I've sacrificed them, for God. I offer all those things in the service of other people.'

She seemed very young, although she was the eldest of eleven children. Another sister of hers was also a nun and would soon be joining her in Spain. 'Our parents could spare us,' reasoned Josefa. 'In Spain now the birthrate is so low that families are less willing to let their children join orders. That is why there are so few vocations. Young people aren't attracted by this way of life.'

Sister Carolina was very worried about the young in Spain. 'You hear them in the street, swearing. They do not have a happiness that fills them. Happiness is more than what society can offer, it is feeling yourself loved by a superior being.' She was using computers to try to get this message across to schoolchildren and students. 'People find all kinds of ways to evangelise nowadays. If the media can be used to lower morals, we should use it to fight back by raising them.'

An example was *Sisters* – a popular new television sitcom about nuns. In the last episode I had watched, a nun was held captive by a burglar and his pregnant girlfriend who suddenly went into labour. The baby was named after the nun, who helped with the birth. 'It isn't bad,' said the Mother Superior, 'but it doesn't show the reality. It doesn't show how things really are.'

'Nothing is ever as it seems', said Antonio, chewing thoughtfully and perhaps he was thinking of the women of Salamanca, so outwardly respectable, so thrillingly deceitful beneath their fur coats.

CHAPTER SIX
Is Anything *Real?*

Nothing is ever as it seems. Don Quixote fathoms giants out of windmills, he sees two flocks of sheep meet on a road and imagines they are armies entering into battle. His delusions throw into confusion the meaning of basic objects. Some readers see this as a device to examine life's tenets and institutions. By mistaking a horse trough for a baptismal font, says Nabokov, Quixote questions the purpose of a font. Is it really no more sacred than a horse trough?

The trouble with this argument is that Quixote is not consistent about his misinterpretations. Sometimes he gets things bafflingly right – taking an inn for an inn, to Sancho's relief – or admits that he has been wrong, perhaps blaming his mistake on the enchanters who deliberately confuse him. Occasionally he is prepared to compromise. In chapter twenty-one, he and Sancho spot a barber going to an appointment by mule, wearing his basin on his head for convenience. Quixote sees the basin, gleaming in the sunlight, and decides that it is really the helmet of mythical hero Mambrino – he attacks the barber and carries off his trophy. Later the knight and his squire have an argument about the identity of the object, finally agreeing to call it neither basin, nor helmet, but something like 'basmet'. Here the knight settles neither for truth nor illusion but a combination of both, a distinctly quixotic third way.

Elsewhere, Quixote can be uncharacteristically reasonable about his misinterpretations. One night, not long into their journey, Sancho and Quixote hear a great thrashing and clanking. Quixote suspects giants may be at hand, and wants to go and investigate but Sancho, terrified, gets an attack of wind. Baring 'a pair of ample buttocks' under cover of darkness, he tries to disguise the ensuing stream of farts by grinding his teeth, but since Don Quixote has good hearing and a keen sense of smell, 'and the odour ascended almost perpendicularly', he cannot escape detection. Quixote drily remarks that Sancho has become overfamiliar. 'Pay more attention in future to your person and to the respect that you owe me.'

The next morning the source of the frightening noise is revealed as six fulling hammers at a watermill and Sancho mocks his master's mistake. Quixote is furious. 'They could just have easily been giants,' he says, but when Sancho suggests that there is no harm in laughing this off Don Quixote grudgingly agrees, and even apologises for his bad humour. Exchanges like this one become more frequent as the friendship between master and servant evolves and deepens. Quixote is progressively less inclined to be dogmatic, more willing to trust Sancho with his doubts about reality. Sancho is even able to question him about the inconsistency in his delusions, whereupon Quixote settles on a trusty scapegoat. 'It is simply that there are always a lot of enchanters going about among us, changing things and giving them a deceitful appearance, directing them as suits their fancy, depending on whether they wish to favour or destroy us.' So Quixote's delusions are not as straightforward as they seem. What he sees depends on the caprices of the 'enchanters'. If a windmill always looked like a giant and a tavern a castle, at least you would know where you were. When even unreality is unreliable, life becomes frightening.

On the street where I lived with Carmen and Alvaro there were women who were really men. There were men who were in the process of becoming women. There were housewives who turned into prostitutes at night, a man who pretended to be Dracula, a child with a Cyclops eye. Although we were thousands of miles away from the sea, pirates plied a trade in fake designer clothes and jewellery, in drugs and documents, from half-lit rooms behind shuttered windows. Each day, a small army of blind men and women descended on our area, white sticks tapping along the pavements, on their way to the National Organisation of the Spanish Blind to collect the lottery tickets they were licensed to sell.

The drug-dealers patrolling our street resembled Italian fashion designers. They were well dressed and softly spoken and their murmured offer of 'chocolate' – the slang for cannabis – sounded harmless. The dealers' preternatural thinness – they were heroin-addicts themselves – gave them a sinister elegance. They seemed taller and moved with an unworldly grace, almost as though, through their choice of drug, they had joined a different order of life, one whose cycle was brutal and short. At first sight, these glamorous men and women bore no connection to the scraggy creatures who crouched on doorsteps or among rubbish bags, injecting themselves in full view of passers-by. Yet, as the months passed, I was able to observe the dismal metamorphosis of the first group into the second. They dwindled slowly but inexorably until, like the finale of some illusional trick, they disappeared completely.

The people I lived amongst sometimes seemed like the fabulous cast of an epic novel. The man who ran the local launderette, for instance, was deaf and mute – how could be run a business? Yet he managed not only to communicate with his customers but to row with them. When I complained to him about the state of a shirt that had been spoiled in the wash, the furious, arm-flapping response could only have been interpreted as yelling.

A woman who lived in one of the flats opposite ours was fascinatingly indiscreet. Carmen and I thought she might be an actress because she never usually opened the shutters before noon.

Then she would wander around her room in a grubby bathrobe that was apt to lag or fly open, exposing a white dimpled buttock here, a bit of breast there. Each display caused Carmen and me great excitement and hilarity, not so much because of what was exposed, but because of the unpredictability of the exposure and the pleasure of waiting on tenterhooks. Sometimes a couple of weeks passed without a hint of flesh, then one day, as we were lunching, we might be rewarded with the glimpse of her shadowy figure flitting naked across the back of her room.

One day we saw the woman, in the murky depths of her bedsit, open her door to a male visitor. He stepped sideways into the room like a man with a mission and not much time to accomplish it. They did not greet one another with kisses, as would have been usual, but it was clear that some sort of hurried negotiation took place. Then the woman approached the window and the man followed close behind; before she could close the shutter, he placed his hands on her shoulders and turned her round to him. He kissed her on the mouth, not as if he wanted to, but as if the kissing were necessary, then he drew her robe aside to reveal her breasts. These he handled inconclusively for a few moments, as if weighing up discounted fruit on a market stall. At that point, the woman closed her shutters, excluding us from the scene. Carmen and I were speechless with excitement about our voyeuristic coup, but months later I had a greater one.

It was a sunny afternoon and I was sitting on the floor of my room reading essay notes. The balcony doors were open to provide an intense square of sun into which I had stretched my legs to brown. Looking up from my notes, I saw the woman opposite sitting close to the open doors of her own balcony. Her head, wrapped in a turban made of bath towels, was thrown back to take a good spread of the sun across her face, her eyes hidden under wedges of cucumber. Her bathrobe was hitched up to reveal legs that glistned with oil. The tops of her thighs were surprisingly bulky, compared with her skinny calves and knees, and there was a mottled play of purples and pinks about them. A veined cartography identified the territory behind her knees. Latin-American music rattled from the room behind the woman, and the gentle rise and fall of her chest suggested a light slumber. A pile of magazines lay on the ground beside her chair and a cigarette dangled from her right hand, its mounting ash caught in a game with gravity.

On the next-door balcony Juanito, the sort of child who might divest a fly of its wings, was absorbed in his own gravity-game. For ages now, he had been tossing his yo-yo over the railing, challenging it to keep breaking the laws of physics with its weary upwards roll. The chubby hand released, clamped shut, released, clamped shut on its toy. His innocent right eye followed the yo-yo's roll up and down, but his Cyclops eye seemed to dwell hungrily on his neighbour's exposed thighs.

I thought how strange it was that the three of us should be physically so close, and yet so confident of our separation in space and time, free to inspect one another from the demarcated areas of our balconies. It was not just the three of us, either: within a limited radius were Carmen lying asleep on the sofa and Juanito's mother, probably watching soap operas in the room behind her balcony. Underneath my room, the shoemaker had shuttered up his business and could just be heard listening to a sports commentary on the radio; he imagined himself alone. At the Windmill the prostitutes who worked the siesta shift would be sweating away at some kind of intimacy. How might their clients perform if they brought to mind the nearness of their neighbours? Each of us had the illusion of privacy, but the truth was we were, millions of us, living together, beneath and on top of one another, literally under one another's noses.

I was busy thinking all this when the woman opposite made some tiny movement, perhaps to swat an insect or scratch her knee. The grubby robe fell open – just for a second, but it was long enough to see that she was not after all a woman – not yet, anyway. Her womanhood was an illusion, perhaps even a delusion.

The neighbours, though disconcerting, came to seem part of that area's kaleidoscopic pattern, so much coloured plastic shaken into different patterns every day. The junkies and postitutes did not bother us, knowing that we were not in the market for anything they could sell, although the brothel-keeper never lost hope of adding Carmen to her troupe. It was easy enough to adjust to the local ways, not to carry a bag that could be snatched, a flashy watch or jewellery. We did not have any of these things anyway. I learned to avert my eyes from the junkies in the hallway, but I never stopped being frightened of them. It was bad enough finding them downstairs, but once I left the flat to find a man injecting himself on the stairs outside our front door.

Around the corner was a small square, picturesque in the Spanish style. Boxed in on three sides by crooked, balconied houses, it featured a demoralised fountain in the centre around which a few old benches were placed by way of encouragement. Cannabis-dealers sometimes used the fountain to wash their knives after cutting a deal. On the fourth side of the square, cars passed down the narrow street which was, in fact, a continuation of the stretch I could see through my bedroom's cracked wall. At night I sometimes heard the feline purr of cars cruising down that stretch; Reina and the other transvestites were their prey.

Otherwise the traffic was human. On sunny days, Carmen and I sometimes sat at one of the parasoled tables, drinking coffee and watching people drift through the square. If there was a nip in the air, we might add cognac to our coffee, to ward off colds. At midday, when much of the neighbourhood was still asleep, this was the preserve of young mothers and pensioners. As the afternoon progressed, past lunch, and the siesta, the picture changed; the mothers and pensioners moved on, and the transvestites came to pick up a sun-tan. Later the drug-addicts lolloped through to buy cigarettes and newspapers.

On the other side of the square, the warren of narrow streets continued, but the atmosphere was noticeably smarter. Ornate balconies, sometimes entirely boxed in with glass, hung like family jewels on the faces of the old buildings. Thanks to the nearness of an important avenue, an insidious upgrading had taken place over the last few years. Dozens of tiny boutiques had opened, so exclusive that you had to ring the bell before you were permitted entry. Their interiors, glimpsed through windows that took up most of the front wall, were minimalist spaces in which a few flimsy garments were displayed like *objets d'art*. The thought that these precious pieces might be handled, or even purchased by the wrong kind of client, seemed to distract the angular women who presided over them, deterring all but the boldest customers from ringing the bell. There was also a handful of small very select nightclubs in the area. In the evening, men and women, known to gossip columnists by an English phrase, 'the beautiful people', arrived on motorbikes, to dance in them, and, if they were famous, to be photographed coming out of them. These people never crossed the square, past the transvestites and the junkies, into our neighbourhood, and only on rare occasions did we venture into theirs.

They were great times to be young in Spain. Madrid was still in the grip of a post-Franco backlash known as *la movida*, or 'the commotion'. The word expressed the ceaseless activity of a city that had spent too much of the century asleep and now refused to go to bed. The nights had become a disproportionately long counterpart to days. Even at four o'clock in the morning, on a weekend, there were traffic jams in the street below our balcony. Madrid was now, officially, the noisiest capital in Europe.

One of the most popular records of the day described the difficulty of getting out of bed after a weekend of partying. In Spain there was not the pressure to drink and get drunk you find in Britain, but certainly there was a pressure not to sleep. Going to bed was seen as a kind of failure, a renunciation of life. Perhaps that was why, the morning after a particularly hectic night, people invariably claimed to feel *fatal*. It was bad luck to draw things to a close, so Spaniards never ordered 'one last drink', but rather *la penúltima*.

One night Carmen and I got chatting to a man in a bar and had a few drinks with him and his friends. At about three o'clock in the morning he said he had to go home. Everybody remonstrated with him, and the man agreed to a *penúltima*, before finally insisting on leaving. 'I'm an eye-surgeon,' he explained to us. 'I have an operation to do in about five hours' time.'

How could *madrileños* perform operations, manage machinery or in fact, do any sort of work at all? It was a mystery when they slept. Even though shops and businesses closed for a three-hour siesta every afternoon, for many, that time was taken up travelling home for lunch, then back to work. In Spain, where family took precedence over work, the idea of forfeiting lunch at home for a sandwich at the desk would have struck most people as too brutal an efficiency.

Democracy was well established in Spain, but the memory of dictatorship – and a recently attempted coup – was alive enough to give an edge to the new freedom. There was a sense of cool on the streets. *Madrileños* were stylish. Miguel, in his squeaking leathers, strutted down the street with Carmen on his arm. 'Sweet motor', he would murmur at the glossy-hubbed bikes that had proliferated since the end of the dictatorship. Young Spaniards seemed to want everything, even speed, to excess. Although Franco had been dead for a decade, his presence still stood for energetic rejection. A friend of mine dropped a coin while paying for drinks in a bar. Stooping to pick it up, he saw that it was one of the old ones, still in circulation, that bore Franco's face. 'I'm not picking up that bastard,' he said, and kicked it under the table.

~~ ~~ ~~

On Friday and Saturday nights Carmen and I would start getting ready to go out at about eleven o'clock, trying on clothes in Alvaro's bedroom – which we were expressly forbidden to enter – because his wardrobe had a full-length mirror. Once we were out we did not expect to come home again until dawn, when we would have a hearty breakfast before retiring to bed. In the intervening hours we met friends of Carmen's in different bars around town. Carmen's friends had names like Annunciation, Miracles and Immaculate Conception. Spaniards were expected to take a religious name at baptism and Mary, Joseph or Jesus did for both sexes. Thus José María, a common name among boys, could simply be reversed to provide María José, a popular choice for girls. Some women were called María Jesús, and some men Jesús María. Later things changed, and even Hollywood names became fashionable, but people were wary of abandoning the religious names altogether.

In our area the streets were crowded all night, and cannabis was readily available on street corners. The bars served beer and spirits cheaply and in extravagant measures, but it was unusual to see scenes of drunkenness or violence. That would have been behaviour fitting only to a British *jooligan*. There was an atmosphere of excess, but with little accompanying aggression. In the murky depths of some bars, couples could be seen trying out ingenious sexual acts. One night, in some bar or other, a girl in the ladies asked me to hold her bag while she removed her sweater, then she asked me to hold that while she took off her shirt. Passing me the shirt, she took off her bra and gave me that too. Then one by one, the items went back on again, apart from the bra, which she put in her bag. 'I hate feeling restricted,' she explained, on her way out.

If Madrid was a centre of convergence for all Spaniards, it was also a magnet for students and exiles fleeing the turbulent regimes of South America. They did not always mix easily with the Spanish, but their presence gave Madrid an extra dynamism. One night at a party to defend human rights in Peru, Carmen and I met a Chilean with wild curly hair and a knack for flirting. Some musicians were there, playing Andean pipes and we all danced into the early hours of the morning. The Chilean, who had seemed quite cheerful when we first met him, grew increasingly morose as the party approached its end. Finally, in an eruption of tears, he revealed that his father, a colonel in the army, had recently been poisoned by General Pinochet, during a meal in which he thought he was about to get a promotion.

'He was a fascist, but he was still my father,' wept the Chilean.

I asked if there was anything I could do to help, at the same time fascinated by the idea that General Pinochet might preside personally over the poisoning of his enemies. I could not resist a macabre reconstruction of events: the two military men leaving the sitting-room where they had been drinking gin-and-tonic for the dining-room, the last room one of them would ever admire and compliment; an agreeable curdling in the stomach of my friend's hungry father as warm bread rolls were brought out, and butter on a china plate.

'Stay with me tonight!' the Chilean had howled. 'Don't leave me alone!' His glossy ringlets had fanned out beautifully as he slumped, like his father perhaps, over the restaurant table.

Carmen and I brought him back to the flat and put him to bed in Alvaro's room, but during the night he skulked away, obviously disappointed that his story had not drawn a more romantic response. The next day we spent half an hour returning Alvaro's bed to a pristine state before he came home.

A few weeks after moving in, we decided to have a flat-warming party. On a Friday afternoon we tidied up, bought cheap wine, spirits and crisps, and locked away our valuables – mostly Alvaro's – in his study.

At ten o'clock we sat down to wait for our guests. From our own building we invited the Dutch jazz-lovers and the jobbing Dracula, but not the muse or the Chinese family, who certainly would have fleshed out the numbers. It was an hour before Alvaro's friends, the ones who were trying to avoid military service, arrived and took up their accustomed place on the sofa, and another hour before anyone else came. From then on the flat filled up steadily, mostly with people who had not been invited. Our neighbour who played Dracula arrived with some women he had met at another party. Rufus came with one of his girlfriends who wore an array of protest badges, variously promoting the rights of bulls, Basque Nationalists and women. Her eyelids, heavy and veined, fluttered unattractively over her grey eyes, like venetian blinds in the hands of an experimenting child.

As I passed them, Rufus said, 'I hope you don't mind, I've invited some friends.' Steadily, the flat filled with people and smoke. Some Irish friends of ours arrived and were immediately offended when Rufus sang the praises of the IRA to them. On the sofa, a woman I had never seen before gave herself up to the devouring kisses of one of Alvaro's friends. Some time after midnight a gentle squeaking announced the arrival of Miguel. The party had been going for a few hours when I saw that Rufus had been joined by the man I had first seen at his flat, the revolutionary.

'Did you save the world in the end?' I asked him, shouting above the noise.

The revolutionary looked confused until I reminded him of Rufus's fulsome introduction, then he roared with laughter, an over-generous reaction to my comment, which I felt, for a flattered moment, must have been very witty.

'I haven't had a chance to save it yet,' he said and his expression switched very suddenly to one of elaborate sadness, as if this were a genuine apology. 'Something else came up.'

I enrolled at the Complutense, one of the largest universities in the world. It was founded in 1506 at Alcalá de Henares – the town thirty kilometres east of Madrid where Cervantes was born – the Latin name for which is Complutum. In its time it had been a highly distinguished institution. Scholars working there under the auspices of the Grand Inquisitor Cardinal Ximénez de Cisneros, produced in 1517 the world's first Polyglot Bible, incorporating texts in Hebrew, Latin, Greek and Chaldean.

The university moved to Madrid in 1836 and was nowadays far from being the intellectual powerhouse of the sixteenth century. The faculties sprawled, a series of resentful, brooding lumps, over an area, to the north-west of Madrid, that had been a battlefield during the Civil War. It was through the University City that General Mola and his men advanced on Madrid in November 1936. Morroccan soldiers, fighting alongside Spanish National-ists, were met by the 11th International Brigade comprising volunteers from Britain, France, Germany and Poland. Also fighting on the Republican side were a column of anarchist volunteers and one of German communists. Hugh Thomas, historian of the Civil War, described an atmosphere in which a 'babel of tongues, the frequent multilingual singing of the

"International", the insults exchanged between the nationalists and republicans, added to the macabre confusion. The marching songs of the German communists brought to the crumbling masonry of the laboratories and lecture halls a teutonic sadness.'

As the armies met, hours of artillery and aerial bombardments around the faculties were followed by hand-to-hand battles to control single classrooms. The German communist battalion placed bombs in the lifts of the Clinical Hospital to explode in the faces of the Moroccans on the next floor. The Moroccans made themselves ill by eating inoculated animals being kept for experiments. Though some of the African Army managed to advance towards the centre of the capital – where they were killed – the Republican occupation of the Philosophy and Arts buildings held the rest of the Nationalists at bay. At the end of November the two armies dug trenches, built fortifications and Madrid found itself in a state of seige. Franco, who had told one journalist that he would rather see Madrid destroyed than leave it to the 'Marxists', began a bombing campaign designed to bring about a rapid surrender by targeting the capital quarter by quarter. Although the Second World War would see similar bombardments, this was the first campaign of its kind, and it was a failure: Madrid held out.

The university blocks in which Sciences and Arts were taught were ranged down a long avenue, at one end of which stood a monumental arch, pock-marked by mortar bombs. Three times a week I walked the length of the avenue, past couples smoking on concrete benches, on my way to lectures on modern Spanish literature.

Some ten thousand men had died at University City; revolution was etched into its foundations, yet there was no sense of debate, no controversy there; the place bred boredom. Some of the courses were so oversubscribed that students had to arrive an hour in advance to be sure of a seat in the lecture hall. Lecturers often seemed moody, or merely defeated by the numbers of students and the bureaucracy. Knowledge, grudgingly imparted to those students who bothered to turn up and fight for a chair, spread among the rest via photocopied notes with key words or sentences highlighted in lurid yellow or blue. Young men and women poring over these photocopied notes were a common sight in the cafés of Madrid, but for all the studying they did, the undergraduates advanced very slowly. The process of acquiring a university education took many years, with fewer than half of all students finishing their degrees in the normal time. Many would be in their thirties by the time they graduated.

As in any other university, the students wore denim, but here the fabric was stripped of its anarchy: jeans were neat and straight, lovingly ironed into creases. Women often carried their notes in folders dedicated to Snoopy, while the men had well-washed hair and wore boat-shoes.

The first class I attended was not inspiring. I gathered that the students were meant to have read *The Family of Pascual Duarte*, by Camilo José Cela. The novel, written shortly after the war, was ground-breaking for the violence of its imagery, its questioning of human motivation and a depiction of Spanish rural life as backward and squalid. Our lecturer asked if any of the students could summarise the points she had made the week before. Judging by the silence that followed, none of them could. After ten minutes the teacher pulled out a classroom cliché: 'I'm waiting.' The twenty or so students stared at their books, their fingernails or out of the windows at the landscaped gardens that had once been battlefields. Nobody said anything. More time elapsed, our tutor reminded us that she was still waiting, and the silence was now excruciating. At half past the hour our teacher's pinched face juddered into tears and, muttering inaudibly, she turned on her heel and marched out of the lecture hall. The students took this show of petulance in their stride. After waiting a few minutes to see if she would return, they resignedly gathered up their books and shuffled towards the door and the café.

The university was dull, but it had one great advantage – the revolutionary was also studying there, in the same faculty. It was his habit to meet friends for lunch in the Philosophy and Arts faculty restaurant. A student lunch which might, in Britain, consist of a bag of crisps and some biscuits, was a three-course meal with wine in Spain, and did not cost much more. In the restaurant, waiters wheeled among the students carrying steaks and dishes of lentils and chickpeas. Dessert, for some reason, was always Crème Caramel, which Spaniards call 'flan'. When a friend and I arrived to eat at the restaurant at the same time as the revolutionary and his friend Arturo it was only logical that we should all sit together.

Arturo was the anarchist who had once lived with Rufus and left his room there covered with slogans. Since leaving Rufus's he had been sharing a flat with the revolutionary where he continued to write anarchist poems in a beautiful script on the sitting room walls. Everywhere Arturo went, he scattered slogans. Even his jeans bore anarchist insignia in felt-tip pen. He was studying to be a film-maker so that he could make anarchist films. The revolutionary told us little about himself, other than that he had studied English at a course in Bournemouth. I thought perhaps he was joking: I could think of no more incongruous setting for a Peruvian revolutionary.

After lunch the four of us agreed to meet that Friday evening, and so began a new social pattern to my weekends. From then on I saw less of Jesus, Mary and Joseph and more of the revolutionary and his friends. These included a number of South American students, some of whom were communists, like the revolutionary, though others were right-wing, or not political at all. There were also several Basque Nationalists who wore black and were moodily good-looking. Although they consented to speak Spanish

85

in mixed company, among themselves they spoke Euskera, one of the least intelligible languages on the planet. They were also proponents of a revolution, to emancipate the Basque Country from Spain.

Now that I was finally keeping the sort of idealistic company I had hoped for when first arriving in Spain, there were days when I would have agreed with Ernest Hemingway, that Spain was the *only* country. The weather was often very cold, but the skies were cloudless. It was possible to talk about politics and idealism without sounding pretentious. Britain seemed banal by comparison. Thoughts of home summoned up images of DIY megastores, newsagents packed with chocolate bars, tidy parks and television programmes about animals. I imagined old people sitting on park benches which bore little plaques immortalising the many other old people who had preceded them there. I thought of the bored chattering of its blonde-streaked shop assistants – 'So I turned around and said . . . so he turned around and said, so I turned around . . . he turned around.' A swirling of shop assistants, turning around and turning around: this would be a shopkeepers' revolution, an English revolution.

～ ～ ～

Spaniards – and South Americans to a lesser degree – do not believe in beating around the bush. If they want something, in a shop, or at the dinner table, they ask plainly for it, dispensing with 'please' and 'thank you'. Nicknames also go straight to the point. Fat people are called 'fatty', bald people 'baldie', with no offence meant or taken. Once I was on a bus with just one black passenger, who had asked the driver to let him know when the bus reached his stop. In due course the driver called out: 'This is your stop, *negro*.'

Cervantes would have seen no shame in his moniker – The

Great One-Handed One. The Greek artist Domenikos Theotoko-poulos was cut down to size when he settled in Spain and became El Greco. The idea of tempering truth with kindness is anathema to most Spaniards. They are not good with innuendo or euphemisms. Why waste time on platitudes? If you are fat or in need of psychiatric help, they will tell you so. Any woman who really wants to know if her bottom looks big can find out in Spain.

In our new-found group, everyone had a nickname that went straight to the point. Carmen was called La Negra, whereas my Anglo-Saxon roots earned me the derogatory Gringa. El Chino, a Peruvian student of Politics, was so-named for his oriental look.

El Doc was a paediatrician who had come to further his studies in Spain for a year. He loved his job, and often spoke about his work with the poor in Peru. Western morals appalled him. Instead of lavishing money and attention on their pets, he said, Europeans should adopt children from poor countries. El Doc did not believe that there were problems in the world that were not to do with money or health, that it could be possible to suffer in the western world, where people had so much.

The revolutionary's particular friend was Ernesto, a short Peruvian Indian with a round belly which the others were wont to pat affectionately. Ernesto would have met with discrimination in Peru but in Madrid a topsy-turvy hierarchy was at work: he commanded respect by virtue of his Indian blood. Ernesto was good at cooking, though his passion was for fast food. This was the sort of vice he could not confess in front of our more radical friends. One of the prettier Basque Nationalists had announced that she could never kiss someone who drank Coca-Cola. Nobody, least of all Ernesto, wanted to cut down the chances of being kissed.

Ernesto sometimes came to our house to cook meals which we would all share around the broken sitting-room table. The conversation was of politics, Marxist theory, of the evils of capitalism and the racism of Spanish police. My new friends had strong ideals and believed in all kinds of duty except, perhaps, a duty to do the washing up. Carmen and I usually did that.

~ ~ ~

The urge to turn private detective must be contagious. On my last evening in Salamanca I followed a trail of my own. I was walking in Calle Concha, close to the university, when I heard a woman announce into an entry-phone:

'I'm going to see the virgin – are you coming?'

'Actually, I'm not feeling very well,' answered the voice.

'It might make you feel better.'

'I don't think it will,' the voice wavered.

'Well I can't hang about,' said the woman and she took off at a brisk pace. Curious, I took off after her. I followed her as she strode across the square in front of the vast New Cathedral and through some ramshackle back streets down to the River Tormes. Together we crossed the Roman bridge and walked along the far river bank, before entering a residential area of new houses. This estate was very bare and empty, as if it had only just been finished. The absence of hubbub, or any vegetation made trailing my quarry through the quiet streets difficult, especially as she walked fast. I wished I had the private detective with me to offer advice, and perhaps chewing gum.

Soon we emerged on to a busy main road. The woman kept up a brisk pace and after we had been walking for twenty minutes or so I began to feel tired and in need of a double cheeseburger. After half an hour, I was annoyed with her for choosing to visit a virgin at such a distance from the centre of town – surely there were closer ones? It crossed my mind to turn back, but I had already come so far and now I saw that we were not alone, there were other groups of people walking in the same direction. As we progressed, the numbers swelled until it became clear that this was some sort of pilgrimage, but to what? Caught up in the throng, I felt I must carry on.

In our knots and groups we trailed through a small park and on to another main road; a voice could be heard now on a microphone. I could not make out any words, but a tone of barely checked excitement suggested that he was offering a bargain – cheap virgins? As we got closer I saw that we were approaching a small funfair. Roadside stalls were selling the confectionary you find at any Spanish fiesta: caramelised nuts, sunflower seeds and piles of sweets.

But the funfair was only a sideshow. Hidden behind the amusements was a small, unattractive church into which dozens of people were squeezing themselves. At the portal our throng met with a scrum of people collected from different parts of the city. Together we all pressed, gasping, into the church. Inside, an elderly woman was standing at a microphone intoning Hail Marys over and over again. Looking around, I saw that hundreds more elderly women made up the bulk of the congregation. And there was the Virgin, a statue placed at the front of one set of pews; with finely drawn eyebrows and shining cheeks, she looked like the Queen of a minor European royal family, at a Gala function. Presiding over the other set of pews was a baby Jesus, dressed in a white silk dress and wearing white woollen tights. With curly blond hair and red lips, *he* looked like a little girl at a party. Women were approaching both statues, murmuring all the while and adding flowers to the piles that surrounded both mother and child.

'Hail Mary, full of grace, the Lord is with you,' said the woman at the front of the church over and over again into the microphone. 'Blessed are you among women, and blessed is the fruit of your womb, Jesus.'

'Why is everyone here?' I asked the elderly woman to my right.

'To be cured of illnesses,' she said. 'By the Virgin of Good Health.'

'And by the Baby Jesus of Good Health,' said another elderly woman, adding under her breath, 'As if you could be cured of old age.'

She embarked on a litany of aches and pains which, since it was whispered, and was set against a noisy background of Hail Marys, was hard for me to follow, but I got a general picture of sore joints and hypertension and extrapolated it to the ageing congregation in front of me. In fact, the grey heads were testament to an extraordinary progress – Spaniards were very much more likely to reach old age now than they had been a century before. They were the longest-living nation in the European Union, thanks to their diet and high standard of health care.

The chanting soon became oppressive. I scanned the crowds for my red-coated quarry, but she was lost in a sea of pious women. I slipped outside and trudged wearily back to the city centre and the refuge of a fast-food joint.

That evening, I walked once more around the Plaza Mayor. As usual, it was full of people. The Tuna was there singing medieval ballads and a group dressed in regional costume was demonstrating traditional dance steps. As I drifted among the milling crowds I could not quite shake off the sensation that I was being watched. It was a feeling that dogged me during the rest of the time I spent in Salamanca, and I was never again able to eat a double cheeseburger without looking over my shoulder.

CHAPTER SEVEN
Pastoral Scenes in Avila

In the last line of *Don Quixote*, Cervantes says that the entire purpose of his book has been to do away with Spaniards' fondness for chivalric literature. For about a century readers took him at his word. Why not write a complex, thousand-page attack on a literary genre that showed nothing more dangerous than knights rescuing weeping damsels and shepherds writing poetry? In 1654, Edmund Gayton hoped someone might do the same for Britain's current obsession. 'The Don's passion for *knight-errantry* was not more ridiculous than our own countrymen's infatuation with the bubble of *Alchymy*. If *Quixote* sold his lands to purchase books of *chivalry*, we have sold our estates and beggared posterity in our fruitless researches after the *Philosopher's Stone*.'

Since the start of the sixteenth century, romantic books about chivalry had been immensely popular across Europe, as much with kings and queens as with the illiterate people who crowded into inns to hear episodes read aloud. The best-known heroes were as much a part of daily life as the characters in today's soap operas. When the conquistadores, led by Cortés, got their first sight of Tenochtitlán, the Aztec capital, their instinct was to compare it to the enchanted city in Amadís of Gaul, one of Don Quixote's favourite novels.

The immense popularity of chivalric novels had some advisers to the Inquisition proposing their inclusion in the Index of prohibited books – not so much to ward off moral danger, but as a way of encouraging Spaniards to read better literature. Then again, who would dare to deprive a nation of its favourite entertainment? The Inquisition left it well alone.

Walter Scott claimed that Cervantes had sounded the death-knell of the chivalric era with *Don Quixote*. If so, said Lord Byron, it was no bad thing. 'I fear a little investigation will teach us not to regret these monstrous mummeries of the Middle Ages.'

In fact, the penchant for chivalric novels was already tailing off by the time Cervantes penned his most famous work. Rather than seeking to finish off a dying genre, it is more likely that he chose it as a device through which to explore his ideas about reality. While he was writing *Don Quixote*, Galileo, Bacon and Descartes were still alive. Europe had recently learned that the earth revolved around the sun, that there was another world beyond the Atlantic Ocean. Objective truth was the new prize and Cervantes was one of several Spanish writers to discuss the difficulty of attaining it. Calderón de la Barca wrote that 'life is a dream'. Mateo Alemán, a friend of Cervantes, argued that 'everything deceives'.

At the end of Part One, a friendly canon with an interest in literature asks how Quixote finds it possible to believe in 'all those palfreys, all those wandering damsels, all those serpents, all those dragons, all those giants, all those extraordinary adventures, all those varieties of spells, all those battles, all those desperate encounters, all that fine raiment, all those love-lorn princesses, all those squires who became counts, all those facetious dwarfs, all those love letters, all that wooing, all those courageous ladies and, in fact, all those monstrous absurdities contained in books of chivalry?'

In replying that it would be *blasphemy* not to believe it Quixote demonstrates the unreliability of absolute beliefs. Who decides what is true?

He claimed to hate chivalric literature, and yet Cervantes imitated some of its worst excesses in *Don Quixote*'s pastoral passages. Every time Quixote and his squire come across love-lorn shepherds, or distressed shepherdesses, the narrative descends into absurdity. Virginia Woolf confessed herself 'sinking in the sand' during some of these stories. One translator, J. M. Cohen, advises 'judicious skipping'. Nabokov also takes the author to task for his romantic vision of nature: 'In point of fact,' he says, 'sheep and goats stink.'

Cervantes loved his shepherds, as if they were pieces of Dresden china adorning a literary mantelpiece, while the modern reader can only see them as chintzy clutter. The puzzle is that Cervantes, inventor of a way of writing that would revolutionise literature, wanted so much to prove himself in the outmoded, romantic style.

The train south from Salamanca to Avila swept across a plain that was vivid with wild flowers, after an unusually rainy spring. Bloody splashes of poppies stood out amid the crops. In one field a woolly square moved against the grass; it was a flock of sheep, penned and under the guard of a mastiff. This region of Castilla y León, covering the northern half of Spain's huge central plateau, is austere, but beautiful none the less. The huge plains are backed by mountain ranges. Ochre landscapes are dotted with the sandy-coloured castles, thousands of them, that originally gave Castile its name. It is a far cry from the pretty pastures in which Cervantes – who was perhaps sick of empty plains – liked to imagine his shepherds. There *are* fountains, but they are provided by irrigating machinery. Seventy per cent of farmland in Spain relies on irrigation; this is no easy land to cultivate. As for the woods in which Quixote and Sancho often take shelter – Spain was once so densely wooded that, it is said, a squirrel could travel from the Mediterranean to the Bay of Biscay without touching the ground. Eighty per cent of Spain's original forests have been destroyed since then.

There were not many people in the train carriage – nowadays in Spain it is more usual to make long journeys by coach. One elderly man in a beret shouted to his embarrassed grandson about the convenience of the modern refrigerator. His harangue was liberally dotted with swear words. The Spanish love to swear. Although 'coño' refers to the female genitals, it is not deemed offensive in Spain, in fact it seems to be favoured by the old, perhaps because it is relatively easy to say with few teeth. Altogether toothier is 'Hostias' which describes the communion wafer and is a more shocking expletive.

One stop short of Avila, another very elderly man in a beret got on, and the two recognised one another with a stream of delighted abuse. The second man was carrying a wilted flower. He proclaimed, to all of us in the carriage, 'This flower smells of a woman, although it's lost its bloom – not unlike my mother, who lies resting in her tomb.'

'You're no poet,' growled the first beret and the two cursed and shouted to one another for the rest of the journey.

As we reached our destination, the magnificent walls that completely surround Avila's old town came into view. The mile-long rampart, completely undamaged, looks as fantastic a structure as you might find in a chivalric romance. It took Muslim prisoners nine years to build, after Alfonso VI captured the city from the Moors in 1090.

A novel by Miguel Delibes described sermons in which the local priest bids the congregation to think of the city wall at Avila, apparently resistant to all incursions, and to make of their souls a similar fortress against evil. Like many Castilian towns, Avila is a bastion of conservatism. For all the indignant graffiti that covered it, Franco's name still honoured one of the main streets. Here, as in Salamanca, the shop windows offered polite displays of stationery, hosiery and leather bags. Sweetmeats made from egg-yolk, a local delicacy, were arrayed in neat rows. Posters around town advertised memorial masses for men and women who had been dead for many years.

Avila is the capital of a large, underpopulated province that has seen much migration to the prosperous cities in northern Spain. At the beginning of the twentieth century about two-thirds of Spain's population lived and worked in the country. In 1950 almost half the workforce was still engaged in agriculture. By 1990 the figure had fallen to twelve per cent. The leader of Avila's agricultural workers' union told me that life in the country was getting harder. Part of the problem, he said, was the low birth-rate. There were no children to help with the work or inherit plots. What young people there were wanted to leave for the city. Spain's member-ship of the European Union was a life-line, he said. 'It's always a good thing to hold the hand of someone who is stronger than you.' He was not so keen to hold the hand of the East European countries that would soon be joining.

Laura, a 24-year-old agricultural engineer who worked at the union, took me to one of the outlying villages to meet Enrique, a shepherd. Although the village was only a few miles from Avila, it felt bleak and remote. On a bench by the side of the road three elderly men sat almost entirely motionless.

'This is the life,' exclaimed Laura. 'Those people have all the time in the world. They don't feel the stress and grind of the city.'

I could not share her enthusiasm. The locals looked large and toothless, and greeted our arrival with curiosity, asking for news of the 'capital' as if they had never heard that there was a much bigger city than Avila, capital of the whole country indeed, only an hour or so down the road. We asked after Enrique and someone said that he had gone to wash his hands. Five minutes later he was striding along the dirt road towards us, slim and athletic, with teeth that were still good enough to say 'hostias'. We walked across the village to the barn where his flock had been resting until our arrival in the yard provoked a startled tinkling. Enrique's sheep were quite different from any sheep I had ever seen before. Their long faces wore a quizzical, anxious expression, and they were nervily thin. British sheep would look smug by comparison.

Enrique said that all the men in his family, for generations back, had been shepherds. In the summer, his father and grandfather used to go away for days or even weeks at a time, seeking something edible for the flock in the lusher lands of the north-west. Sometimes they spent five or six months away from home. 'They slept where they fell down,' said Enrique. 'It was a hard life and the jealousy put paid to many a good marriage.' Nowadays the returns were ever more meagre. Wool fetched such a low price that Enrique sold it only for a token price to the shearer. He said that Spaniards preferred to wear synthetics.

I asked Enrique what he did while he was watching over his anxious flock. 'I used to read quite a bit and think, but the transistor radio is the great enemy of thought and I've lost the habit of it now,' he said. 'I wish I wrote more. If you don't practise your writing you lose the facility for spelling. I get mixed up with "v" and "b".'

Enrique had read *Don Quixote* at school and, although it seemed like a punishment to start with, in the end, he said, he found it meaningful. He thought it said a lot about life, but he agreed that the portrayal of shepherds was far-fetched. We laughed about the way they were always drifting around La Mancha talking about love.

'Being in the country, looking after sheep is hard work,' said Enrique. 'There are no holidays – I can't even take a day off to go to a wedding or a fiesta.'

'It's not as if you have much time to write poetry,' I quipped, but Enrique pulled me up short.

'As a matter of fact I do write poetry,' he said.

'Really?'

'It kills time. I don't write as much as when I was younger and I still believed in women – I was more idealistic then. How happy I was.'

The flock, as though sensing the melancholy that had come over their master, issued a subdued tinkling. There are eighteen million sheep in Spain and nearly twice as many people, but the steady migration of people to cities means that in many places sheep are gaining the upper hoof. Spain, which tourists may still think of as an agricultural society, is now very much an urban one: although ninety per cent of the territory is rural, more than eighty per cent of the population live in cities. In the twentieth century the level of migration was such that several thousand Spanish villages have now been entirely abandoned by their inhabitants.

There is a movement, still in its infancy, to reclaim some of these towns and develop them as havens for artists, or the disabled, but many of them are so far from roads and services that they will never again be inhabited. In a sinister devleopment, one abandoned town has been taken over by neo-Nazis. In others, a handful of elderly people remain and flocks of sheep wander among the crumbling houses. In many parts of the country, sheep rule, or at least they could rule, if they had the personalities for it.

Enrique would not elaborate about the women who had ruined his ideals. He said that at eighteen he had tried to give up the family business and moved to the city to get a job as a builder. 'I had to give it up because I missed all this' – he swept his arm across the dazzling Castilian plain. 'I'm happy now. When I was a builder I was always worried about the time. Now my watch is decorative, I barely ever look at it.'

'You're really happy?'

'Well, quite happy. I think you have to have a vocation to be a shepherd, or a priest,' said Enrique. In Spanish both professions can be described with the same word: pastor.

Hearing about his poetic inclinations and his disillusionment with women, I was beginning to feel that Cervantes' cultivation of the pastoral genre was not so ridiculous after all. Enrique would not seem out of place wandering across La Mancha in a toga, his crestfallen flock tinkling behind him.

After we had seen the sheep, we went back to the bar and drank a glass of wine with a plate of piglets' ears and another of sheep's large intestine. 'People say that food in England is, well, a bit disgusting,' said Laura, apologetically. 'I had a friend who went on an exchange to an English family. They made her eat – what do you call it? – "pudding".'

'I think the food's better now than it was,' I said. 'We have tapas bars all over the place.'

'There was an Englishwoman here in the village once,' said Enrique. 'She was married to a shepherd, but she couldn't take the life and one day she disappeared back up there.' His hand vaguely motioned north. 'It was sad, because she took their little boy with her. She was too lonely here. The country life is very hard.'

We went to the other village bar and had more wine, this time with a plate of olives. Somehow, we embarked on a conversation about women's rights. Laura said that she, her brother and sister were all still living at home, but her brother was not expected to help with any domestic chores. After meals he relaxed in a comfortable chair while Laura and her sister cleared the table. Enrique said that that was wrong, but in general he thought that Spanish society was changing for the better. There was no doubt that women had got a bad deal in the past. A row of red-faced men leaning against another angle of the bar formed, like Enrique's sheep, a watchful, ruminative and faintly sceptical audience.

'I don't clean out the bath after I use it,' admitted Enrique, 'but only because my mother would take that as a criticism of her ability to do the same job.'

Everyone in the bar pondered this, and after some hesitation one man nodded, as if seeing the logic in the argument. 'If I ever get married,' Enrique pressed on, 'I will, of course, expect a fair division of the chores.'

'You'd go so far as cleaning the bath?' asked one of the men.

'Of course. If my wife didn't insist on cleaning it herself.'

The man shrugged and carried on chewing impassively. Enrique commanded enough respect in the village to get away even with this rather dubious theory.

For all his talk of equality, Enrique refused to let us pay anything towards the drinks and tapas. Before Laura and I left the village, he went to fetch me a copy of one of his poems, dedicated to the memory of his father.

Shepherd

Your skin is weathered by winter's cold
when the North Wind caresses your face.
The blanket hanging from your arm
is an inseparable companion

you tell us stories
about your mastiff dogs
of drovers' roads and cowbells
of long treks to distant pastures

When you drank water out of horns
from springs along the way
and dined on rice with cod
in ancient roadside inns

At night you slept beside your sheep
alert to the howl of a wolf

Shepherd, the winter wind has roughened your face.

The weather of the great Castilian tableland is famously cruel: nine months of winter, three months of hell, they say. Don Quixote's skin, which is white from the years of confinement with his romantic books, turns brown and leathery just a few days into his first expedition. The sun can be punishing, even when it is very cold. On days such as these, the locals like to issue warnings about the danger of developing catarrh.

Castilians are fascinated by catarrh and the phlegm it produces – you might even say they were proud of it, judging by the skill and dexterity with which they conjure and dispose of it. Ideally phlegm is summoned in a brusque, noisy manoeuvre from the channels in which it has gathered to the back of the throat, then, in one splendid eruption it is ejected on to the pavement, or some convenient corner in a train carriage. For maximum effect, men make this violent exercise in the dark winding streets that are so typical of Spanish cities. To find yourself alone in one of these alleys with a catarrh-sufferer walking close behind you can be disconcerting. Castilian women are either not prone to catarrh or learn to deal with it less flamboyantly.

Dr Juan Huarte, who identified the weather as an influence on character in his 1575 book on psychology, might have argued that the sun damaged Quixote's brain as much as the books did. How does it affect today's Castilians? They are reputed, especially among other Spaniards, to be closed, braced against emotion as they might be against sun or wind. Jan Morris, who travelled around Spain in the 1960s thought they seemed 'pursued by some mighty preoccupation'. It has been said that the excess of light makes Castilians too extremist in their beliefs. They fear doubters.

Castile is a region much associated with the mystic writers Saint Teresa and Saint John of the Cross, and you can see how the landscape might induce someone with the right temperament to experience visions. 'The immense plains affect people,' Ana had told me on our night out in Salamanca. 'With weather and a landscape like this, the only option is to go mad or become a mystic.'

Don Quixote took the first option; Saint Teresa, who also loved chivalric literature, took the other and became Spain's most famous mystic. She was born in Avila in 1515. As a girl she enjoyed a spirited rapport with God, often scolding Him and saying it was no wonder He had so few friends. 'Life', she once complained, 'is a night in a bad hotel.' She laughed when friends warned her to be wary of the Inquisition.

At the age of seven, perhaps fuelled by too much romantic reading, Teresa ran away from home hoping to achieve martyrdom at the hands of the Moors. Later she tried her hand at writing romances of chivalry, but acknowledged the hobby to be a dangerous distraction. Saint Teresa is nowadays revered for more pious work: the reformation of the Carmelite order, the foundation of dozens of convents and some of the most important mystical writing in the Western canon. You can see the spot on the road outside Avila where her uncle caught her, and put a stop to her planned martyrdom. At her birthplace, now a convent, you can see one of her blackened, gnarled fingers; the nail on it is said still to be growing. You can also see the very staircase, at the Convento de la Encarnación, where the Virgin Mary appeared to Saint Teresa.

You cannot see the nuns who live there. 'There is nothing I can tell you that Teresita does not say better,' said a voice behind a familiar oak door. 'I recommend that you study her teachings.'

Instead, I took a guided tour around the convent with two priests who were overwhelmed to be so close to the spirit of Teresa. 'Isn't it amazing?' one or other of them kept saying to me, and each time I felt them scan my face for signs of amazement. These two were old friends and met each year to make a spiritual journey to a Spanish city. One was a teacher in a seminary in Madrid.

'You know', said the shorter one, 'that after Saint Teresa died, her body was cut up and bits of it sent all over Spain? General Franco had an arm in his office.'

'Don't take that the wrong way,' his taller friend said to me, quickly. 'It makes Franco sound bestial. He wasn't that bad.'

'He did have her arm, though,' the shorter priest remonstrated. 'He took it off the Republicans after the war. He never went anywhere without carrying it with him in a suitcase. When he died it was by his bedside. The Order used to write to him asking for it back, but he never would send it.'

'¡Hombre! There were bits of her all over the place! Why should Franco be the only one to send his bit back? They've got it now, anyway.'

The priests offered me a lift back to the centre of Avila, so we piled into their old Seat and rumbled up the hill. The Seat is so much a part of Spanish cultural history that I felt nostalgic climbing aboard. Sitting behind the two grey heads was like stepping into Graham Greene's novel, *Monsignor Quixote*, in which two friends drive around Spain in a Seat called Rocinante. It was, however, an uncomfortable ride: every cobblestone we crossed had ambitions to dislodge vertebrae. The priest who was not driving turned and said to me:

'What hope do you think there is of a reunification of the Catholic and Protestant churches?'

'I don't know,' I said. 'Do you think it's important for them to be reunited?'

'Of course! It must be our most pressing goal.'

When we arrived in the centre of town, one of the priests went to buy some stamps, while I waited by the car with the other. Suddenly a large group of schoolgirls came running up to us and surrounded us completely. It was unnerving, as if a flock of birds had descended on us from the sky.

One of the girls, the ringleader, jigged around in front of us. 'Is he your boyfriend?' she asked.

'No,' I said, alarmed by the girls' sudden arrival and the intimacy of the question.

'Is he your husband? Is he your boyfriend?'

'I'm a priest,' said the priest. 'Now go away.'

The girls flocked away just as suddenly, but in those few seconds, they had changed the relationship between the priests and me. We said embarrassed goodbyes, and they climbed back into their Seat to make another pilgrimage.

〜 〜 〜

In the evenings, Avila's main square was full of parents and children, the latter calling the shots, while the former could do little more than feebly negotiate. Spanish children are always beautifully dressed and seem well-loved, yet a report in that day's newspapers suggested that the incidence of sexual abuse was high, though concealed in close-knit families. As I crossed the square, I watched a mother chasing her infant around with his little jacket, like a torero in pursuit of an escaping bull. From where I was sitting I could hear her shrill cry: 'Come here child – you're going to catch catarrh!'

I was on my way to a lecture on 'Spain and the Challenges of the Twenty-First Century'. The lecture was supposed to start at eight, but we waited upstairs for a quarter of an hour while the organisers had a smoke and a bit of a laugh in the courtyard downstairs. As we waited, it occurred to me that one of the most pressing challenges facing Spaniards might be punctuality.

Although the lecture was to be given by one man, four others came to sit with him at a long table on the stage.

'This end of century will be totally different to any that has come before,' said the speaker, 'not just because it is the end of the millennium, but because at the close of previous centuries, Spain has lost prestige and standing. This time things will be different. We are now one of the most open countries in the world. A profound social and economic change has taken place with enormous dynamism and speed. The process of internationalisation of companies is finally happening. Services are beginning to improve. Five million people have mobile phones now.'

Indeed Spain was one of Europe's leaders in telecommunications. Spaniards' love of being in the street and their addiction to talking made mobile telephones an irresistible accessory.

Behind me, a businessman was tackling the challenge of catarrh in a horribly liquid fashion.

'We are facing a magnificent opportunity, though we still have some problems,' said the speaker. 'We have to make structural reforms which go against our traditions, the labour market is protected and over fiscalised. Why should services continue to be provided by the public sector? They should be provided at the best price by the private sector. Laws of competition should replace legal restraints. Bureaucracy slows a lot of things down. The state must shrink. The unemployed are overprotected and not willing enough to move about. Public provision needs to exist, but why shouldn't it also be provided by the private sector? Beveridge said that provision should never be a disincentive to work.'

The audience shuffled uncomfortably during the lecture and at the end of it, one man asked irritably:

'Wouldn't you agree that there are some things more important than capitalism? What about workers' rights?'

'The hardest thing will be for us to adapt ourselves mentally, but we have to change,' insisted the speaker. 'The recipes of the past no longer work. Things are going to be very different.'

It was strange to hear this sort of rhetoric issue from the mouth of a Spaniard. If it had not been for the battle with catarrh going on behind me, and the pall of smoke hanging over the proceedings, we could have been listening to the same lecture in Britain, fifteen years earlier.

If the increasing homogeneity of European countries seemed inevitable, perhaps it was a comfort that the service economy was not yet fully installed in Spain. The notion of the customer always being right would take some selling to Spaniards when it was obvious to them that the customer was not only often wrong but stupid as well.

At the small *pensión* where I was staying in Avila, I had complained on arrival to the cleaner that my room smelled strongly of smoke and the window would not open. She stepped into the room, sniffed the air and agreed cheerfully, as if our shared verdict on the smell were a cause for celebration.

'Tell you what,' she offered, 'I'll leave you the ambient odoriser and you can spray it as much as you want'.

'Thanks.'

I kept spraying it until I had transformed my room into a synthetic Spring Meadow. After watching a chat-show about relationships I went to sleep in this twenty-first-century pastoral idyll.

Student outings in Madrid had a habit of snowballing so that an excursion with two or three friends might become a gang event by the end of the night. That meant that, although my evenings out now usually included the revolutionary, I barely ever got the chance to speak to him. As our growing group processed down the streets, as we squeezed into bar after bar, I tried to devise strategies for ending up beside him. So often, though, I found myself stranded on the wrong end of the group, with some bore who wanted to practise his English or boast about his mother's cooking – Spanish men are tediously loyal to their mothers. I watched the revolutionary talk to other people, with the same generosity of expression I had imagined was meant just for me at our party, wondering if it was really necessary for him to laugh so readily, as if everyone were amusing.

To see him laugh with other women was galling. It was worse to see him dancing with them at the Latin-American salsa bar where we sometimes spent our Friday evenings. The revolutionary had various female admirers, the most dogged of whom was called Isabel. People said that she had loved him for years. If he would only say the word she was prepared to drop her fiancé, a businessman, like a hot brick. It was unlikely that he would ever say that word to her, or anyone else, but Isabel waited and kept her businessman dangling. One day she would give up, and marry him.

I had seen the revolutionary leaving the salsa bar with Isabel. I had seen him flirting with various women. His friends joked that he was a womaniser. Even so, I sought him out. In between weekends, if I had not seen him at the *facultad*, I would go to the university library that specialised in South American literature – partly because I knew there was a chance of seeing him there. The walk to the library was full of apprehension. The anticipation of seeing him made me feel as nervous and uncomfortable as would the prospect of an exam. To endure the walk, then spend an afternoon at the library, not seeing him, my heart jumping every time the doors opened to admit someone else, was draining.

In the end, I decided that it was a waste of energy. Then, just as I had resolved to forget about him, some accident of planning landed us together in a bar one weekend. Now here I was, the sole recipient of his attention, and I had no idea what to say to him. We must have made some sort of conversation, but afterwards I was at pains to remember any of it. From then onwards, we were often thrown together, and increasingly I was the object of his flirtations. I supposed that he was flirting with other women too, so I was surprised at the end of a long evening when he asked me out. 'Why don't we go to the cinema tomorrow?' he said.

I spent the afternoon before the film in agonising anticipation of our date. On the way to the cinema it kept crossing my mind to turn back: perhaps he would not be there. But when I got to the cinema, I found him waiting at the door and half-way through the film he took my hand and held it for the remaining time. After the film we walked up the Gran Vía, still holding hands and when we came to my turn-off, he kissed me. He said, 'See you soon,' and I was too nervous to ask when that might be, but the next day, he was standing under my balcony, asking if I wanted to go to lunch.

In Spain there is a kind of restaurant that is so cheap and homely it is simply called a *casa de comidas* – an eating house. Every day millions of Spaniards go to one of these restaurants and ask for the 'menú del día', usually a three-course meal with bread and wine. People tend to go to the same restaurant every day, the waiter becomes a friend, the cook makes adjustments to meet her client's dietary needs. That first lunch the revolutionary took me to El Castillo – The Castle – a *casa de comidas* in the same street as my flat. During the meal he bantered with the waiter, Jesús, while I pushed food around my plate. The strain of wanting to be attractive, entertaining and fluent, all of it at once, killed my appetite.

Away from home, in a culture that I loved, I was all too susceptible to romance. So I fell in love with the revolutionary, and it was a hard fall. I wanted to see him all the time and anything else I did was measured out as time not spent with him. The hours between our meetings lagged, but then as the time approached to see him again I would start to feel sick with nerves – there was nothing comfortable about my infatuation. The brown nape of his neck, the smooth angle of his arm, our fingers intertwined – the discovery of these fragments was as perfect to me as the identification of a stray jigsaw piece to Alvaro.

He was not only remarkably good-looking but firey in defence of his cause. He wore home-spun Peruvian waistcoats with knitted llamas on them and among the university books he carried everywhere, there was always a sheaf of documents pertaining to meetings. In fact, one of the most exciting things about him was the sheer number of meetings he was required to attend. As representative of the Peruvian revolutionary communists, he had been invited to meet young activists in the Soviet Union, and to attend conferences in Paris.

I loved what I took to be his revolutionary zeal. I was still hazy on the details of his commitment – I knew that the revolution he planned for Peru would provide housing and sanitation for the poor, land distribution and education. I was less sure how these goals would be achieved, and what part he would have to play, but I decided not to worry about that. The point was that he had goals, he had a consuming passion. And I, who had a passion, but nothing to consume it, was happy to be taken over by him and his cause. I was so exhilarated, I felt sick much of the time.

One lunchtime, when Ernesto was showing me how to make a Spanish tortilla, he told me that he had friends who were already 'militating' in Peru. One of them had joined the notorious Shining Path terrorists. He hinted that he and the revolutionary would also be returning to Peru to 'militate'.

'When do you think you'll go?'

'It could be quite soon,' Ernesto confided.

Perhaps the imminence of his departure also lent attraction to the revolutionary. He was merely using Madrid as a base from which to launch an assault on the forces of evil in Peru.

The first time the revolutionary spent the night with me, he peeled off his jeans to reveal footless woollen tights, made of alpaca wool, which had been darned at the knees by a motherly hand. I had realised that his legs would be thin – but not as thin as all that.

CHAPTER EIGHT
Love in a Cold Climate

It is not hard to fall in love in Spain. The climate, landscape and architecture connive at romance. Any visitor to Spain may be intrigued to see how much kissing goes on in the winding alleys of its ancient cities. In the narrowest streets the balconies pout hopefully at their opposites. Cafés welcome lingerers and, after dusk, the parks rustle with fornicating youths. Juan María, the Communist who lived next door to Carmen and me, boasted that he and his girlfriend had made love in the garden outside the opera house. He joked about hitting his top 'C' at the same time as the soprano.

Spanish legends are all about lovers escaping across rivers or being persecuted for daring to cross the boundaries of faith and race. Love and courtship are couched in superstition. In Toledo there is a dark alley where a shrine to the Virgin Mary is set in one of the walls. Young women who leave a hair-clip here increase their chances of marriage within the year. Another way to get married fast in Toledo is to go to a small church outside the city, pull the bell-rope inside, then run outside in time to see the bell swing.

In fact, there are dozens of tricks and enchantments at the disposal of would-be brides. Nowadays, though, Spanish girls who may once have murmured incantations at dawn, or eaten special foods or otherwise made fools of themselves in the hope of finding the right husband, are opening their eyes to the advantages of putting marriage off, perhaps indefinitely. Once I asked a friend if she was thinking of having children. 'I don't really need them,' she said. 'My sister has some.'

The first time I went to Spain I was sixteen and at a summer school in Andalusia, a region of white-washed houses and spectacular Moorish architecture. Having never visited the country before, my language skills were poor and the Andalusian accent is probably the hardest for a foreigner to understand. The couple in whose modest home I was lodging sometimes resorted to writing notes to me. The rest of the time they shouted, in the hope that at least the gist of what they wanted to say would be understood.

Rafael was a few years older and a student of Aeronautical Engineering. We met at a party and although we were able to communicate very little, he and I sustained a week-long romance fuelled by Rafael's flamenco guitar-playing. The day before he left to return to university, we wandered, love-lorn and tongue-tied through the streets of Córdoba in the pouring rain. We wept when we said goodbye, and having seen him off on the train, I spent another hour wandering in the rain, purely for the melodrama of the occasion. The next day I had a raging temperature. My landlady stood at the end of the bed looking worried, then passed me a small package containing a wax tube; with a meaningful look, she withdrew from the room. I examined the mystifying tube before putting it in a drawer and drifting off to sleep, to dream of Rafael.

Later my landlady and her husband returned to the end of the bed and shouted incomprehensibly, before passing me a note. 'Do you know how to use the suppository? DO NOT EAT IT!' I realised then what it was they wanted me to do with the wax tube, but I could not bring myself to comply. The next day I seemed so unwell that the director of the language institute was called to remove me from my lodgings. While they waited for him to arrive my landlady and her husband made their last, desultory attempts to communicate. Inevitably, these were abandoned in favour of a note: 'You are ill. We do not wish you to die in our house.'

Madrid has little outstanding architecture, but it was made romantic for me, at twenty, by other things. I loved the noise and the smell of the streets, the clatter of shop gates closing as the siesta hours began. After a quiet few hours, the city came back to life in the late afternoon, shops and cafés buzzing, at a time when other Europeans would be leaving work and trudging home to the television and something from the microwave.

There seemed also to be a surplus of poets. Engagingly despondent in black clothes, and carrying battered satchels, they circulated around the cafés of the centre, dropping little photo-copies of poems on to the tables. Sometimes the poems were illustrated with forlorn drawings. Once a distribution was completed, the poet did the rounds of the tables again, gathering up all the poems that had been rejected or ignored – but the charitably minded gave him a few pesetas and kept the poem. Poor people did something similar with pictures of the Virgin Mary. Perhaps the poets got their idea from the poor.

One day, soon after I had met the revolutionary, on some street corner I passed a man sitting upright at a table with his hands folded in his lap, as meekly as if he were waiting to be served dinner. In front of him was a pile of folded papers and the sign: 'I am hungry. Please buy a poem.'

The man was quite different from all the other poets I had seen. Far from being scruffy, he offered a visual lesson in probity. Everything about his person was righteously aligned – his trim haircut neatly accommodated a pair of large ears that lay obediently close to his head. His feet, in shiningly well-polished shoes, were carefully placed together, his cardigan buttoned to the top. He sat at a folding table, of the kind children eat at in gardens, behind piles of folded coloured papers. I felt that the folding exercise could be taken further. The poetry-seller himself looked as if he could be folded along the dotted line of his buttons, his hands and feet tucked neatly in behind his ears, and, along with his folded table and folded poems, slipped into a pocket of Madrid at the end of the day.

'What are the poems about?' I asked.

'Some of them are about love or loss,' said the man quietly. 'Some are about nature. The different colours represent different themes.' I paid for a poem written on yellow paper, but it was only when I opened it at home and recognised a bit of Keats that I realised Madrid's poets were not all that original.

To be in love with a revolutionary, albeit one untested by revolution, was the most exciting thing that had ever happened to me. Even if I did not know what the chief reasons for revolting in Peru were, I could imagine there might be plenty – the country's name alone conjured images of unrest. The revolutionary described the streets of Lima as battlegrounds, where confrontations between civilian demonstrators and the police sometimes ended with dozens of deaths.

He had been a member of a Christian youth movement in Peru, before becoming a communist. Such a route to militancy was not unusual in South America – where a number of 'red' priests had been defrocked on the orders of the Vatican – nor indeed was it in Spain. Juan María, our neighbour, had studied for the priesthood in Toledo before becoming a communist. He was proud of his party affiliation. 'They'll have my name on a list somewhere,' he said, as we both leaned on our balconies, never suspecting that communism would so quickly become a spent force.

'When you're used to seeing dead bodies in the street, your whole attitude to life changes,' the revolutionary told me. 'People in Europe are very spoilt, they have no idea what it is to live in the Third World.' The revolutionary and his friends had no time for well-meaning euphemisms like 'the developing world'. They were proud to call themselves *tercermundistas*.

Once, when we were lying in bed, he showed me an indentation between his ribs. 'A souvenir of the police in Lima,' he said.

'That's terrible! It could have gone into your heart. Did it puncture your lung?'

'No, no', said the revolutionary with a terse expression that happened to suit him very well. He would not be drawn on the details of this injury.

I embraced him as effusively as the cramped conditions would allow. The revolutionary frequently felt cold and complained bitterly about the crack in the wall, which admitted an icy wind. Even in the spring, when the days were growing warmer and the transvestites' skirts got shorter, he would still be huddled in a denim jacket which was buttoned to the neck and covered in protest badges.

One day I returned home from lectures to learn from Alvaro that the revolutionary had been round earlier and left a present. His beard bristled with excitement as he suggested I look in my room. I went there and found an electric fire perched at the foot of my bed, its fraying wires trailing to a socket behind the wardrobe. It was the revolutionary's indication that he expected to be spending the nights with me from now on. I was happy about that, though unhappy about the wiring.

Even with the fire floating dangerously above us, the revolutionary felt the cold and often he had to borrow clothes of mine to sleep in – he was small enough to fit into most of them. Once, when he had forgotten his footless tights somewhere, I even had to lend him some of those. It never occurred to me, at the time, to ask where he had left his own tights, or perhaps it was simply that I would rather not know.

Our relationship grew quickly in affection. Sitting in the park on a sunny afternoon, the revolutionary's head lying in my lap, I thought that I had never been happier. We often met for lunch at El Castillo, then sometimes we spent the afternoons together at the library or reading in my room. I was used to students making a virtue of laziness, but the revolutionary worked hard. When he was not studying, he was always busy with some project or preparing for a political meeting. He edited a newsletter for South American political exiles living in Spain, called ¡Urgente! With its stark print on cheap paper, this had the look of a banned political pamphlet. Arturo had drawn a design of barbed wire around the masthead. While the newsletters awaited distribution they were stacked in my capacious wardrobe, and their presence there made me feel that I was involved in some clandestine activity.

At the weekends we often went to a communist bar and crouched on low stools at rudimentary tables with friends of the revolutionary. Everyone drank beer from bottles, or we would buy a big, litre-sized glass and pass it around the group, like an alternative chalice. Some of these co-religionaries drew inspiration from the anarchy movement that had been so powerful in Spain during the first few decades of the twentieth century. They believed in self-education, free love and even aspired to a kind of androgyny. I was told that one day everyone would be bisexual and that it was 'bourgeois' to think otherwise. The women frowned on make-up and uncomfortable shoes. They were avid proponents of nudism. Some were vegetarians, which was otherwise unusual in Spain at the time. All these 'libertarian' ideas had been discussed in weekly pamphlets published in their thousands by anarchist organisations in the years before the Civil War. The Franco regime later held them responsible for 'poisoning three generations of Spaniards'.

The walls of the communist bar were covered with posters of

Che Guevara and Fidel Castro. Several of the people in our group had been to Cuba to help with the coffee harvest. There were banners bearing the slogan 'No Submission!' referring to Spaniards who refused to do either military service or the civil equivalent required by the state, and thereby courted a prison sentence. In practice, their chances of imprisonment were small – the need for recruits was not great enough to justify the bother of chasing up every objector, but every so often the courts chose to make an example of an *insumiso*. The Basque Nationalists we knew were all *insumisos*, arguing that the Spanish state had no authority to enlist them (they always called it 'the Spanish state', rather than 'Spain') to fight for a power they regarded as foreign. When the Basque Country won independence, they said, it would not have an army anyway. Who would ever want to invade them?

The Basques lived in an attic flat behind the Gran Vía, though really it was no more than a tiny room, hidden beneath the rafters of an eighteenth-century tenement. The room contained a rudimentary shower and cooking facilities and it was possible to crawl from it into two cubby holes where the Basques slept. One of these had the best view in Madrid, across patchwork red rooftops to the buildings on the Gran Vía. Looking at the statues and adornments on these grand buildings from behind was like standing back-stage, watching some glittering cast from an unexpected angle. There was a bakery at the bottom of the tenement with a ventilation tube that met the sky outside the Basques' window. A smell of baking bread, so powerful that it appealed directly to the stomach, poured out of this tube twice a day, interrupting whatever talk had been going on, with an urgent call to eat.

The Basques took their politics seriously. In Spanish, when referring to a mixed group of male and female people, or things, the male plural adjective is used. The Basques, to show that they were feminists, often used the female form which, however laudable, made them seem faintly ridiculous. When blaspheming they demonstrated their atheism by prefacing 'God' with 'their', rather than 'my'. Their lavatory, which also had a fantastic roof-top view, was covered in obscene observations about the Pope. When we argued about British history, the monarchy and the Falklands War, my friends said that I was an imperialist and bourgeois – but they delivered the insults with affection.

Basque resistance has been a model to the left-wing young in Spain since the days of the dictatorship. The anarchic look of the Basque language which is littered with 'k's and 'x's has also been adopted by some 'alternative' groups who substitute 'k' in words usually spelt with a 'c' or a 'qu'. Thus, anarchy becomes *anarkia*. Squatters live in *kasas okupadas* and are called *okupas*. Sometimes we showed our solidarity with the squatters by going to parties in the *kasas okupadas*. It meant sitting in dirty rooms, listening to punk music, sometimes sung in Basque, and sharing lentils from a communal pot. I hated the parties. My friends told me that was because I was bourgeois.

Once, a group of us including anarchists, communists and Basques set off on a weekend trip to Cuenca, which is about ninety miles south of Madrid, in the region of Castilla-La Mancha. Cuenca is set in marvellously dramatic surroundings. The old part of the town clings to a high ridge, pincered by deep gorges over which some of the houses hang precipitously. One of these 'hanging houses' is home to the Museum of Abstract Art, which must be among the most strikingly presented collections in the world. We were going to visit this, then the Enchanted City, where the bizarre rock formations look like fantastical, invented creatures. A capitalist friend had been persuaded to take us all to Cuenca in his van – the availability of a capitalist friend was often essential to our plans. On the journey someone farted and an argument broke out, with the communists demanding that the offender own up, while the anarchists saw no reason to allocate blame. The Basques said nothing.

The many decades of dictatorship in Spain had spawned a vibrant counter-culture. In some way or other, everyone I knew was involved in flouting convention. It was almost as if Spaniards still found it easier to react to an authority than they did to participate in a democracy. Several of my friends had lived their childhoods in a context of mute repression. One of the Basques had been brought up studying his language at secret classes in the cellar of his house, because it was forbidden to speak it publicly. During the dictatorship, notices in telephone boxes warned occupants to 'speak Christian' – that is, Castilian – on the telephone. Perhaps because Franco had branded all dissent 'subversion', there was now a confusion between useful opposition and posturing. The antagonistic behaviour of the police meant that many young people hated them as though this were still a military state. It would be inconceivable, for instance, to ask a policeman for directions. When Carmen lost the national identity card all Spaniards were obliged to carry, she was genuinely frightened about what might happen to her.

Perhaps Madrid's burgeoning drug problem was part of that need for rebellion. Spaniards could claim to be in shock as a result of the rapid change in their circumstances, and refuge in drugs was a way to deal with that. Perhaps it was simply that so much was now on offer that had previously been prohibited that there was a tendency to make a run for all of it. One of Carmen's close friends was an eighteen-year-old who had been sent to live with her grandmother while she studied in Madrid. Irene was bright, but her determination to escape the constricts of a traditional Spanish bourgeois family knew no bounds. She took drugs, dated illegal immigrants, had sex with strangers in lavatories, then returned in the evenings for a polite supper with her grandmother. If she was late back, she was punished with a weekend's curfew, so Irene kept her rebellion strictly within hours. (By the time I returned to Spain at the end of the 1990s, public consumption of drugs had been criminalised – though its private use remained legal – and bars which had once been cloudy with cannabis smoke had posted signs warning their patrons not to light up. In the intervening years, however, the drug problem had become acute. Spain had the highest AIDS rate in the European Union.)

One afternoon Carmen told me that Miguel smoked heroin. It was not an addiction, she said, merely a habit. There was a big difference between smoking the stuff and injecting. She said she had not been worried about it at all until she accompanied him one day to buy his drugs from a dealer working in a delapidated house not far from our street. I knew the house she meant: its exterior was dismal, covered in graffiti, but Carmen's picture of what was going on inside was hellish. She described young people lying around the rooms in a drug-haze. There was writing scrawled all over the walls and rubbish decaying everywhere. At the top of the house, Carmen said, there was an old woman measuring out and selling the heroin. I found it almost impossible to associate this terrible vision with Miguel, always so polite, so neat in his squeaking leather clothes. Carmen said she had told Miguel he must give up his habit, and he had agreed to try, but the long nights working alone as a security guard were hard to fill.

Rufus was the most ingenious of the law-breakers I knew. The poet had found new and lucrative work running an illegal telephone service. It was a simple scam: using one or other of the false passports he kept hidden under the sitting-room rug, he would rent a flat and install telephones in different rooms. He hired out the telephones by the hour, mostly to homesick South Americans, at a very competitive rate. When the telephone bill arrived, he simply abandoned the flat, taking thousands of pounds with him. Then he used one of the other passports to rent another flat and the whole enterprise began again. Rufus spread the word about his *locutorio* via business cards that offered his services as a medium. Perhaps everyone who received the card instantly recognised it as a coded advertisement, but it may be that some people turned up sincerely expecting to communicate with their dead relations. If so, Rufus would simply persuade them to talk to live ones instead.

The *locutorio* was a convivial place to spend an evening, being full of South Americans who were cheerful about a long-awaited opportunity to call home. We often spent an hour or two there, chatting to them as they waited. Sometimes someone whipped up a meal, a Spanish omelette or a Cuban rice dish, in the kitchenette. Once, when we were at the *locutorio*, a Guatemalan woman started reading palms. She examined the revolutionary's hand and said 'You will die young, away from home.' She must have been infected by the Spanish gift for straight-talking because she did nothing to soften the blow. The revolutionary seemed to pale momentarily, but then he smiled and shrugged and made some joke about it.

On Sundays, Carmen and I usually spent the morning at the Rastro, Madrid's great, sprawling flea market. The revolutionary had a stall there selling second-hand books on politics and Marxist theory and Arturo sold handmade jewellery. I had heard them joke that it was a great way to meet girls.

One sunny afternoon, after we had been at the Rastro, the revolutionary told me that he did not believe in monogamy. We had been drinking vermouth in the square near my flat, watching the transvestites sunbathing and the drug-dealers washing their knives.

'Are you trying to tell me that you're seeing someone else?' I asked.

'At the moment I'm not seeing anyone, but if I wanted, then I should be able to,' said the revolutionary.

'Then so should I.'

'Of course,' said the revolutionary, though with less conviction. 'The notion of "fidelity" was invented by the Church, to induce fear and obedience in the proletariat. It's absurd that we fetter our relationships according to arbitrary and unworkable rules.'

'I don't really want to see anyone else, though.'

'Neither do I,' said the revolutionary, 'but things may change. You can never be sure.'

He told me that he could not be faithful to me because it was against his principles. He gave the impression that this was an inconvenient principle, that a monogamous relationship would be preferable, but untenable. He also said that he never usually went out with someone for more than two weeks.

'But we've been going out more than a month.'

'I know,' said the revolutionary. 'I can't explain that.'

Although fidelity is also a sticking point for Don Quixote, his principle is a mirror-image of the revolutionary's. Exclusive, binding love is a part of the deal for a knight errant. The love of a princess is as indispensable as a shield or lance. Quixote knows this, and he creates Dulcinea from a formula. She is a princess by numbers, with golden hair, eyes like amber, eyebrows like rainbows. Even her 'hidden parts' Don Quixote suspects to be peerless (that reference was too much for the Portuguese branch of the Inquisition, which had it excised in 1624).

Dulcinea is beautiful but untouchable, a sort of hologram, and she might for ever have remained that way if it were not for an apparent slip-up of Don Quixote's. In Part One, he mentions the names of Dulcinea's parents, allowing Sancho to identify her as Aldonza Lorenzo, no princess, but a peasant girl he happens to know in a small town, called El Toboso. Delighted by this discovery of a mutual acquaintance, Sancho cannot stop chatting about Aldonza, describing her in terms we know risk puncturing Quixote's delusions. According to Sancho, Aldonza is a 'brawny girl, well built and tall and sturdy'. She smells of garlic; she has hairs on her chest, is able to compete in athletic events with the strongest men, and is 'not at all shy'. Her lungs are so powerful that she has been known to climb into the bell-tower and summon men working in the fields several miles off just by yelling.

Hearty, bad-breathed, loud and hairy – the real 'Dulcinea' is the opposite of what Quixote would have her be. However funny, Sancho's description cannot be read without concern for the knight whose dream-girl is being torn apart before his eyes. We know that his belief in Dulcinea is a delusion, but it is one we want to protect, for his sake.

Yet Quixote's reaction is surprisingly robust. Far from being deluded, his answer shows that he is perfectly in control of his created Dulcinea. Most women in chivalry novels are invented, Quixote reasons, purely to serve as love-objects in poems and ballads. 'For what I want of Dulcinea del Toboso, she is as good as the greatest princess in the land . . . I imagine all I say to be true, neither more or less, and in my imagination I draw her as I would have her be, both as to her beauty and rank.'

If he is happy to admit that Dulcinea is an invention, how can he love her? You cannot sustain real love with a hologram. Samuel Taylor Coleridge thought the knight was frightened of women. 'In Don Quixote there is no shadow of sensuality,' he wrote in 1811. 'His very dreams of Dulcinea are chaste. We may take it that in his heart of hearts there lurks no hope of ultimately possessing Dulcinea; rather would it seem that he has a certain dread of such a union.'

Yet it cannot be true that Quixote has no amorous instincts. Towards the end of the novel he is taken to a dance where some women persuade him to try out some steps so that everyone can have a laugh at him. 'It was a sight indeed to see the knight's form, tall, lanky, lean and sallow, tightly encased in his clothes, so awkward and, even worse, by no means nimble.' As the women goad Quixote, their flirtations are so relentless that he cries out 'Leave me in peace, unwelcome thoughts.' Finally, 'wearied and shaken' by the dancing, he has to be carried up to bed. Don Quixote may not have the stomach for a relationship with a real woman, but the 'unwelcome thoughts' are there, all the same.

In Part One of *Don Quixote*, the knight's delusions have tended to be checked by real life; he recognises the contradiction and sometimes even accepts that he is wrong. In Part Two it becomes harder to distinguish reality from fantasy. While some of the people he meets in Part One quickly tumble to his lunacy and exploit it to their own ends, in the second part, everyone is in on the act – even Sancho dupes his master. In one scene he and Don Quixote have arrived at El Toboso, looking for Dulcinea's house. Quixote waits outside the town and sends Sancho to look for Dulcinea, a preposterous mission since both of them know that she does not exist in the form he has described her.

Sancho sits alone and ponders the absurdity of his position. 'I am going to look, as you might say, for nothing.' He rationalises Don Quixote's madness as the kind that always mistakes one thing for another, black for white, sheep for soldiers, windmills for giants. Why not, therefore, play to Quixote's madness by substituting the first peasant girl who comes down the road for Dulcinea? When three suitable candidates approach, riding donkeys, Sancho runs back to Quixote to tell him that he has found Dulcinea, who is on her way with two serving maidens. Quixote is excited by the news, then flummoxed when he sees the peasant girls. Where are Dulcinea and her retinue?

'Can it be that your worship has eyes in the back of your head that you don't see that these are they, coming along shining like the very sun at noon?' asks Sancho.

'I can see nothing, Sancho,' said Don Quixote, 'but three village girls on three donkeys.'

Sancho persuades Quixote to address 'Dulcinea' in courtly language, which merely earns him an earful of abuse and finally the girls go on their way. Afterwards the knight is particularly miserable – why has he been singled out for punishment by the enchanters who allow Sancho to see Dulcinea's beauty? He quizzes Sancho for details of her appearance. The squire obliges, describing Dulcinea's beauty as 'enhanced and perfected by a mole she had on her right lip, like a moustache, with seven or eight red hairs like threads of gold more than nine inches long.'

One might expect Don Quixote to fall gratefully on this information about the woman he loves. Instead, he queries it. 'Hairs of the length you indicate are very long for moles,' he tells Sancho. Nor does he believe that Dulcinea's eyes could have looked like pearls. 'Eyes like pearls suit a sea-bream better than a lady. According to my belief, Dulcinea's eyes must be green emeralds, full and large, with twin rainbows to serve for eyebrows. So take these pearls from her eyes and transfer them to her teeth, for no doubt you got mixed up, Sancho, taking her teeth for her eyes.'

The fact that Quixote is bold enough to contradict Sancho's description and even to amend it, shows, again, how he controls the illusion of Dulcinea. Here, we begin to see how Sancho and Quixote connive at creating an unreal world for themselves. As the novel proceeds, they increasingly work together in this way.

∾ ∾ ∾

Cervantes reflected the real-life success of his first volume by having it play an important role in the second. Don Quixote and Sancho hear about the book's publication, and are pleased to know that their exploits have been recorded (Quixote always suspected that a friendly sage was keeping track of them). They also get wind of Avellaneda's scurrilous plagiarism and meet one of its principal characters, Don Alvaro Tarfe. When Quixote finds a copy of the apochryphal sequel in his hands, he leafs through it with great restraint, merely pointing out a few inaccuracies. But after a cheerful evening together, the knight persuades Don Alvaro to sign an affidavit to the effect that he, not Avellaneda's creation, is the true Quixote.

In Part Two, Quixote and Sancho come across people who know them, having read the best-selling Part One. None are as cruelly exploitative of Quixote as the Duke and Duchess in whose castle he and Sancho stay several nights. This aristocratic pair orchestrate a number of elaborate pranks, including a mock inquisition, in which Quixote is made to wear a cape painted with flames. Unknown to them, the staff also plan and carry out 'jokes' of their own.

One night, as Quixote is undressing, about two dozen stiches burst on his stocking. Upset about his ruined hosiery, hot and unable to sleep, he opens a window on to the beautiful garden and hears two women apparently discussing the love that one of them, Altisidora, feels for Don Quixote. The knight is immediately thrown into a quandary. The young woman is very attractive and Quixote 'trembled at the thought that he might yield, but resolved in his mind not to let himself be conquered'. He sneezes, anyway, to let them know that he is there and Altisidora takes this cue to sing an absurd love ballad, in which she reveals, among other things, that she is fourteen and walks without a limp. She makes a romantic proposal:

> 'Oh, that I were in thy arms,
> Or, if not, beside thy bed,
> That I might but scratch thy head
> And of dandruff rid thy hair.'

Don Quixote goes to sleep perplexed by thoughts of Altisidora – 'like fleas, they would not let him sleep or rest for a moment, but mingled in his brain with thoughts of his torn stockings.' The next day, our knight asks for a lute to be put in his room, so that he can soothe Altisidora and that evening, with almost all the people in the castle secretly listening and stifling giggles, he sings a return ballad about his need to be faithful to Dulcinea. While he is singing, however, a rope with a hundred sheep bells attached to it and a sack full of cats are thrown in through the window. The din and chaos are so tremendous that Don Quixote is 'dumbfounded with fear'. Thinking that a gang of sorcerers is trying to attack him, he draws his sword and makes stabs at the window. He succeeds in chasing all the cats away apart from one which jumps at his face, digging its claws and teeth into his nose, 'whereupon Don Quixote began to roar his very loudest in pain'.

The Duke and Duchess, regretting their joke, rush to his room, but Quixote refuses all help: 'Leave me to deal with this devil, this wizard, this enchanter hand to hand. For I will teach him myself what it is to deal with Don Quixote de La Mancha.' Finally the Duke intervenes, to the knight's annoyance, and Altisidora tends to his wounds, with more provocative comments about adoring him. The Duke and Duchess go away feeling guilty about their prank. Don Quixote takes five days to recover from his bewilderment and his fear of the enchanters.

It is terrible to picture Don Quixote, alone in his room, his torn tights lying crumpled in the corner, his nose throbbing and his heart confused. Nabokov can draw only one conclusion: 'Back to the torture house'.

But is Quixote ever long out of the torture house? Writers are divided on the question. Thomas Mann, troubled by Cervantes' intemperate cruelty, wonders if it reflects a kind of self-hatred on the part of the author. 'He gets endless beatings . . . And yet his creator loves and honours him. Does not all this cruelty look like self-flagellation, self-revilement, castigation?'

'Yes, Don Quixote is laughable', admitted Ivan Turgenev, at the end of the nineteenth century. 'But our laughter has in it a conciliatory balm, a quality that makes amends.'

For Michel Foucault, the humour is in keeping with its period, but readers have changed too much in the interim to appreciate it properly. 'It is incongruous, even indecent, to make fun of a madman, as our ancestors loved to do; and we perceive as tragic the loneliness of the hero that Cervantes shows us misunderstood by everyone.'

Milan Kundera, on the other hand, believes that the humour in Don Quixote does not spring from its cruelty: 'We laugh not because someone is ridiculed, mocked or even humiliated, but because suddenly the world shows itself in its ambiguity, things lose their apparent meaning, people are revealed to be different from what they themselves thought they were.'

The revolutionary and Arturo shared a flat with two other Peruvians. One of them was the son of a right-wing MP who took a merciless ribbing from the others. Lucho was so slight that it was a wonder he had sufficient muscle even to keep himself upright, let alone to propel himself to the university and back every day. The other was a large, hairy man, with startlingly blue eyes, called Julio. His nickname was 'El Mago', which means magician, or enchanter, because he seemed to have strange powers. For instance he could make things levitate. Carmen and I were at the flat once when he put this power to the test. One person sat in a chair while four others, Julio included, held it with their fingertips. He made us close our eyes and concentrate our energies on to the chair, and it really did lift and hover in the air. A sceptical friend of mine said this must just be an illusion, really we were lifting the chair with more strength than we realised. But I had taken turns both as levitator and levitatee. I knew the feeling as the chair lifted, wavering off the ground and I was convinced that it was not an illusion. I did not believe in magic, exactly, but I thought that Julio had some sort of power.

One day he decided to lead the others in a trick on the hapless right-wing flatmate. Someone had got hold of a blonde wig and, while Lucho was at a lecture, they arranged it on the pillow of his bed. A body was improvised out of cushions, under the bedding and the blind lowered. When Lucho returned from university Julio met him in the hallway and told him about the blonde girl lying in his bed. She was a distant relation who had arrived from Peru, but she was very tired and needed to sleep off the jet lag. Lucho was soon beside himself with excitement. What did she look like? They told him she was very pretty, and opening the door a crack, he saw the blonde hair cascading on the pillow, the curvaceous body imaginable under the covers. Lucho waited excitedly in the sitting-room trying to concentrate on revising for the exam he had in a few days' time; it had been years since he had had a girlfriend, if indeed he had ever had one at all. Before she had gone to sleep, the others told him, she had mentioned that she was very much looking forward to getting to know Lucho.

By night-time, the mysterious cousin had still not woken, so he slept on the sofa in the sitting-room. The next morning, when she was still alseep, Lucho began to be worried, but he went to his lectures as usual, persuaded that the blonde might just be unusually tired after her trip. When he came home that night, and she was *still* in his bed, and seemed not to have moved, Lucho became hysterical with worry. This relative, whom he did not even know, had come all the way to Europe and died in his bed. He started ranting at Arturo and the revolutionary, both of whom were in on the joke. The police would have to be called and he would be held responsible for her death, he might go to prison and his life and career prospects would be ruined. Julio tried to calm him down, suggesting that they attempt to rouse the girl. Lucho, crying, and sweating, did not dare, but finally he was persuaded to venture into the room. Julio led him by the hand towards the bed, Lucho at each step crying and shaking. They approached the bed, pulled back the covers and Lucho discovered the illusion. His face, the revolutionary told me afterwards, changed colour several times as shock, relief and rage registered on it. It would have been fair enough never to forgive his flatmates, but Lucho wanted to go further. 'When I am president of Peru,' he warned them, 'I'll have you all slung in gaol for this.' It was no idle threat: with his connections, Lucho probably would be president of Peru one day. 'We'll have toppled you before you get a chance,' countered the revolutionary.

~ ~ ~

The revolutionary was an excellent, amorous dancer. Unfortunately, he was amorous with everyone, not just with me. To watch him partner a succession of besotted women was a torment. One weekend, at the salsa bar, I matched each new partner with a Cuba Libre and got drunk enough to be taken home by taxi. I leant back in the car and let the lights of the bars and cafés we passed blur into neon streakers. The revolutionary gave instructions and the driver, curious about his accent, asked where we were from. The revolutionary explained that he was from Peru, and that I was English.

'Well now, there's a combination,' said the driver. 'What brings you both to Spain?'

'We're students at the university,' said the revolutionary, but I leaned forward and enunciated with inebriate care: 'He's waiting for a revolution.'

'A revelation did you say?' asked the driver.

'A revolution,' I said, 're-vo-*lu*-tion.' I felt a bubble of hilarity rising in my throat.

'I was going to say,' the driver said. 'I mean, if you're waiting for a revelation, well, you could be waiting a bloody long time.'

CHAPTER NINE
A Question of Faith

Five boys, about eight years old, sat in the row in front of me. One of them was dark skinned and looked Moroccan. All banged their legs against their chairs in a fashionably bored way. I thought I could tell which of the boys had started the exercise: there was a confidence about one of them that marked him out as a group-leader. The North African boy's leg-banging, on the other hand, looked imitative, desirous of fitting in.

I was in Madrid, at a non-stop reading of *Don Quixote* to mark the anniversary of Cervantes' death. The reading was expected to take about forty-eight hours. Celebrated writers, politicians, trade unionists, actors, singers and at least one South-American president were taking part. A number of live link-ups to other countries had been arranged, including one to a ship at sail on the Adriatic Ocean. The Confederation of Deaf People would be contributing, in sign language. Prisoners would read live from their gaols.

The pregnancy hormones must have been getting to me again: I found the celebratory coming together of all these groups, especially the last two, absurdly moving. Prisoners are supposed to feel a natural affection for Don Quixote, if not because Cervantes was on various occasions imprisoned, then because he seems not to judge the various villains he depicts. In one chapter, Don Quixote and Sancho come across a group of slaves who are being taken in a chain gang to work on the galleys. One is an old man with a bladder complaint, had up for procuring. 'All I wanted was for everyone to have a good time and live in peace and quiet.' Another is a Latin scholar, there for 'having too much fun with two girl cousins of mine, and two other cousins who were not mine'. The most malevolent among them is Ginés del Pasamonte, a thirty-year-old with a squint who has committed so many crimes that he has to be heavily shackled.

Don Quixote is appalled by the men's plight. 'What! Men forced? Is it possible that the King uses force on anyone?' Sancho's argument that the king has a duty to mete out justice holds no sway. Quixote attacks the sergeant and the prisoners break the chain. Quixote commands the newly freed men to set off for El Toboso, where they can pay tribute to Dulcinea, but Ginés argues that this is impractical – why not substitute a few Hail Marys which they can handily do on the run? Quixote is enraged by this insolent suggestion but worse is to come: on Ginés's wink the others stone and strip him and Sancho.

Readers have debated whether Quixote's freeing of the slaves is an act of justice, or plain stupidity. For Unamuno, Quixote is a kind of Messiah, enacting the will of God and therefore beyond reproach. Virginia Woolf thinks the scene very sad, but is troubled by Cervantes' motivation: 'Did C. feel the whole of the beauty & sadness of that as I feel it?' Borges sees in the knight's defiance the great strength and weakness of the Hispanic character: Spaniards and South Americans would rather show solidarity with a fellow, he says, than respect an authority. Byron takes the romantic view that Quixote's aim is noble, but doomed:

I should be very willing to redress
Men's wrongs, and rather check than punish crimes,
Had not Cervantes in that too true tale
Of Quixote, shown how all such efforts fail.

Presidents, criminals, the deaf and the blind: All in, it was going to take some 2,500 people to read both parts of *Don Quixote* all the way through. When I arrived on the second morning, the reading had been going on for more than twenty-four hours and the readers were making a start on the second part of the novel. The opening pages show the priest and barber going to visit Don Quixote a few months after he has been returned to his village in a cage. They are relieved to find that he is much improved from his delusions and the three engage in a conversation about the issues of the day. It is only when Quixote suggests that the king could see off the Turkish threat by convening all the country's knight errants that his friends realise he is not quite 'cured'.

Dignatories and celebrities having started the reading, it was now the turn of Madrid's schoolchildren and there was chaos in the ballroom of the Centre for Fine Arts. As one school finished, its pupils' crashing exodus clashed with another school's crashing arrival. Every seat was full and more people continuously pressed through the doors. No nation is worse at queuing than Spain. At bus stops the aim is always to get on first, whatever obstacles may be in the way, and the same principle applied here. I heard one of the teachers reprimand her students for not pushing harder. 'If we could keep everyone else out, we'd have a better chance of getting in ourselves.'

Inside the hall bright lights doused the audience, making them camera-ready. The presence of all the television aparatus fed the children's exuberance, and those who approached the podium were much less interested in what they were reading than in how they might read it. Some tried to put on funny voices, others were almost tongue-tied with nerves. On the stage was a long table at which various people sat looking officious. A woman, smoking, controlled the length of each reading by cutting it off with a curt 'Muchas gracias'. She was either incompetent, bribed or biased, because some patently bad readers were allowed double the length of other, better ones. Many of the teenagers wore expressions of studied boredom. One chewed gum. One peeped flirtatiously through tendrils of hair. A very pretty teacher drew a chorus of wolf whistles. Reader 314 came to the podium on the mobile phone, broke off his conversation to read a few paragraphs, then cheekily continued it as he walked back to his seat. Reader 315 tackled the scene at the beginning of Part Two, in which Don Quixote and Sancho discover that a book – that is, Cervantes' Part One – has been published about their exploits, and that they have been made famous. From now on, the characters they meet will recognise them as literary heroes. People will marvel at the fact that they are not fictions, but real, flesh and blood. Don Quixote and Sancho will often find themselves drawing attention to their true existence, as opposed to other literary representations. In a post-modern twist, they will refuse to be taken for mere fictional characters. Number 315 read:

'Don Quixote was very thoughtful as he waited for the Bachelor Carrasco, from whom he expected to hear how he had been put into a book, as Sancho had told him. He could not persuade himself that such a history existed, for the blood of the enemies he had slain was scarcely dry on his own sword-blade. Yet they would have it that his noble deeds of chivalry were already about in print.'

'Muchas gracias.'

Number 316, a tall, nervous girl, read on: 'Nevertheless he imagined that some sage, either friendly or hostile, had given them to the Press by magic art; if a friend, to magnify and extol them above the most renowned actions of any knight errant; and if an enemy, to annihilate them and place them below the basest ever written of any mean squire – although, he admitted to himself, the deeds of squires were never written of. But if it were true that there was such a history, since it was about a knight errant it must perforce be grandiloquent, lofty, remarkable, magnificent and true.'

'*Muchas gracias.*'

'With this he was somewhat consoled,' said 317, who was short with surprisingly bushy eyebrows. 'But it disturbed him to think that its author was a Moor, as that name of Cide suggested. For he could hope for no truth of the Moors, since they are all cheats, forgers and schemers.'

'*Muchas gracias.*'

'He was afraid too that his love affairs might have been treated with indelicacy,' offered 318, 'which would redound to the disparagement and prejudice of his lady, Dulcinea del Toboso. For he was anxious that it should be declared that he had always preserved his fidelity and reverence towards her, scorning Queens, Empresses, and damsels of all qualities, and curbing the violence of his natural appetites.'

'*Muchas gracias.*'

I wondered if the little Moroccan boy had noticed the reference to Moors, and what he made of it. Observations about the untrustworthiness of Moors, of the kind made by Cervantes' narrator were still commonly heard in 1990s Spain. In fact anti-Moroccan feeling was on the rise, in response to growing immigration. There had recently been a rash of violent, unprovoked attacks on Muslims and in the fruit-growing areas around Valencia, tension among the poorly paid immigrant workers was running high. Graffiti on the city walls and in the metro trains was blunt: 'No Moors'.

Undeterred, thousands of Africans tried to cross the straits of Gibraltar every year. Many were Moroccans, but some had made their way on foot from sub-Saharan Africa. Crossing the straits in *pateras* – flimsy vessels that were liable to capsize – many of them died in the attempt. In Tenerife, where they often arrived at night, the morning patrols found their drenched clothes lying on the beaches. As soon as they made land, they changed into dry clothes, hoping to blend in while they organised forged documents to carry on northwards. Their destination was not necessarily Spain but 'Europe': Britain, Germany or France.

Not so long ago, Spain might have been regarded merely as a place to travel through on the way to rich countries – some Africans knew nothing of the country itself, because there were so few immigrants there to send news back. These days Spain itself was rich enough to stay in. There were 200,000 legal African residents in Spain, and maybe another 100,000 illegal ones, but the Spanish government had recently announced that another million would be arriving over the next three years. Even so, it would be twenty years before this became a properly multi-racial country. Would Spain be able to become once more a country where different races and religions worked harmoniously together?

'We want to integrate into this society, while maintaining our own culture,' a spokesman from a Moroccan organisation told the national newspaper *El País*. 'Public opinion must know that some things are not negotiable, such as the attempt to convert Muslims to other religions.'

'Is Spain ready to meet this challenge?' asked *El País*. 'Has the xenophobic gene that provoked the expulsion of the Moors five hundred years ago been purged from the Spanish system? . . . Are we racists?'

Spain, at the end of the sixteenth century, was preoccupied not so much with race as with religion, and specifically the fear that Lutheran Protestantism might take root in the peninsula. The century since Columbus first set foot on South American soil had been one of extraordinary endeavour. Thanks to the successes of the conquistadores, the Spanish empire was the greatest in the world. Spain itself was a vital centre for learning and debate.

Encouraged by the New World's apparently inexhaustible supply of silver, Philip II embarked on ever more ambitious enterprises, such as the sending of an 'Invincible' Armada to England. But the wealth was illusory. Only a quarter of Philip's revenue originated in Latin America. The rest was borrowed from foreign bankers, or collected in ever higher taxes by bureaucrats like Cervantes. By the end of Philip II's reign, Spain's debt was eight times as high as its annual income.

Beset by financial worries, Philip II overreacted to the discovery, in 1558, of Protestant groups in Valladolid and Seville. The Inquisition had reckoned Spain to be safe from northern Europe's 'heresy' – now suspicion fell on the popularity of Erasmus among Spanish intellectuals. His doctrines were not technically heretical and he had many followers at court and in the Church. However, the Erasmian emphasis on inward aspects of religion, at the expense of its outward expression, began to look uncomfortably close to the ideas of Luther and other Protestant sects.

Erasmus also seemed to highlight the difference between those two groups – the 'two Spains' – that would wrangle over the country's destiny for centuries to come, right up to the outbreak of the Civil War. While his followers welcomed the flow of ideas from Renaissance Europe, his detractors saw them as anti-Catholic and anti-Spanish. The first group wanted to open Spain to ideas from abroad, the second was inclined to hunker down in memories of the glorious past. On this occasion the second group won, by successfully tarnishing Erasmus with heresy. By the time Cervantes was born, there were few of his followers left in Spain.

Under the rule of Philip II, the climate of suspicion that had led to the expulsion of the Jews, flourished once more. Foreign study was banned. The Inquisition's Index of prohibited books was widened to take in most of the great Europeans writers, including Dante, Rabelais and Machiavelli. Spain was still much more racially diverse than its European neighbours and that diversity, which had so enriched the country, came once more to be perceived as a threat.

Christians had hitherto been largely sympathetic to the population of Muslims and of Islamic converts to Catholicism, called Moriscos, living among them. One Christian archbishop even encouraged Moriscos in his congregation to sing Arabic hymns at mass. But undoubtedly some Spaniards were irritated by the Muslims' lifestyle: they would not eat pork, the most common meat in Spain, and lived apart in separate communities. Even habits such as sitting on the ground and eating couscous were seen to be provocative. In 1567 Philip II prohibited all Muslim customs – 'above all that most un-Christian, most peculiar oddity of taking a daily bath' – provoking a revolt in Granada that lasted two years. The ferocity of the conflict swung public opinion against the Moriscos and accordingly the Inquisition stepped in to repress 'crimes of Islam'. In 1605, the year the first part of *Don Quixote* was published, the number of Moriscos burned at the stake rose dramatically.

In 1606, a courtier called Pedro de Valencia submitted to Philip III his report on the problem, 'A Treaty on the Spanish Moriscos'. Valencia had a reputation as a humanist and a classics scholar. He had already made a study of mental illness and written critically about the Inquisition, whose method of trying witches in public he thought risked corrupting normal women. 'If they find out that there are ways of flying, of becoming invisible, or being prostitutes or enchanters of their enemies . . . they'll think that fornication, adultery and any other kind of sin is child's play by comparison.'

Valencia's treaty on the Spanish Moriscos is a sympathetic document about a community he accepted was not foreign, but Spanish 'given that they have lived here for nearly 900 years'. Valencia agreed – expediently perhaps – that the Moriscos were only interested in 'lying to us, cheating us, robbing us and killing us, in whatever way they can', but he also suggested that such an attitude was not surprising, given that these people lived in fear of being tortured and executed at the hands of the Inquisitors, or at the very least of losing all their property.

His study of the Moriscos' way of life showed that there was much to admire. Christians, though 'loving, trustworthy and well-meaning', were also lazy and vain, devoting themselves to 'begging, or gambling, or hunting and other pleasurable pastimes'. Moriscos, on the other hand, were hard-working, serious, abstemious and physically fit. Valencia thought that they were also more resistant to extremes of temperature, fatigue and hunger.

All this was part of the problem, for then, as now, Spain was worried about a declining birthrate. What if the hard-working, fast-breeding Moriscos threatened the socio-political balance of the country?

Even more worrying was the prospect of Moriscos becoming agents of the Turkish Empire. Spain had been victorious at Lepanto in 1571, but the Turks were still a threat, the greatest threat of all, as far as Pedro de Valencia was concerned. 'There are not ten, nor a hundred, nor a thousand, nor a hundred thousand but many more spies and soldiers of the Empire and faith of the Ishmaelites at work in Spain.' In spite of his admiration for the Moriscos, Valencia could reach only one conclusion: 'It isn't possible for us to live safely with them.'

Valencia's document discussed various solutions to the problem: genocide he deemed too cruel; slavery, dangerous because of the risk of an uprising; expulsion, particularly hard on children and impractical because no other European country would want to take in such a large number of poor and bellicose migrants; seclusion in ghettoes, unworkable; castration, cruel. Valencia's preferred solution was for the Moriscos to be dispersed around Spain and integrated into Christian communities.

In the event, Philip III chose one of the crueller, though not the cruellest of Valencia's options: mass expulsion. In 1609, 300,000 Moriscos were ordered to leave Spain.

Six years later, Cervantes registered a protest. In Part Two of *Don Quixote*, Sancho runs into Ricote the Moor, his village shopkeeper before the expulsion. Ricote has smuggled himself back into Spain to look for some buried treasure he was forced to leave behind. They have a meal together and Ricote talks about the 'terror and dismay' provoked by the expulsion of Moors. Cervantes plays the scene cautiously, with Ricote demonstrating an improbable respect for Philip III's decision. 'It was with good reason that all of us were punished with exile,' says Ricote, but 'wherever we are we weep for Spain.'

~ ~ ~

If all Muslims were, as Pedro de Valencia put it, liars and cheats, why did Cervantes choose to have the story of Don Quixote filtered through not one, but two Muslims? The answer has to do, again, with the value and interpretation of truth.

The narrator of Don Quixote's first eight chapters is, ostensibly, Cervantes himself. He claims to have discovered an anonymous text about Don Quixote's adventures in some archive in La Mancha. Unfortunately the chronicle ends at chapter eight, right in the middle of a scene in which Don Quixote is fighting a Basque. The two are actually frozen mid-jump, leaving the reader on tenterhooks.

Cervantes has been unable to discover anything else about Don Quixote's exploits, but convinced that there must be more, he turns detective and heads for the great book market at Toledo. He does not have to hunt for long: at one stall he finds a lad selling a bundle of parchment papers covered in Arabic script. On the first page of the manuscript there is an illustration of the pose we have left Don Quixote and the Basque striking in chapter eight. 'Both were shown in the very postures the story describes, with swords aloft, the one covered by his shield, the other by his cushion, and the Basque's mule so life-like that you could tell from a mile off that it was a hired one.'

'Mark how neatly', says Nabokov, 'the description of the attitudes in which they froze at the breaking point is now made into a picture. Whereupon the story is picked up again, the picture becomes alive, the fight goes on – like those movies of football games stopping and then again coming into motion.'

Arabic speakers were ten a penny in Toledo in those days and Cervantes easily finds a Morisco interpreter to cast an eye over the manuscript. When the boy laughs at a note in the margin, a joke about Dulcinea's pork-salting skills, Cervantes knows that he has found his quarry. What he has in his hands is the continuation of the story of Don Quixote, written by an Arab historian called Cide Hamete Benengeli. He buys the manuscript and goes with the interpreter to the cloister of the cathedral where he strikes a deal for the translation – fifty pounds of raisins and three bushels of wheat. Then the two go to Cervantes' house, where the interpreter takes six weeks to translate the manuscript.

Don Quixote will now be a story told by an Arab and translated by a Morisco, a convert. Cervantes also remains in the frame, to comment, either disparagingly or admiringly, on the narration. If the novel is about the difficulty of separating truth and illusion, Cervantes complicates things by placing his story with this new 'untrustworthy' team of narrator and translator. Cide Hamete Benengeli is apt to cry out to Allah when he cannot believe Quixote's antics. Just as Cervantes was not sure where Quixote was born or what his real name was, Benengeli is taken to task for a failure to be precise about details such as the type of tree under which Quixote and Sancho fall asleep. Sometimes Cervantes excoriates him as a 'liar and a hound', other times praising him as 'a flower among historians'. Where once there was one unreliable, middle-aged narrator, now there are two: a Catholic and a Muslim.

I took a new, fast train from Madrid to Toledo, packed with tourists on their way to see El Greco's house, the synagogues and the other treasures of Spain's erstwhile capital. On the way, we ran alongside fields of sunflowers that caused the passengers to marvel and swivel their heads in unison. One or two reached, belatedly, for their cameras.

Sitting across the gangway from me was one of those ubiquitous travelling nuns, looking strangely out of place in the modern train. Opposite her sat a northern European woman with her young son. The woman was wearing a backpacker's garb: a pair of cotton shorts, a sleeveless T-shirt and easy rubber sandals on her feet, whereas the nun was entirely covered, from wimple to leather shoes. The tourist was tall and large. Her flesh moved lazily to the rhythm of the train, her thighs rolling on the seat. The nun was contained, and almost motionless beneath the folds of her habit. Every so often these incongruous travelling companions exchanged a polite smile. Finally the nun produced, from the depths of her shoulder bag, a sweet for the little boy. His face lit up at the offering but as he sucked it disappointment quickly set in. Having known similar disappointments in Spain, I guessed that the flavour was aniseed. The boy held the sweet in his cheek, and tried to ignore it there, but it was too revolting. Finally his tongue protruded with the sweet stuck on its end, whereupon his mother plucked it off his tongue and popped it straight into her own mouth. She smiled a cheerful apology at the nun, who had watched the exchange with bemusement. I wondered if she envied what she saw: the exposed flesh, the intimacy of motherhood.

The Plaza de Zocódover, the marketplace in Toledo, was nothing like it must have been in Cervantes' time. There were no stalls groaning under manuscripts, no sign of Arabic traders or translators. There was, however, a fast-food outlet. I joined the queue behind four American teenagers whose sweatshirts proclaimed that they were on a mission to spread the word of God. Each one of them wore a name-tag: 'Brother Pete', or 'Sister Tracey', as if the donning of a sweatshirt and a badge were an acceptable short-cut to becoming a nun or monk. They were evangelists, come from the New World to rescue the teenagers of the old one. All of them looked tired, as if the promotion of God were proving to be hard work. They might have come to McDonald's to look for converts among the teenagers or, more likely, they were looking for the restorative properties of a quarter-pounder and fries.

I asked for a double cheeseburger and an ice-cream.

'We don't have any ice-cream,' said the girl. 'The machine's broken.'

'Just a double cheeseburger, then.'

'What about the ice-cream?'

'I thought you said you didn't have any?'

A look of very distant understanding drifted across the girl's face. She realised that there had been a failure in our communication, but decided to attribute it to me, rather than to herself. 'You don't want one then?' she asked, with just a little exasperation.

'I suppose not.'

I ate the cheeseburger at a table overlooking the Plaza de Zocódover. *Zoco* is the Arabic word for marketplace. The Moors arrived in Toledo in 712. For the next three centuries, under Muslim rule, Toledo was a vital trade centre and home to a thriving mix of three cultures, Jewish, Muslim and Mozarabics (Christians living under Moorish rule). After the city was captured by Christians in 1085 – with the help of El Cid – the tolerant commingling continued and its new ruler, Alfonso VI of Castile, even styled himself 'Emperor of the Three Religions'. At one time there were seven synagogues, of which two still survive. At the

School of Translators, founded in the twelfth century, scholars made invaluable contributions to European culture with their translations of Arab philosophical and scientific treatises.

In Cervantes' time, when Toledo was still the seat of the monarchy, the Plaza de Zocódover was the hub of the empire – justice was administered, kings were proclaimed here. The monarchy's move to Madrid in 1560 saw Toledo start to decline. Four hundred years later, the city that had been home to some of Europe's greatest minds had one of its most shocking illiteracy rates.

The streets of Toledo hold the memory of Moors, Jews and Christians, but they also belong to the fresher ghosts of Republicans and Nationalists. It was in the formidable Alcázar fortress, the Spanish infantry officers' school, that 1,300 Nationalists lived under siege from Republicans for seventy days. Though the walls of the fortress were almost destroyed around them, they held out in subterranean chambers, eating their horses, when other provisions ran out. One woman even gave birth there. The siege at the Alcázar took on such a symbolic value for Nationalists that in September 1936 Franco made a diversion from his march towards Madrid to liberate the captives – crucially giving Republicans enough time to prepare for the capital's defence. Ironically, in the city that had once been Muslim, it is said that the besieged Nationalists knew they were saved when they heard Franco's Moroccan troops speaking Arabic outside the walls. The massacre that followed the liberation was terrible. No prisoners were taken and, in retaliation for the murder of two Nationalist airmen, Franco famously made the city's main street run with blood.

In the shadow of the Alcázar I found an old people's day centre and asked a helper if there was any veteran who might tell me what it had been like to live in Toledo at that time. To my embarrassment she interrupted a game of pool with a cheerful invitation to 'chat about our Civil War'.

'There's nothing to say,' said one man angrily. 'We were all fighting one another,' he motioned at three other men at the pool table. 'We never talk about it now.'

'I spent the whole bloody thing in a trench,' muttered one of the others.

As I was making my way to the exit feeling foolish, another veteran caught my eye and beckoned me to the seat beside him. Barely had I sat down when he started whispering to me.

'My father and I had gone to hide among the rocks outside the town, but I got caught and I had to enlist with the Nationalists. My brother and I ended up on different sides just because of that. It was terrible, because we loved each other and neither of us knew what we were fighting about anyway. We were never interested in politics. Then I was wounded in the chest and I was taken off duty.'

'What about after the war?'

'We were the closest of friends for another fifty years, until he died. I still have a war pension for the injury,' he said, patting his chest proudly. He was in his eighties, but for a moment I could picture him as a frightened young man, quaking behind one of the giant boulders that dot the hills outside Toledo.

〜〜〜

Toledo's cathedral is huge, yet somehow elusive. You can get lost looking for it, then drop down an alleyway to buy a marzipan and suddenly find one of its great façades staring you down. Spanish cathedrals are often this surreptitious: they crouch in the centre of a web of streets, suddenly to surprise the unsuspecting sinner with their massive proximity. Close to the cathedral I bought a postcard which depicted the crucified Christ in three dimensions. If I held the card one way, Christ gazed imploringly heavenwards. By tilting it, I could make his head suddenly swing downwards, his eyes closing in a grimace of despair – an agonised hokey-kokey.

Inside, the air of the cathedral was heavy with history. A plaque boasted about the expulsion of the Jews. The mozarabic mass – the Latin rite used by Christians living under Muslim rule in Toledo a thousand years ago – is still celebrated here every morning in a tiny chapel decorated with scenes from the victory of Queen Isabella and King Ferdinand over the Moors at Granada. This was probably not the mass attended by the Virgin Mary, who is said to have made a lightning visit to the cathedral in 1658, accompanied by a celestial choir. The room is very small and on the day I went there were only three of us in the congregation. A celestial choir would not be easily accommodated.

Toledo's archbishops, Spain's primates, were once second only to the monarch in authority. Tomás de Torquemada, a Jewish *converso*, was the first Inquisitor-General, appointed here by Ferdinand and Isabella in 1483. He presided over the bloodiest years of the Inquisition, when 2,000 people – most of them *conversos*, like him – were burned alive and 17,000 mutilated. His successor, Cardinal Ximénez de Cisneros, founded the University of Alcalá in 1506 and sponsored work on the first Polyglot Bible. It was Cardinal Martínez de Guijarro who introduced, in 1547, the Purity of Blood Statute, the first step to making freedom from Jewish blood a prerequisite for holding important office. The Inquisition issued the necessary certificates. Cervantes had to obtain at least fifteen of them during his lifetime.

'The Inquisition was not as bad as it has been painted,' an unfriendly priest told me in a dark ante room close to the main altar. 'Religious conflicts have been common all over the world, not just in Spain, and other countries were also driven to take drastic measures. You have to set the events in their context.'

'But Spain had previously been notable for its tolerance. It's hard to understand why the fear of *conversos* took root so quickly.'

'Spain is still tolerant,' said the priest, brusquely missing the point.

What he really wanted to talk about were the immoral, sensation-seeking ways of teenagers. He harped so tediously on the word 'sensation' that I had half a mind to strike back with it; I had heard that the Archbishop of Toledo was encouraging the viewing of an explicit anti-abortion video in local schools. Outraged parents had also complained that the video was 'sensationalist'.

Listening to this unattractive character rail against sinners, I could understand how so many Spaniards had felt oppressed by the Church, and its prurient interest in their private lives. My Toledan friend Juan María had told me about his sister who, going to make a confession for the first time, at the age of eleven, was stumped for sins. The priest tried to coax her with some ideas, but to no avail: she had been kind to her parents, good at school, could not recall any churlish thoughts. 'In the street,' probed the priest, 'do you ever look at men's laps?'

'No', said the little girl, intrigued. It had never occurred to her to look at men's laps before. As soon as she left the church, of course, she started looking at them.

At any rate, the priest was right about one thing: after Torquemada, the Inquisition was not as terrible an authority as has been portrayed in numerous gory narratives and engravings. It is likely that over three-quarters of all those who died under the Inquisition in the three centuries of its existence, did so in the late 1400s, when worry that the *conversos* were secretly still practising Jews and that their separate identity threatened Spanish security had reached fever-pitch.

Thereafter, Spain was not more ruthless with heretics than other European countries. The Inquisition did, however, encourage a spirit of denunciation and petty revenge: ordinary Spaniards, like private detectives, learned to look out for anyone who might be leading a double life. One man was denounced by a neighbour for eating bacon on a day of abstinence, and a woman was alleged to be a heretic because she had smiled at the name of the Virgin Mary.

The only line that the Spanish Inquisition made Cervantes remove from *Don Quixote* was about the value of public piety. 'Remember, Sancho, that works of charity which are performed feebly and half-heartedly have no merit and are worth nothing,' says the Duchess. This apparently innocuous line seemed to support Luther's doctrine of interior faith. On the other hand, Cervantes was able to write, without fear of censorship, a satirical chapter about the 'inquisition' held in Don Quixote's library, in which various chivalric books are denounced as heretics and sent away either to be burned or held under lock and key.

Back in the main body of the cathedral, in front of one of the altars, a smartly dressed, middle-aged woman was lying spread-eagled on the floor, drawing attention to her piety in a way that would have pleased Torquemada and horrified Luther. It was a controlled prostration: the woman's dress rode neatly above her knees, not a hair was out of place and she kept a firm grip on her handbag. Her shoes were smart, possibly Gucci. It would have been fascinating to know what, if anything, she was praying for.

~ ~ ~

In the Plaza de Zocódover there was a blind man selling lottery tickets. I asked him if he knew a native Toledan who would be willing to show me round the city. He directed me to the National Organisation for the Spanish Blind. ONCE was founded in 1938 to offer employment to the blind – who were much more numerous after the Civil War – as lottery ticket-sellers. In recent years it has become one of the country's most powerful institutions, providing a range of services, education and bursaries for its 40,000 members. Two-thirds of ONCE's members sell lottery tickets. Nowadays, some of them earn nearly twice the average national wage.

At ONCE's smart Toledo office I met Miren, a partially sighted young Basque woman who organised events for the members. Miren told me that she had myopia. 'I can see your hair and a blur where your face must be, but I can't make out any expressions.'

She said she would show me around Toledo with Valle, her 24-year-old flatmate. Valle had gone totally blind two years previously, as a result of diabetes. She had lived all her life in Toledo but when she went blind she had to get to know the city again, by feel and ear alone.

That evening, as we walked down the winding main street towards the cathedral, Valle explained how she distinguished streets by the different noise of traffic, the textures on the wall. She knew the bars and cafés by the various noises of their coffee machines, and the clatter the cups made on different surfaces. Smell, noise and touch were her guides. The worst enemies of the blind were the bollards that the council installed on pavements without warning. She called them *mataciegos* (literally 'blind-killers'). 'They put them everywhere for the sole purpose, I think, of catching us out.'

As we neared the cathedral cloister where Cervantes went to negotiate a fee with the Morisco translator of *Don Quixote*, Valle showed me how the texture of the stones in the wall changed and roughened. She described how the quality of sound changed, as we approached the large open area in front of the cathedral.

'Wherever I walk in Toledo, I feel its medieval past,' said Valle. 'Making your way down one of its alleys on a cold night, you can imagine some knight with a sword and cape stepping out of the shadows. This city is drenched in history.'

'The streets are so narrow you have to squeeze into the doorways to let cars pass, and there are so many alleys, it's like a labyrinth,' said Miren. 'If you're blind, it's easy to get lost.'

Miren and Valle wanted me to experience the city 'blind'. They had brought a folding white stick and led me to a narrow street in which to practise.

'Don't cheat', said Valle and I closed my eyes and started to feel my way along the path with the stick. I could hear our voices reverberate – as the alley became more narrow, as if it were actually closing over our heads, but when I tried to touch the walls on either side – inexplicably – there was nothing there.

'Rely on the stick,' said Miren.

It was in one of the labyrinthine alleys hereabouts that the Nationalists arriving with Franco had brought Republicans to be shot, though in other cities bullrings had been used for executions. It was possible to imagine the sound of gunfire ricocheting around these walls, the panicky departure of birds overhead. And while the story of blood running down Toledo's streets seemed melodramatic, here it would certainly be possible. The passages were narrow and steep.

'I'm always veering into the wall,' I said. It was terrible to think that what was an experiment for me, was for Valle a way of life.

'Tap the base of the wall with your stick, and you'll keep the right distance,' said Valle.

'I feel claustrophobic.'

'We're nearly there.'

We progressed slowly up the alley, the blind leading the blinded, until voices of young men could be heard at the other end. Their conversation was punctuated with laughter that sounded threatening, and, without the evidence of my eyes, I thought they might be jeering at us. Immediately abandoning my solidarity with Miren and Valle, I opened my eyes to get my bearings.

'You're doing well,' said Valle, and I was tempted to pretend that she was right.

'I've already opened my eyes,' I confessed to the other two. 'Sorry, I give in.'

After our experiment, we went for a drink and a sandwich at one of Toledo's bars. The girls mused over the handsomeness of the waiter, whom Valle could not see at all, though Miren could make out a blur she thought might be appealing. 'I'll go to the bar and get a closer look at him,' said Miren.

While we waited for her to glean this important information, I asked Valle what it had been like to lose her sight.

'It happened overnight. I had to learn everything again. I could have got very depressed about it, but I didn't see the point. How would it help?'

'Is there anything good about it?'

'I've met a lot of friends through ONCE, and there's always someone to go and have coffee with, but no gains I've made were worth the loss of my sight. If I could have it back tomorrow, I'd jump at the chance.'

We went on to another bar, where we were joined by Valle's cousin, Esther. This bar's owner had bought it as a near-derelict lot a few years back and when he started to strip the walls, he found intricate carvings and decoration, suggesting that it had once been the home of an important Moorish family living under Christian rule. The original artwork had now been preserved, though not, the owner sniffed, with any sort of grant. 'You don't get money for that sort of thing in Spain, just officials breathing down your neck.'

Friends of Miren and Valle were going to be putting on a display of belly dancing here. Soon after we arrived, in fact, the lights dimmed, music began and the dancers made their entrance. Two beautiful women took it in turns to undulate around the room, stopping to wiggle provocatively in front of some of the men. Valle, Miren and I stood together at one side of the area. The plan was that Miren would give Valle a myopic version of what was happening on the dance floor, and that I would fill in the details. We would be two narrators, unreliable in our different ways.

'The first dancer's wearing a silver shimmering material.' Miren nudged me: What does it look like?

'It's a sort of spangly bra, then gauzy veil. She looks very thin to be a belly dancer.'

'She's dancing around the room, waving her arms, Valle,' said Miren.

'She's making intricate movements with her hands and rippling her stomach,' I added, 'though to be frank, there's very little to ripple.'

The music and the surroundings rekindled for a few minutes the atmosphere of a prosperous household in Moorish Toledo, before the Christian reconquest. After the dancers had finished their performance, they moved among the tables greeting people they knew, but since their teacher was sitting with us, ours was the table at which they finally alighted. They told us about the years they had spent studying their art, including several months at a school in Cairo. One of the girls said that learning to dance had taught her about Spain's Arabic heritage.

'So few of us are in touch with that side of ourselves. It's something that's been hidden, suppressed.'

In fact, more and more Spaniards were rediscovering their Arabic heritage. Franco's insistence on Roman Catholicism had forbidden other religions to advertise their services or publish literature, but the constitution of 1978 gave Spaniards the unequivocal right to worship as they pleased. Since then, hundreds of Catholic-born Spaniards had converted to Islam. Madrid had a park named after its founder, Emir Mohammed, and a synagogue in which King Juan Carlos had attended a service of reconciliation on the 500th anniversary of the expulsion of the Jews.

Both the belly dancers were expansive, sentimental and breathlessly sympathetic towards Miren and Valle. 'It must be so hard to have reduced, I mean diminished, or rather *impaired* visibility,' said one, struggling to remember the politically correct term.

'It's all right – you can say "blind",' said Valle.

'We could come and do a display at ONCE,' suggested the other one. 'We could let the blind people touch our tiaras.' Around our table there was enthusiasm for the idea, but Valle said, 'I wouldn't risk it. That's not all they'd touch. There are some quite randy ones.'

Miren mentioned that I was pregnant and suddenly all attention switched from the dancers' bellies to mine.

'How wonderful!' cried one of them. 'I must feel it!'

I acceded with some embarrassment. After all, I had so much more of a belly than either of them.

It was about two o'clock in the morning when Valle suggested we drive to a vantage point outside the city from which all of Toledo could be seen, floodlit. The belly dancers were delighted with the idea and we all piled into the cousin's car and took off. Valle, the only one of us who could not see at all, gave her cousin precise instructions about the best way to reach a perfect look-out. She seemed to remember every boulder along the route and told us about legends that attached to the different landmarks, stories of Moorish princesses, of sorcerers and fantastic creatures.

Finally we all got out of the car and stood looking across at the city, bathed in light. On one side of it was the Alcázar fortress, a massive reminder of Franco's determination. Nearer the other side, the hidden cathedral sent a spire up towards God. Cranes were poised over many of the old buildings, evidence of the spirit of restoration that had gripped Spain.

The blind girls stood together, Valle listening attentively as Miren told her about any changes that had been made to the skyline. The belly dancers sighed, their tiaras glittering in the moonlight. 'It's so beautiful,' they said, 'it really is.'

And it really was.

It was three o'clock in the afternoon of a Spring day in 1988, and Madrid was at rest. Oil and onions, dictators to whom the city had been subjugated for the last hour or so, had been toppled by the pungent forces of grinding coffee beans. Heat buzzed in the air, like a note caught on a vibrating string, constant against the insubstantial din of television sets that emanated from dozens of darkened sitting rooms.

Alvaro had gone to have his coffee in the corner bar with an ex-army officer who claimed to know the magic combination of string-pulling necessary to release him from military service. Carmen, who was avoiding coffee for her skin's sake, was asleep on the sofa, a book of English irregular verbs tossed on to the floor beside her. The prostitutes were dozing, the transvestites were flicking through magazines. The *barrio* was quiet.

The revolutionary and I were lying on my bed, with the balcony doors open and the blind pulled down so that slits of light fell across the floor. The crack on the wall, which had been widening over the months, allowed a distant hubbub. We had not been to have lunch at the *casa de comidas* as a protest because Jesús, the waiter, had been fired for stealing. The communists believed he had not been paid enough; the anarchists thought the restaurant should be run as a collective. Someone joked about occupying the restaurant and turning it into a People's Canteen.

We had been reading, but the revolutionary had turned his back to me. I thought he was going to sleep, but suddenly he murmured, 'Perhaps you don't really love me.'

'I do love you!'

'Perhaps one day you'll decide to go off with someone else.'

'Of course I won't do that!' I put my arms around him, pleased by this display of vulnerability. Psychological adventurers, women want to reach a man's essence and stick a flag in it. Having arrived quite unexpectedly at that secret domain, I began to feel more confident of our relationship, now three months old. The revolutionary was still a flirt; it was true that he had told me about his political opposition to monogamy, but I had managed to forget that, or disregard it as a principle that appeared to mean nothing in practice, since he was always with me. I felt that we were happy together. Sometimes it crossed my mind that he might ask me to go with him to Peru. I had rehearsed the arguments for and against abandoning my studies and thought that I might, in the right circumstances, be persuaded to go.

So it was with a cheerful anticipation of the same warm affirmation I had given him that I replied: 'Perhaps one day *you'll* suddenly decide to go off with someone else.'

'I probably will,' conceded the revolutionary.

CHAPTER TEN

Is Burgos Boring?

In 1930 the writer and intellectual, Manuel Azaña, addressed a women's literary association in Madrid. His lecture purported to be about *Don Quixote*. Really it was about the failures of Spain. Azaña reminded the women of an incident, at the start of the book, when Don Quixote makes himself a cardboard visor. He strikes it with a sword and it immediately breaks. Distressed to see his handiwork so easily undone, Quixote makes another visor, and resolves not to test it this time. The lesson he has learned is not to reinforce his defences until they are trustworthy, but rather never to test them. Reality will not impinge on him if he refuses to let it come close. Quixote's visor, said Azaña, was like 'so many values in this country, ancient or modern, it looks prestigious, but it only survives on the understanding that it never be used'. At some point in the preceding centuries, Spaniards had lost their critical faculty, fooling themselves into believing in the unreal; they had become quixotic.

In the defeat and disillusionment of Quixote, said Azaña, it was possible to see the very failure of Spain, a country that had been in decline for four centuries. Cervantes had been 'crucified' on the cross of that decline. 'Although Cervantes believes in the value of life and tries to conceal the bitterness of his personal failure and that of the society that surrounds him, his cheerful expression cannot hide his melancholy. If the destiny of Spain had been otherwise, perhaps we would not be so aware of the sadness in Cervantes' spirit, but . . . history has borne out and consolidated all that Cervantes, as a Spaniard, felt beginning to happen around him. It has turned into a crucial problem what was then simply a matter of conscience.'

A year later, in 1931, Azaña himself had an unprecedented opportunity to address the crucial problem of Spain's failure. He became the prime minister of the second Spanish Republic. Save for one short-lived republican experiment in 1873–4, this was Spain's first chance of democracy and the auguries were good. There was a palpable desire for change in the country. The dictatorship of Primo de Rivera had ended bloodlessly; Alfonso XIII had taken himself off into exile. Anti-clerical feeling was strong, not just among the agricultural workers in the south – many of whom had joined anarchist organisations – but in the middle classes. Here was the chance that the Regenerationists had been looking for: Spain might finally become a modern, secular democracy, along the lines of France or even the United States.

Perhaps no one was more surprised by this turn of events than Azaña himself. A deeply introspective man whose instinct was to bury himself in books, he had been born and brought up in the university town of Alcalá de Henares – where his father was the mayor – in a house that was wedged between two convents and diagonally opposite Cervantes' supposed birthplace. He might rather have stuck to cultivating his roses or to writing books which, by his own admission, were of no interest to anyone, 'even to me who wrote them'. However, a conviction about Spain's need to change, not just its government, but its national character, led Azaña into politics. 'The Spanish people never learn from their mistakes,' he had said in 1923. 'Although the nation is old, and hardened by misfortune, the discontinuity of its culture, which always appears sporadically in isolated groups, makes it a people without experience.'

Azaña's aims were consistent with those of most liberal, moderate Spaniards. He believed that Spain had to develop a democracy with independent institutions, a proper civil service, a church and army that were subordinate to the State. Eventually there might be a culture in which it was possible to debate, and to *compromise* – anathema to most politicians at that time. His immediate goals included the creation of thousands of new schools. Education was terribly inadequate, with only two-thirds of Spaniards literate. Land reform was needed to improve the lot of millions of impoverished peasants who worked on vast estates run by absentee landlords. Azaña also planned the scaling down of the army to a more technical role, absorbing enough to keep its officers' minds off plotting and politics. Voluntary retirement was offered to officers, with the warning that they would be made redundant if they did not accept. As an efficiency measure, Azaña ordered the closure of the military academy at Zaragoza. Its director, whose name was General Francisco Franco, would not forgive him for that.

The new constitution of 1932 made a number of revolutionary changes to Spanish life. Universal suffrage was introduced. Men and women received the right to divorce by mutual consent, a provision not introduced in Britain until 1971. Most controversial was to be the disestablishment of the Church, whose domination of daily life had made it the object of widespread hatred. From now on, to the Church's dismay, Spaniards would enjoy freedom of conscience. Cardinal Segura, Archbishop of Toledo, asked Spanish women to fight against the new regime with a 'prayer crusade'.

Shortly after the election, the Minister of Justice made a speech in the Cortés in which he accused Catholicism of having strangled the life of the nation since 1492. Where the Church had constantly stood against human rights the Republicans were the 'descendants of the followers of Erasmus, the descendants of those whose dissident conscience was stifled for hundreds of years'. His speech was greeted with a rapturous ovation, but it had an unfortunate consequence: prominent Catholics in the government felt obliged to resign, so widening the gulf between religious and non-religious Spaniards.

The political groups supporting the Republic ranged from conservatives who wanted to create a modern, capitalist democracy, to anarchists who wanted no state but a full-scale ideological revolution. Azaña's own prejudices prevented him seeking an alliance with the centre-right-wing party – together they might have formed a moderate government capable of quashing extremists on the left and right.

His atheism, the result of an unhappy education with the monks of the Escorial, led him to take a heavy hand with the Church. In the early days of the Republic, decrees were issued to enforce the withdrawal of crucifixes from classrooms, the secularisation of all cemeteries and the prohibition of religious burial – unless it was provided for in the will of the deceased. Henceforth only civil marriages were to be recognised. A decree banning monks and nuns from teaching created a serious shortage of teachers, but Azaña said it was essential to the *defence* of the nation, as if classrooms were battlefields.

These measures struck many otherwise sympathetic Spaniards as petty and antagonistic, at a time when it was vital to heal the rifts between political groups occupying the centre. Azaña alarmed right-wingers especially with his blithe announcement that 'Spain has ceased to be Catholic.' The 1933 elections returned a right-wing coalition which wasted no time in reversing Azaña's reforms. In 1934 a powerful Catholic party entered the government. Amid fears that Fascism was coming to Spain, there was a rash of strikes and protests, sometimes brutally put down.

As a result the left won elections in 1936, and Azaña became president, but by then talk of a civil war was already in the air. The government was now constantly undermined by strikes, on the part of workers who felt the pace of reform was too slow, and by street battles between left and right. In vain Azaña warned the extreme left parties to control the rising radicalism in their ranks. When mass audiences greeted his speeches with clenched fists, he refused to return the salute. As the violence grew daily, Azaña wrote of his 'black despair'.

Finally the military coup came. On 17 July 1936, the Army of Africa, led by General Franco, rose in Morocco and was joined by garrisons across Spain the next day. But in many parts of the country the coup failed and was met by a savage backlash. Churches were looted and burned and the mummified bodies of nuns shaken from their coffins. In the following weeks some 7,000 priests, monks and nuns were murdered behind Republican lines. The violence was not confined to cities – there were stories of parish priests being crucified, of a woman who was stifled with her own crucifix.

Azaña was devastated by the violence: 'This cannot be! This cannot be!' he exclaimed to a colleague in August 1936, after Republicans had massacred prisoners attempting an escape in Madrid. 'I am sickened by the blood. I have had as much as I can take; it will drown us all.'

Azaña thought that the Republicans could not win a war against the Nationalists, but the loyalty of large sectors of the army, the enthusiasm of civilians, trade unionists and foreign volunteers meant that what the Nationalists had planned as a walkover became a three-year-long war. In Madrid's Plaza de España, crowds gathered around the statue of Don Quixote, shouting 'death to fascism'. Quixote's lance was said to be directing the Republicans to storm the Montaña barracks where the rising had started. Later Nationalists took issue with that interpretation of Quixote's pose, pointing out that his hand was outstretched in a fascist salute, not bent with a clenched fist.

During the war that followed, both sides would sometimes claim to be fighting for the survival of 'Cervantes' Spain'. A copy of the English Language News Bulletin of the International Brigade, dated 15 October 1937, and circulated round the trenches of Guadarrama, features on its editorial page the scene from *Don Quixote*, in which Sancho tries to relieve himself without his master noticing. 'Don Quixote was a Spanish hero and adventurer,' notes a commentary, 'you in your privations are adventuring with him – and so perhaps are heroes too.'

If the Republican violence, uncontrolled and abhorred by the authorities, was mostly confined to the first few weeks of the confict, behind Nationalist lines violence was part of a deliberate policy to overcome resistance. As they advanced, Nationalist troops systematically massacred government officials, trade unionists and known Republican sympathisers in their thousands. By 1939, when Madrid finally fell and the war ended, some three and a half million people had died, tens of thousands more had gone into exile – and Spain's attempt to build a liberal democracy was finished.

'Why did the centre fail – fail not merely to govern but even to be born?' asked Salvador de Madariaga, a minister in Azaña's government and, like him, a Cervantine scholar. His conclusion: 'First and foremost because of the unyielding and absolute nature of the Spanish character. This is the psychological root-cause of all Spanish troubles . . . So while Englishmen who think differently are nevertheless always within sight and hearing of each other and of the parting of their ways, Spaniards are always out of each other's mental reach and must shout to each other, and always run the risk of misinterpreting a gesture of acquiescence or doubt as a gesture of threat, and of mistaking a pipe for a revolver.'

Forty years later, when Spaniards once more had a chance to

forge a democracy, the ease with which politicians put aside their differences and worked together struck observers as almost miraculous. 'In the days of the Republic,' said the veteran communist leader, Santiago Carrillo, 'you would never have talked to anyone from "the other side".'

The truth was that everyone working on the 1976 constitution kept the memory of the Civil War at the forefront of their minds. The Hispanist Ian Gibson later wrote: 'This, for the first time in the history of Spain, was to be a consensus Constitution, the result of dialogue and compromise, with no bullying, no impositions and the stress on national reconciliation. The word *consenso* could be heard on everybody's lips in those days.'

~ ~ ~

Did that mean that Spaniards had finally learned to listen to one another? Visitors to any major Spanish city might think otherwise. Spain is reputed to be the noisiest country in the world, after Japan. A report published while I was living in Madrid claimed that 20 per cent of Spanish adolescents suffered impaired hearing caused by excessive noise in discos and bars. Whereas Japan's noise may be industrial, in Spain much of it is human; Spaniards love to shout. I had one friend whose home-life seemed to consist of endless shouting matches with his mother. 'I wish you two wouldn't row so much,' I said once, to his evident surprise. 'We're not rowing,' he replied, 'we're chatting.'

If you observe any group of Spaniards talking, says Gibson, 'you will notice how they switch off, or become intensely impatient, when anyone holds the conversational stage for too long.' In 1982, when Pope John Paul II presided over an open-air mass in Madrid, the crowd's inability to keep quiet forced him to raise his voice: 'The Pope would also like to speak,' he remonstrated.

During my journey around central Spain I often watched chat shows on television disintegrate into rows because one or more of those taking part always refused to give ground, to *stop chatting*, in other words, and let someone else have a go. The pretty but helpless presenter of one show was regularly reduced to shouting 'One at a time' at her guests and punishing them with the withdrawal of their microphones. But even with the microphones switched off, the hullabaloo continued. When the noise grew particularly fierce the presenter instructed the studio band to drown her guests out with music, but you could still see the mouths moving furiously. Her last resort, one I saw enacted several times, was to stop the show for a long advertisement break. Even then, when it came back on the air the participants would still be yelling at one another. It made for oddly compelling television, though completely incomprehensible, because nobody's opinion could ever be heard over the din. It was not that the topics were particularly controversial, but simply that Spaniards are not happy to be confined to slots or sound-bites, and that they hate to give way to others, to cede ground.

One afternoon in Burgos, in 1998, I watched a much quieter show, on local television. It was a debate on the subject, Is Burgos Boring? A young man proposed that it was, while his female co-presenter protested that it was not boring at all. Then they sat in a television studio taking calls on the subject. Everyone who rang in thought that Burgos was boring. Defending her city, the young woman became increasingly indignant. 'My life isn't boring! I go out with friends, I go to the cinema. I read books.'

'All those things are quite boring, though, aren't they?' said the young man.

'There's a folklore festival featuring regional dances on at the moment!'

'*Bor*-ring!'

My guess was that the people of Burgos, perhaps especially the young ones, had a complex about the conservative history of their city. About 150 miles north of Madrid, Burgos was the capital of the kingdom of Castilla y León for 500 years, and also the birthplace of El Cid, the hero who led the conquest of Arab Spain and whose tomb is in the cathedral. During the Civil War, it was a nationalist stronghold and the seat of Franco's military operations.

In the historical archive I scrolled through old copies of the *El Diario de Burgos* on microfilm. Those published just before the Nationalist uprising had a cosmopolitan flavour. There were articles on dating agencies and exhibitions. In June, just a few days before the war broke out, a columnist warned against the 'psychosis of fear'. Another made a plea in defence of the Republic:

> Today to be a republican, purely republican with no fascist or communist adulterations, is to believe in tolerance, transigence, respect for ideas, the superiority of reason over strength, peaceful processes and good manners, in other words it is to believe in a liberal spirit that is the crowning achievement of centuries of civilisation and culture ... We cannot suppose that all that humanity has learned will be swept away by Marx, Lenin and Mussolini. We have to believe, if we want to preserve our faith in the higher destiny of man, that today's fascist and communist movements are fleeting and superficial, a moment of barbarism in the history of our civilisation.

The writer could not have known how easily, and for how long, those moral values would indeed be swept away. Even before the war was over, General Franco wasted no time in reversing the Republicans' legislation in the Nationalist zone. Divorce was made illegal and all those that had taken place during the Second Republic were immediately rendered null and void. The offspring of any remarriages that had taken place would henceforth be regarded as illegitimate. A secular education was no longer possible.

The change of regime had devastating consequences for women. During the days of the Republic, wrote the novelist Carmen Martín Gaite, it had been possible for a girl to imagine a future as a researcher, a politician, maybe even a vamp. 'We had seen their pictures in magazines, smoking with their legs crossed, driving or looking at bacteria through a microscope. We had heard about strikes, arguments in Parliament, emancipation, lay education, divorce, we knew that not all newspapers say the same thing, that not all people think the same way and that, of course, when we grew up it would be possible to choose among those theories that people argued about.'

In Franco's new regime, girls' access to higher education was limited. Married women lost the right to dispose of their own property, to inherit, to go anywhere in the company of men other than their husbands. Article 57 of the Spanish civil code stated: 'The husband must protect his wife and she must obey her husband.' Women needed the permission of their husbands to make long journeys, to get a job, buy a house or open a bank account. Leaving the family home, even for a few days, could constitute desertion, so if a battered woman took refuge in the home of a friend, she risked legal action. Adultery was always a crime when committed by a woman but only in certain circumstances when the offender was male.

In 1945 the *New York Post* protested that the position of women in Spain had returned to that of the Middle Ages. But for Franco the liberalism promoted by the Republic had been a disgusting aberration. 'We must all commit ourselves, for life, to a determination not to let those old ways return,' he said, on gaining power in 1939. 'Nothing that happened three years ago is possible any more, that way of life perished on the weapon of its own indecency.'

The diminutive Generalísimo wanted to be Spain's new El Cid, at the head of a holy crusade to liberate Spain from communists, freemasons and foreigners.

Where would the crusade lead? Franco had no clear ideas about that. To start with, he only knew that 'The state I want to establish will be the opposite of what the Reds want' – hardly a lucid strategy. Franco's reason for agreeing to the military uprising – which he had initially rejected – was the preservation of Spain as a nation, which he believed would otherwise break up. His first steps were therefore to reverse the autonomy that had been awarded the northern regions: Catalonia and the Basque Country. The massive support that Franco had received from the Church ensured his loyalty to that institution, though he was not himself as devout a Catholic as his wife. The priorities of the new regime were thus 'Re-Spanishification' and 'Re-Catholicisation'.

Later a fuzzy picture emerged of adherence to 'traditional' values – religion, nation, property, family and social responsibility (one of Franco's subordinates complained that he mentioned the word 'order' *ad nauseam*). Estimates of the number of executions held after the Civil War vary wildly, but by the very lowest estimate, ten people were shot, on average, every day, between 1939 and 1945. The highest figure multiplies that number by seven. Prisons could not cope with the vast increase in inmates. Under the new regime it was not only a crime to have supported the Republicans, but a crime *not* to have supported the Nationalists.

The Generalísimo accrued more power than any other Spanish leader since Philip II, whom he much admired. Indeed Franco believed that the rule of Philip II, together with that of Isabella and Ferdinand, the 'Catholic Monarchs', represented the most glorious moment of Spanish history. After that, he thought, everything had gone wrong. Spain had been opened to the nefarious ideas of the Enlightenment, liberalism and modern democracy; foreign ideas had corrupted the country. The Escorial, a large and lugubrious monastery from which the reclusive Philip II had ruled the empire, was, for Franco, a 'profound and perfect symbol' of Spain's heyday. Architects were encouraged to emulate it, as an act of patriotism. There was much rebuilding to be done after the war and whole towns, or town centres were modelled on the Escorial. It was ironic that Franco should find inspiration in the building where Azaña had once been such an unhappy student.

Franco even matched Philip II's paranoia about foreigners, seeing them as responsible for all Spain's woes. He became morbidly obsessed with freemasons and Communists. In 1946, after the United Nations passed a motion condemning the Spanish regime and recommending the severing of diplomatic relations, he convinced many Spaniards that they were victims of an international conspiracy of masons and Communists. Moreover, 'pseudointellectuals' were at work within Spain, trying to undermine its peace and prosperity. In 1952 Franco published, under a pseudonym, a quixotic book on freemasonry, a 'gigantic fantasy', in the words of one biographer, about the way in which masons manipulated international affairs.

'Since the times of Philip II, whenever Spain has asserted herself, she has been attacked,' said Franco, 'and the more she asserts herself, the more independent she shows herself, the more vigorously she tackles a cancer or an illness that afflicts her, the more foreign hostility grows towards Spain.'

The Generalísimo's paranoia was lovingly nursed in the press. An article from that time declared:

Let our friends, our servants, our girlfriends, or children be Spanish. Let there be no customs other than ours on this blessed Spanish soil. And if that is ferocious nationalism, so be it. And if anyone who defends the idea is an absurd retrograde, better still. We don't want progress, the progress of romantics, liberals, capitalists, bourgeois, Jews, protestants, atheists, masons and Yanks. We prefer the backwardness of Spain, the backwardness that leads us to believe that there are fundamental values for which material interests should be sacrificed.

This notion of 'blessed backwardness' dominated 1940s Spain. Those brilliant minds that had tried to take Spain forward, among them the artists Pablo Picasso, the composer Manuel Falla and the film-maker Luis Buñuel, went elsewhere. The innovative poet Federico García Lorca had already been executed by Nationalists, in the first year of the war.

Franco's sacred Spain was an illusion, because there never had been 'one Spain'. The regions of Spain boasted different languages, traditions and even, in the case of the Basque country, an overwhelmingly different blood type. Nevertheless, the Generalísimo succeeded in making Spaniards so obsessed with 'Spanishness' that they sincerely feared losing it, whatever this quality was. The fear was still palpable in the years after Spain joined the European Economic Community in 1982. Friends of mine foresaw a future in which bars might be forced to close early, because other countries – 'foreigners' – said they should. They imagined Margaret Thatcher intervening personally to stop a bullfight.

Since Franco had placed Spain's unity at the heart of his regime, opposition to it was bound to focus on the right of Spaniards to be disunited. For that reason, towards the end of the dictatorship, there was considerable popular support for the Basque terrorist group, ETA. In fact it was ETA that signalled the end of authoritarian rule by assassinating Franco's right-hand man and likely successor, General Carrero Blanco, in 1973. Carrero Blanco had vowed that nothing would change in Spain after Franco's death: 'My programme can be summed up in one word: *continuar*.' He had said that allowing Spaniards to experience democracy would be tantamount to offering the keys of a drinks cabinet to an alcoholic. His assassination finally signalled that things were going to change.

～ ～ ～

The train I had taken to Burgos from Madrid was one of an old and dying breed. Like Rocinante, it never broke into a gallop, but trundled uncertainly across the plains. After experiencing Spain's impressive new trains, I was consoled to find that some of the old stock, reminiscent of my student travels, still existed. The passengers around me also seemed to belong to an increasingly rare species, the women carrying fans, the men black-bereted. The occupant of the seat next to mine offered to share her lunch with me, a courtesy I remembered from travelling in Spain a decade before. She was a northerner, but had lived in Andalusia for thirty years. For much of the journey she regaled me with anecdotes about the laziness and untrustworthiness of southerners.

The great cathedral in Burgos was being restored with the aid of a grant from the European Union. The bells would be repaired. Cleaners were at work in the various chapels and scaffolding surrounded the great dome, finished in 1567, which Philip II praised as 'the work of angels'. A priest took me, whispering, around the cathedral, as though in awe at the scale of the restoration. We whispered at the tomb of El Cid and at the base of the magnificent golden stairway leading up to the Puerta de la Coronería. The door is closed nowadays, but if you could still walk through it you would find yourself stepping from the cathedral's opulence straight into the poverty of the gypsy quarter. My guide took me to the chapel where Burgos's revered Christ is kept. Made in 1300, this gruesome icon boasts real hair and nails and a skin made from the hide of a water buffalo. He had also come in for a bit of refurbishment.

'We were able to feed a camera through the wound in His side to see what the interior damage was,' confided the priest, between genuflections.

During the day the cathedral was full of workmen painting and restoring walls inside its different chapels. At night, the paintwork continued on the walls outside it. A small gang of Castilian separatists was daubing the city with the slogan ¡Castilla Libre!

I was intrigued by the slogan; historically, Spain's regions have often defined themselves by a desire to be free from Castile, yet here was a group asking for Castile itself to be free – from whom or what? I wanted to meet these mysterious freedom-fighters, but it was hard to track them down. The number I rang was never answered, then I was directed to an address I never found. Finally, I went to the local Communists' haunt. This turned out to be nothing more than a spartan bar, empty and with remorselessly uncomfortable chairs. Downstairs, however, there was a small office containing a photocopying machine and, settled at a table just beyond it, two smoking men. When I came upon this scene, it struck me what an important role photocopiers played in revolutionary politics. I remembered the copies of ¡Urgente! stacked in my old student lodgings and felt a stab of nostalgia. The smell of cheap black tobacco was also strongly evocative of long sessions with the revolutionary's friends, talking about nothing in particular. I told the smoking comrades about my search; they looked me over suspiciously and directed me to another bar, further down the road.

The door to this second bar was forbiddingly graffitied, but I pushed it open and found a familiar scene inside. The walls were plastered with posters advertising solidarity with some groups and repudiation of others. Some kind of punk music was playing on the stereo. A pall of cannabis smoke hung in the air. Two moody youths were playing pool in the back of the bar. Again, I felt a tug of nostalgia for the communist bars I had known in Madrid.

The young man behind the bar was so much under the influence of something that he seemed barely to be conscious at all, but he took me into a back room to telephone one of the leaders of the group. I had the feeling that this was a clandestine communication. Two hours later I was sitting outside a café talking to Carlos, a history student and part-time freedom fighter.

Carlos had long hair, like the boys in the bar, but it was better cared-for, black and glossy. His clothes were clean and looked ironed. His appearance suggested a hidden support system of organised living, devoted mother, regular meals. He was a kempt revolutionary, though no less passionate about his cause or articulate in its defence.

'It's indefensible that we still have streets bearing names associated with Franco's regime. They've changed them in other cities, why not here? We and other organisations demand the renaming of all these streets. Until such a time, we have a *right* to deface them.'

Carlos's complaint was that Castile was not distinct enough as a region within Spain. The constitution of 1978 had designated the regions of Galicia, Catalonia and the Basque Country as 'historic nationalities'. Although these regions were still contained within Spain, their claim to be different was acknowledged, their own languages were officially recognised and they had autonomous governments. When they saw what these northern regions had achieved, people in other parts of Spain began to clamour for self-government too. Andalusia argued that it was distinct from the rest of Spain thanks to the Moorish influence on the region. Valencians claimed to have their own language and heritage. By the end of 1983, every province in Spain belonged to one of the seventeen autonomous regions.

With all its regions claiming to be distinct from Spain, what was Spain, exactly? Many people, like Carlos, felt that it was an unreal construct, suffocating the different characters of the regions it contained. He wanted Castile, too, to be recognised as a 'historic nationality'.

'Franco identified "Castilian" with "Spanish" to our detriment,' said Carlos. 'We are not simply "Spanish" – our culture and way of life are totally distinct from that of the people of Asturias, say, or Aragón. For five hundred years Burgos was the capital of Old Castile, but that historic importance is virtually forgotten. There are old traditional games and customs here that are completely different from those of other regions, but they are going to die out if they are not promoted.'

Carlos thought that Spain should become 'a plurinational Spanish state', a collection of autonomous regions that would look for direction to a European Parliament rather than a Spanish government. He believed also that defence should be a matter for Europe, rather than individual nations.

He could not argue, like the Basques and Catalans, that the region's language was being oppressed, because Castilian is spoken all over Spain and indeed, Latin America, but he believed that popular folklore and traditional Castilian proverbs were falling into disuse because of the globalisation of the language.

'We need to get people to rediscover the old sayings.'

'What sort of sayings do you like?'

Carlos had a think. He blushed slightly. 'I quite like that one, "Tell me who you walk with and I'll tell you who you are."'

'Could you see yourself leading a crusade, like El Cid?'

'El Cid was a conqueror. I think Quixote is a more genial figure.'

In fact Sancho Panza, with his love of proverbs, would make a better mascot for the Castilla Libre movement. His addiction to proverbs regularly causes Quixote to fly off the handle. 'Mark my words,' the knight warns his squire, 'those proverbs of yours will bring you to the gallows one day'.

I could have fancied myself a freedom fighter, daubing the streets with slogans by night, but reckoned I was about ten years too late. If you were younger, and bored in Burgos, you could do worse than throw your lot in with Carlos.

On 12 October, three months after the outbreak of the Civil War, Miguel de Unamuno gave his last public address at the University of Salamanca. The occasion was recorded by a socialist poet, Luis Portillo, whose son Michael would one day be a cabinet minister in a British Conservative government.

Unamuno, as rector of the university, was presiding over a ceremony to mark the Day of the Hispanic Race. Franco's headquarters were at Salamanca, and the audience was full of his supporters, including his wife. Also present was General Millán Astray, who had led the Spanish Foreign Legion against uprisings in Morocco. The Spanish legionnaires described themselves as 'the bridegrooms of death'. Millán Astray was notorious for his perverse battle-cry, '¡Viva la Muerte!' or 'Long live Death!'

When Millán Astray rose to speak, he took the opportunity of this being the Day of the Spanish Race, to declare that more than half of all Spaniards were criminals, guilty of armed rebellion and high treason simply for having supported the elected Republican government. Catalonia and the Basque Country, said the General, were two 'cancers in the body of the nation', but 'Fascism, which is Spain's health-bringer, will know how to exterminate them both, cutting into the live, healthy flesh like a resolute surgeon free from false sentimentality . . . Fascism and the Army will eradicate the people and restore the soil to the sacred national realm.'

Unamuno, a Basque by birth, was not impressed. 'Between the fine curve of his nose and the silver of his Quixote-like beard, his mouth was twisted in a bitter grimace of undisguised contempt.'

Millán Astray went on to fulminate against socialists and communists. 'The public rose reluctantly', wrote Portillo, 'and chanted parrot-like: Franco! Franco! Franco!'

Someone called out the General's catch-phrase 'Long live Death!'

This was too much for Unamuno who, although he had not been scheduled to speak, rose trembling to his feet. 'General Millán Astray is a cripple, let it be said without any slighting undertone. He is a war invalid. So was Cervantes. Unfortunately there are all too many cripples in Spain just now. And soon there will be even more of them, if God does not come to our aid. It pains me to think that General Millán Astray should dictate the patterns of mass psychology. A cripple who lacks the spiritual greatness of a Cervantes is wont to seek ominous relief in causing mutilation around him.'

'Death to Intellectuals!' retorted Millán Astray. 'Long live Death!'

Unamuno went boldy on: 'You will win, because you possess more than enough brute force, but you will not convince, because to convince means to persuade. And in order to persuade, you would need what you lack – reason and right in the struggle. It would be futile to exhort you to think of Spain. I have finished.'

And Unamuno was finished. When news of his insolence reached the Junta in Burgos, Franco is said to have ordered the rector's execution. Some adviser must have warned that this would merely make a martyr of him, so the order was never carried out. Instead, Don Miguel was kept under house arrest until his death, on the last day of 1936. Unamuno's tragedy was that he had lived to see the war he once claimed would be so good for the Spanish Race.

Was Orwell right to think that the spirit of revolution could never desert Spain? A poll carried out by the magazine *Cambio 16* in 1990 made the shocking revelation that only 2 per cent of Spaniards still believed in sacrificing themselves for an ideal. The magazine's proprietor responded with a sharp editorial saying that it was time 'Spaniards stopped believing that our destiny on this planet is to enjoy, enjoy, enjoy and that our problems will be taken care of by others'.

While I was studying at Madrid's university at the end of the 1980s I gave two English lessons every week, one to a business-man in his forties, the other to two eleven-year-olds. The businessman had been a student during the last decade of Franco's regime, and he was typically contemptuous of the present generation. 'In my day when we went on demonstrations we knew that the police would be using live ammunition,' he told me. 'We weren't like the young people today who play at being idealists, sometimes we had to run bloody fast.'

His was the generation that had witnessed Spain's journey to democracy, whereas the eleven-year-olds I taught had been born into it and would have the luxury of taking it for granted. When I returned to Spain ten years on, this was the age-group that seemed most disaffected.

Youth violence was on the rise. The term 'supermarket delinquency' was coined, describing a kind of petty crime that seemed to be linked to the rapid growth in consumer values. A supermarket delinquent was typically aggressive at school, a shoplifter, a truant and in the worst cases, a 'parent-abuser'.

One young journalist, Eduardo Verdú, wrote an essay about his peers in *El País*. 'The youth of the late sixties and early seventies achieved, with democracy, an unprecedented Spain, young like them, with a new constitution, and some great sex shops. But today's young people are living in a society that has gone straight from adolescence to mid-life crisis. We are often accused of having no values, no sense of commitment. Perhaps our apathy is the new way of protest.'

In November 1987 I went with Arturo to an event to celebrate the seventieth anniversary of the Russian Revolution.

The venue looked uninspiring from outside, the sort of place where one might queue for hot-dogs and lavatories. But inside, an anachronistic transformation had been wrought. Images of Lenin and Marx hung on dusty red banners. Posters were strung from the rafters with galvanising slogans in Spanish, Catalan and Basque. There were stalls where you could buy badges saying that 'Nicaragua Must Survive' and T-shirts emblazoned with the image of Che Guevara.

A famous flamenco dancer, violently sinewy, opened the proceedings with an impassioned dance, his 'birthday present' to the Revolution. Speeches by a string of trade union leaders followed, each one mouthing the same formula: admiration for the USSR, contempt for the enemies of the Cuban Revolution. Each of these men had come bearing lengthy lists of names of people who endorsed that formula and wanted their endorsement broadcast. The names were read out.

It was a time-consuming ritual with different sections of the audience cheering the names they recognised, while the rest continued talking, making the scene strangely reminiscent of a television quiz show: the basis of the solidarity seemed much the same. Just as the coach party from Liverpool cheers a contestant because he is a Liverpudlian, so the metal-workers in the audience could be expected to cheer a fellow metal-worker. It was a sizeable crowd, making a sizeable noise. Yet, for all that, the occasion seemed wordless or rather, there were words, but meaning eluded them.

Towards the end of the evening, an old, grey-faced Russian, dispatched from the Politburo, was brought on to the stage to proclaim the glory of the Revolution, with the help of a translator. The Russian was large and looked weary, his journey from the edge of the stage to the microphone embarrassingly slow and creaky. Once he had started his speech, it seemed that he might never stop. He even looked too tired to stop, as if all his other bodily functions had failed and only this verbal barrage stood between him and death. So the words tumbled out, many-syllabled and soporific, yet nothing of substance was said. I pictured a stream of darts bouncing off a dart-board.

At the end of the day we all filed down the stairs and out of the building. As we approached the exit we could see through the windows that a group of young men were milling around outside the door, jeering at the crowd leaving the hall.

'Fascists,' explained Arturo.

Some of the people leaving the building returned the abuse, and for a moment it looked as if a fight would break out, but neither side made a move to raise the stakes. In fact the men had no intention of doing more than jeering, and so the threat of violence dissipated. For a moment, though, I felt my adrenalin pump.

None of us leaving the hall that evening knew that on the same day in Moscow, President Mikhail Gorbachev was announcing the sweeping reforms he called *perestroika*.

CHAPTER ELEVEN
A Little Place in La Mancha

One afternoon the revolutionary left the library, where we had both been working, in a rage because he could not find a copy of Karl Marx's *Das Kapital*. The absence of such an important book was outrageous, he said, but typical also of the tacit censorship that still gripped the university, conspiring against youth culture. After he left I looked for the book again and found that it was in the library, but it was filed under 'Recent Acquisitions'.

By the 1950s, censorship was relaxed in Spain, but the first decade of Franco's regime was gruelling. Thousands of political dissidents, teachers, academics and journalists were executed, exiled or lost their jobs. The 1939 Law of Political Responsibilities saw positions at libraries, institutes, on newspapers filled with bureaucrats who could be relied upon to toe Franco's line. The Book Fairs of 1939 and 1940 were celebrated, perversely, with book burnings, as though the organisers had some crucial misunderstanding about the enjoyment of books, letting flames devour them instead of readers. They showed that they misunderstood Cervantes too, by accompanying these events with readings of the episode in *Don Quixote* when the priest 'purges' the knight's collection. The authorities now had the right to enter private libraries and confiscate books. In more ways than one, the spirit of the Inquisition was revived under Franco.

Dictators know better than anyone the dangers of reading. Spaniards opening their newspapers in the 1940s would have found the content completely free of controversy or debate. Directives issued by Franco's Ministry of Information banned reference to arrests, trials, executions, strikes, the exiled Royal Family, the defeated Republicans, crimes, suicides, bankruptcies, stock exchange falls, devaluations, food and housing shortages, price rises, industrial and traffic accidents, epidemics, droughts, flood or storm damage. Nor was any excitement to be had from the illustrations. Retouchers were employed to cover up cleavages, lengthen hemlines and paint vests on to the torsos of boxers. Reports of Franco's activities, sometimes written by the Generalísimo himself, and reproductions of his speeches had to appear on the front page, under headlines of a size specified by the ministry. Newspaper and magazine editors were hardly likely to demur – they were appointed by the state and had to be members of the Falange, the ideological wing of Franco's regime.

Nothing was left to the dangers of the imagination. In restaurants, a favourite dish called 'Russian Salad' had to be renamed 'national' or 'imperial' salad. Little Red Riding Hood became Little Blue Riding Hood. But the bureaucrats were not entirely heartless: chorus girls were allowed to show their legs in towns where the population was over 40,000. Cabarets were permitted, though the songs and sketches must be scanned for satire and immorality. The star of Barcelona's Moulin Rouge visited the censor's office each morning, with mantilla and prayer-book, to perform for him that evening's repertoire. Foreign films were permitted, but their compulsory dubbing gave censors freedom to excise the immoral or subversive elements of the script. Lovers were sometimes recast as siblings. Displays of adultery had to be avoided at all costs, so that when Lana Turner had an affair in *The Rains of Ranchipur*, the script was amended to show that her husband had been eaten by a tiger. Censors' reports included suggestions such as 'Shorten kiss', or 'Cut thighs throughout'.

With all plays, film scripts, song lyrics and lectures having to be submitted for approval before they could be authorised, the state needed to employ a large network of freelance censors. Drawn from Church, military or civilian ranks, their job was to report on anything that offended Catholic dogma, morality, or the regime. Military censors looked for politically sensitive material whereas the Church, as usual, concentrated on sex. About 500 books a month were processed this way. Even then, material that had been passed by state censors could still be vetoed by local authorities or zealous parish priests. Some priests put up notices in the cinema foyers warning that 'those who watch today's programme are committing a mortal sin'.

High-brow culture was not as rigorously suppressed as popular forms, perhaps because the censors knew they did not pose much of a threat. Works by 'dangerous' playwrights, such as Harold Pinter or Samuel Beckett, might be licensed for one-off performances while poetry was more or less untouched. A surprising number of social realist novels were allowed to be published in the 1950s. Franco's first propaganda chief (who broke with the regime in the 1940s) later suggested that that was because the censors knew the novels' pessimism would only make their readers depressed and apathetic. Even in 1972, when the censorship rules had been relaxed a little, a writer had his passport withdrawn as punishment for a short story that was said to insult the army; his publisher was sentenced to six months' imprisonment.

Reading could make you think too much, and about the wrong things. It could turn you quixotic. If you were a woman, it could make you unmarriageable. Magazines of the 1950s warned young women that, while it was acceptable to read 'pink' or romantic

novels, they should not bother their heads with anything weight-
ier. One published a moral tale about what could happen to a girl
who tried to be 'original':

> She develops a literary and sophisticated education that allows her
> to speak freely, and makes her seem unfeminine and lofty . . . She
> experiments with Surrealism, Existentialism and every other
> fashionable 'ism'. She hopes to fall in love with a superior type, a
> thinker or a writer . . . but at thirty-five she has to make do with a
> nitwit because they are the only ones who give her the time of day.

'Pink novels' made a come back after Franco's death but this time
– although their colour made a wry allusion to more innocent
times – any romance contained between the covers was accidental.
The new pink collection encompassed a range of erotic and
pornographic fiction fit to make Franco's toes curl. Alongside such
classics as the Marquis de Sade's *100 Days of Sodom* and *The
History of 'O'*, were published explicit new works by Spanish
writers such as Almudena Grandes, who became a feminist icon in
Spain after selling more than a million copies of her titillating
novel *The Ages of Lulú*.

In the post-Franco delirium, sexual taboos were broached
quickly and energetically. One of the creative stars of the day was
film-maker Pedro Almodóvar, the son of a petrol attendant from
La Mancha. In 1969, at the age of twenty, he moved to Madrid
and later began making the colourful, kitschy films that summed
up the spirit of Madrid after Franco's death. Through comedy
Almodóvar dealt irreverently with religion and aspects of sexual-
ity, such as transexualism and sado-masochism, that would have
appalled Spain only a few years before.

Now, in their anxiety not to be thought prudish or old-
fashioned, Spaniards were happy to be seen watching risqué films
or browsing through a little light pornography. In bookshops
erotica was stocked under the heading 'Libertinismo'. Vertical
Smile, the most successful of the new imprints, was run by a

publishing house in Barcelona. Each pink book bore a tiny triangular motif that would be obscene, were it not so difficult to decipher. Founded in 1978, the series was marketed with risqué slogans like 'You can read it with one hand'. Each year a prize was awarded to the best erotic tome of the year. The prize was very prestigious. Winners, including Mario Vargas Llosa and the Nobel laureate Camilo José Cela, were invited on to political and cultural debates on television, to give their opinion on the economy and politics. Their columns appeared in the Sunday supplements.

One recent prize-winner, Eduardo Mendicutti, was the respectable, middle-aged director of a firm of business consultants in Madrid. He was also the author of a novel in which transvestites fantasise about doing unmentionable things to policemen, using baguettes.

'When I was at university, just before Franco died, we used to read erotic stories by Cela, for instance, and circulate them secretly, on battered photocopies,' said Eduardo, as we sat at a smart glass table in his company's boardroom. 'After the dictatorship, when erotica first became legally available, all kinds of people rushed to buy it, because everyone wanted to look modern. It didn't matter whether or not you were interested in erotic fiction *per se*. The important thing was not to be thought square, or associated with the ancien regime.'

Eduardo thought that, for all their decades of repression, the Spanish were a pretty erotic race. He had doubts about the British, but was prepared to be persuaded. 'From what I hear about your politicians, British eroticism is interesting. It seems to be quite twisted and there's a taste for strange fetishes, like sado-masochism and transvestism. Spaniards are sexually spontaneous and shameless, but perhaps they are a bit more limited.'

A glance at the back pages of respectable newspapers would suggest otherwise. They were crammed with advertisements offering the sexual services of transvestites, sadists, 'insatiable students' and even a 'super-busty widow'. Now that soft pornography was shown on television, and comedy shows were often tediously bawdy, there was a feeling, among some Spaniards, that the joke was wearing thin. They wanted less, not more sex.

Even Eduardo Mendicutti was a little nostalgic for the days of oppression. 'It used to be fun in the old days, when everything was forbidden. Now the feminists, the gays, the necrophiliacs and the nymphomaniacs have all had their say. There's no one left to scandalise. I think the next big challenge for erotic fiction is going to be literary quality. It isn't enough to shock any more, the prose has got to be good.'

Cervantes favoured clear writing, recommending writers to express themselves 'in simple, honest and well measured words, and make it sound good and cheerful, depicting your ideas as well as you possibly can and stating your thoughts in a straightforward and understandable manner.' It was unfashionable advice in the sixteenth century, when most writers preferred their prose purple.

But even when writing is clear, an enquiring reader – especially one living in a culture of censorship – is bound to lift up the words to see what secrets the author may have buried under them. Subjected to scrutiny, words change shape and meaning, throwing up red herrings as well as hidden truths. *Don Quixote* means different things, depending on the interpretative tool you use. Professor Carroll B. Johnson, who takes a Freudian perspective, has described Quixote's beard as 'an upwardly displaced analogue of the virile member'.

Some readers will go to extraordinary lengths to understand the essence of a favourite book. In 1927 writer Jorge Luis Borges set himself the quintessentially Borgesian task of analysing the twelve first words of *Don Quixote*, an opening line so perfect that he believed 'any modification would be sacrilegious'. The exercise was to discover the *precise* meaning of each word in a given sentence. Here is Borges's assessment of the third word in the sentence:

Lugar [place]. This is the word of location, promised by the particle *in*. Its task is merely syntactical, not adding any representation to the one suggested by the two previous words. To represent oneself 'in' and to represent oneself 'in a place' is the same, as any 'in' is in a place and implies this. You will reply that *place* is a noun, a thing, and that Cervantes did not write it to signify a portion of space, but rather to mean 'hamlet', 'town', or 'village'. To the first I will respond that it is risky to allude to *things in themselves*, after Mach, Hume and Berkeley and that, for a sincere reader, there is only a difference of emphasis between the preposition *in* and the noun *place*; in response to the second, the distinction is true, but only discernible later.

Borges's scrutiny of a dozen words in a book which contains at least half a million more looks zealous. Suppose he had lavished the same attention on every sentence in the book? Even Borges, who was obsessed with infinite projects, did not have the patience for that – but he created someone who did.

One of his short stories concerns Pierre Menard, a French philosopher and writer who sets out to produce a masterpiece: a new version of *Don Quixote* identical in every word to the original. 'He had no intention of copying it,' explains Borges. 'His admirable ambition was to produce pages which coincided, word for word and line for line with those of Miguel de Cervantes.'

Menard plans to *become* Cervantes by learning medieval Spanish, experiencing the wars against Moors and Turks and forgetting the history of Europe between 1602 and 1918. Then he decides that 'to become Cervantes and arrive at *Quixote* seemed less hard – and therefore less interesting – than to carry on being Pierre Menard and arrive at *Quixote* through Pierre Menard's own experiences.'

The narrator, or Borges, marvels at this feat, a much greater one than Cervantes ever accomplished. 'To compose *Don Quixote* at the beginning of the seventeenth century was a reasonable, necessary, perhaps even a fateful undertaking; but at the beginning of the twentieth century, it is almost impossible. Not for nothing have three hundred years passed, full of very complex events, not least among them, the publication of *Don Quixote* itself.'

Menard's undertaking is so huge that he never manages to replicate more than a couple of chapters. Even on this scant evidence, his version is 'almost infinitely richer.' His accomplishment, says Borges, throws light on the potential development of the human mind. 'Every man should be capable of every idea and I believe that in the future he will be.'

Borges thought of *Don Quixote* as an unchanging monument, but a great book is like a house – it has to move, shift in the soil. *Don Quixote* keeps on meaning something different, depending on whether the reader is Freudian or Jungian, Nationalist or Republican, male or female. As the sorrowful knight has travelled across the centuries, inevitably he has evolved. The twenty-first-century Don is no longer the figure of fun of the seventeenth century, nor the Romantic hero of the nineteenth. Where did *Don Quixote* begin? There is a clue in a half-finished church in La Mancha.

~ ~ ~

Don Quixote begins with famously vague words: 'In a little place in La Mancha, whose name I do not care to recall'. La Mancha is a vast, arid and underpopulated area, in the south of Castilla-La Mancha and to the north of Andalusia. Not many people have cause to pass through it, which may be why the inhabitants of various places in La Mancha wish that Cervantes had tried harder to be precise about Quixote's home town – it would do wonders for the tourist trade.

At the entrance to Argamasilla del Alba, a pleasant market town which prides itself on being Don Quixote's birthplace, there is even a large stone monument that seeks to redress Cervantes' absent-mindedness with the words: 'This *is* that place in La Mancha'. The inhabitants have to be assertive about their claim because a town down the road also believes itself to be Don Quixote's birthplace and a clutch of dreary academic studies have been devoted to these conflicting claims. Doctoral students have laboriously plotted the distances between both towns and other landmarks. For instance, the windmills Quixote took for giants decorate a hilltop a few miles away. The site of the inn he mistook for a castle, where he was knighted by the innkeeper, is en route to El Toboso, identified in the book as the home of Dulcinea (or rather Aldonza).

Argamasilla is within a horse's reach of all these places – even if your horse is a plodding Rocinante – but the town's claim rests on a specific reference. At the end of the first part of *Don Quixote*, a series of poems appears in honour of Quixote, Sancho, Rocinante and Dulcinea. The poems are said to have been written by the twelve academics of Argamasilla and some of the names mentioned have been identified as those of men who lived in the area at a time when Cervantes himself is thought to have been imprisoned here. 'We don't go around waving flags or anything,' the mayor of Argamasilla told me. 'We just feel quietly sure that this is the town Cervantes neglected to name.'

It was a blazing day in late summer when I arrived in Argamasilla. Across the huge plains that the knight and his squire once roamed, the air had been heated to a simmering, barely breathable, syrup.

The melon harvest had been over-generous and at every cross-roads farmers were selling off the glut at knock-down prices. I was about six months pregnant now, more Sanchoid than ever, and like Sancho I was hot, worried about my food supply and liable to complain.

The mayor, a small, dishevelled chain-smoker, accompanied me around the town (he was actually the deputy mayor, though promoted for the duration of the holidays). 'Luckily I love *Don Quixote*,' he told me, 'otherwise it would be hard to live in Argamasilla.' He was a scholarly man who had once been a priest and was now working on an Ecumenical Bible to be 'the first of its kind in the world'.

We arrived at the subterranean room, once a gaol, where Cervantes is thought to have been imprisoned, possibly for pestering the daughter of a local bigwig. The cell was small, dank and cold, even on a day of such heat. But it was not entirely cut off from the world. It was possible to hear people going about in the street outside. Some years back, the building around the cell, which may originally have been the home of the offended father, had become a cultural centre. In the courtyard through which the cell was reached a class of little girls was practising for a display of regional dancing. The clatter of castanets echoed round the walls.

Though it is known with certainty that Cervantes was held in the huge gaol at Seville once and possibly twice, the case for his imprisonment at Argamasilla is much weaker. That has not stopped scholars of *Don Quixote*, at various times through the centuries, from locking themselves up in this dank basement to be close to the spirit of Cervantes and the genesis of his great work. Perhaps the most romantic of them was Baron Hartzenbusch who, in 1869, set up a printing press there and produced an edition of *Don Quixote* in the cell itself, as if the pages could imbibe a spirit of Cervantes still hanging in the air. He had the royal Infanta pull the first page from the press.

There was an inscription from Hartzenbusch's edition over the door to the prison: 'In this gloomy prison, in this miserable coffer of lime and stone, the fertile mind of Cervantes conceived the vast idea, sometimes sad, always delightful, of his Don Quixote; from here his marvellous imagination, breaking down the thick walls which imprisoned him, spread itself over the wide plains of La Mancha.'

After we had seen the cell, the mayor took me on to the church, which was far bigger than one would expect to find in a small town. Perhaps its scale defeated the builders; although it was started in the sixteenth century, it has never been finished. The town also boasted an unfinished irrigation system. 'We have grand projects but we aren't good at completing them,' the mayor confessed. On a day like this, of such extreme heat, you could understand how people's enthusiasm for bold schemes might wane.

In the unfinished part of the church, the mayor told me about a concert he would like to hold. He looked up at the jagged, grass-covered walls. 'You could have a small orchestra, and a light show, with lasers.'

'It would be spectacular,' I agreed.

We paused to picture this very unlikely event. At the moment the grassy space was empty except for some sort of animal coop, perhaps a chicken run. During the Civil War Argamasilla's church was sacked by anarchists, although they did not bother setting fire to it, since it was a ruin already. Silver was stolen, the statues chopped up for firewood. The gutted building was used as a garage. Evidently, one of the Republicans was a Cervantist and managed to persuade the others not to take a particular treasure. This was an unusual painting, dating from 1606, that showed the Virgin Mary appearing to a kneeling man and woman, dressed in the costume of the time. The inscription read: 'Don Rodrigo Pacheco, Our Lady appeared to this gentleman he being ill of a grave disease and the doctors despairing of him [on the] Eve of St Matthew 1600. Entrusting himself to Our Lady and promising a gift of one silver lamp, he called her day and night of the great pain which he had from a great chilliness which gripped him within.'

'The story of Don Pacheco's madness was well known in Argamasilla during the time Cervantes was imprisoned here,' said the mayor. 'He is the man we believe was the inspiration for Don Quixote.'

Even now there was a cultural group called the 'Academics of Argamasilla', which comprised the mayor and his two closest friends, the judge and the priest. Recently the three of them had spent a night in the cell, producing a colloquium of essays on Cervantes, a copy of which the Mayor gave me.

After we had seen the church, we went to have a drink in the local bar. 'Why did you leave the Church?' I asked.

'I couldn't accept some of the Catholic doctrines, especially the rule of celibacy. Priests should be able to marry.'

'But you still believe in God?' I asked.

'Oh yes,' said the mayor, 'though I have some terrible rows with the priest.'

Just then, two men passed the bar's open door. They were wearing shorts, each held a tennis racquet in one hand and a melon in the other.

'Speak of the devil,' shouted the mayor. 'The priest and the judge armed with melons!'

The two men looked in and laughed. 'So where's the mayor's melon?'

'I'll be along for mine later!'

The three Academics of Argamasilla laughed and exchanged jokes before the priest and the judge went on their way.

'It's funny that the priest is your friend,' I said. 'There's a novel called *Monsignor Quixote* by Graham Greene about a priest and a mayor from a town in La Mancha who are very good friends and share a love of *Don Quixote*. The mayor in the book studied at a seminary, like you, but then he became a communist.'

'Somebody else told me that,' said the mayor, only mildly surprised at the literary coincidence, 'I've heard of the author, but I've never read that book.'

In *Monsignor Quixote* the priest is always parrying with the mayor on the subject of faith. 'You think my God is an illusion like the windmills,' he says. 'But he exists, I tell you, I don't just believe in Him. I touch Him.'

Alone at night, though, Greene's priest is quixotically unsure. 'I want to believe that it is all true,' he says, 'and that want is the only certain thing I feel.'

~ ~ ~

I had planned a quixotic experiment for my time in La Mancha. I meant to forgo the television chat shows I loved so much and spend my siestas reading 'pink' novels – as many as I could – in imitation of Quixote's passion for chivalric novels. The aim was to see what psychological effect an intensive reading of Spain's popular new genre, combined with heat, could have on a reader. If it drove me mad, a week hence I might be roaming the Castilian plains, not in armour, but perhaps in a negligee and sling-backs. La Mancha was supposed to be an easy place to lose your wits, but how mind-altering was Spanish erotica? Would it have as maddening an effect on me as the romances of chivalry did on poor Quixote?

As it turned out, my experiment was too short-lived to prove conclusive: an endless round of breasts and buggeries very quickly did me in. The fact that pink novels were carnal did not save them from being dull. As Eduardo Mendicutti said, the writing was not very good, nor was the shock value sustaining.

I was distracted by an idea about how people choose to read books, and what effect a particular book, selected at one moment in time rather than another, has on the future life and work of the reader. Many of the world's most famous writers have been readers of Cervantes. To what extent had that reading changed the course of their work?

Flaubert, as has been said, created *Madame Bovary* as a direct result of reading *Don Quixote*. The fact that he was epileptic, and suffered hallucinations may account for his sympathy for the character. Dostoevsky, who also suffered from epilepsy, might have been drawn to the Don for the same reason.

Nabokov, who took up *Don Quixote*'s cause with a vengeance in his lectures for Harvard, shortly afterwards went on to treat a different kind of middle-aged madness in *Lolita*. Franz Kafka, in *The Truth about Sancho Panza*, one of his shortest works, suggested that Quixote's madness was fuelled by his squire, who took pleasure in seeing his master behave ludicrously.

Virginia Woolf was at work on her first experimental novel, *Jacob's Room*, when she read *Don Quixote*, in August 1920. She found it heavy going. Woolf was preoccupied, like so many others, by the suspicion that Cervantes could not have known what he was doing in creating the character of Quixote. She wondered if that uncertainty ought to change the value of the book. 'So far as I can judge, the beauty & thought come in unawares; Cervantes scarcely conscious of serious meaning, & scarcely seeing D.Q. as we see him. Indeed that's my difficulty – the sadness, the satire, how far are they ours, not intended – or do these great characters have it in them to change according to the generation that looks at them?'

In May 1934 Thomas Mann chose *Don Quixote* as a companion for his first transatlantic trip, a journey that was to take him from Nazi Germany to New York. He had bought the German translation in four orange linen volumes and looked forward to reading them in the ship's bar, vermouth in hand.

'*Don Quixote* is universal; just the right reading for a trip to the end of the world,' wrote Mann, on the first day of the voyage. 'It was no small adventure to write it; the passive adventure of reading it will worthily correspond. Strangely enough, I have never gone through the masterpiece systematically, from beginning to end. I will do so on board and in ten days come to the rim of this ocean of a book, at the same time as we come to the other rim of the Atlantic.'

∽ ∽ ∽

One afternoon in 1988, I was sitting under a tree in Madrid's Retiro park, gnawing a stale ham sandwich when a gypsy cursed my love life three times over. If you have to be cursed at all, perhaps it is better to be cursed in love than in health, but a curse of any kind feels like a bad deal. The only thing I had done to provoke the gypsy's bile was politely to turn down the offer of a fortune telling. I was not in the mood to have my palm read: it was a demanding sandwich.

I was in love with the revolutionary and, perhaps thanks to that very gypsy, my love was doomed. We had always had arguments. Once the revolutionary had laughed at me because I did not understand what kind of dessert it was that Jesús was offering me at the *casa de comidas*. I had countered that if he ever found himself in a British restaurant, he might not be familiar with every sort of dessert available there.

'But there's just one kind, isn't there?' he said. '*Pudding!*'

A couple of anarchists and a Marxist had been there and they all laughed uproariously. The word 'pudding' had an explosive effect in Spain.

We had argued, among other things, about the proper definition of a 'reactionary', a term I thought my friends were too willing to attribute to anyone who disagreed with their views. The revolutionary said that it was disgraceful and embarrassing that I did not properly understand what a reactionary was. Once we had had an argument about the right of Russians to defect. The revolutionary believed that educated Russians should stay in the Soviet Union.

'If you belong to a country you don't just leave it whenever it's convenient, you have a duty to contribute to its progress. They shouldn't take the education and the expertise that they have received free in the Soviet Union and use it in another country.'

The argument that did for us was, inevitably, about women. A Colombian had become attached to our group. She had a dramatic past – apparently she was on the run from the police and travelling with stolen documents. The company she kept suggested that she was also involved in drug-trafficking. She was beautiful and looked attractively absent-minded, as though permanently taken up with some complicated brain-teaser. The truth, as we came to realise, was that her brain was not so much subject to teasing as to sustained drug-abuse. When she first went with us to the salsa club the revolutionary danced with her – for most of the night.

I brought up the matter of Lucía when the revolutionary was at my house having lunch, and it prompted a much longer argument about my possessiveness and his right to freedom. It ended with the revolutionary snatching up a cheese sandwich he had made in my kitchen and throwing it out of the balcony windows. We both watched the doughy square somersault slowly past the window of the transvestite who lived opposite, and some intuition told me that we were not watching it alone. Juanito, standing a few yards away in the street, had allowed his yo-yo to dangle while he followed the career of the sandwich. It was somewhere above him, that the bread let go of the cheese, and this heavier component fell quickly to earth, landing at Juanito's feet with a moist thud. Juanito stared at the whitish piece of pumelled fat, nudged it with his shoe and, encouraged by criteria of shape and texture that only children know about, he jumped on it with both feet, eliciting a faint but satisfying pop. Then he trotted away, still trailing the unwound yo-yo.

The argument might have been made up, but fate intervened. I was deliberately prickly the next time we met – my strategy was not to make the peace this time, in anticipation of making it up the time after. Unfortunately, the revolutionary then went away for two weeks. Later I heard that he was back, but busy with university work. By the time we saw one another again, the number of days without speaking seemed too many to bridge. Besides, Lucía was now always by his side.

I had essays to concentrate on and a dissertation about 'the language of democracy as used in Spanish newspapers of the Transition'. Returning home late from the library one day, I rounded the corner into our street and ran into our neighbour, the one who played Dracula. He saw me and came forward to say hello, his white face bobbing in the dark like a satirist's interpretation of the man in the moon.

'Are you on a job?' I asked.

'We're going to one, but there's been a technical hitch,' said Dracula, and he gestured into the shadows at another man, a fellow entertainer who was dressed as a seventeenth-century wench, a *Maritornes* grotesquely made up with lipstick and eyeshadow. Under a plunging neckline, the man was wrestling with a pair of plastic breasts.

'What's the hitch?'

'Raul's dented his body part.'

With one hand up his dress and the other inside the plastic body part, Raul was trying to punch a dent out of the left breast. For all that it was a comic spectacle, the manly concentration of effort in Raul's womanised face somehow made him look tragic. One of his eyelashes had come loose and sweat was streaking the make-up.

'That's bad luck.'

'It doesn't matter. He's got another pair at home.'

As I said goodbye, I looked down the street towards my house and noticed a figure waiting in the doorway. In an effort to deter the junkies, our landlady had finally agreed to install an entryphone, and it looked as if the waiting man was trying to ring our buzzer. I thought it might be the revolutionary, and quickened my pace.

Through the window upstairs, the brothel-owner's dark living-room was periodically convulsed with light, to the muted rat-tat-tat of televised gunfire. I imagined Juanito curled on the sofa, his magnified eye accumulating murders.

As I drew nearer, I realised that there was something wrong about the man waiting at the door. Perhaps it was an unfamiliar stoop, or the arrangement of his limbs. It could have been something as fleeting as a glint of light on metal, or simply the texture of the air between us. I walked cautiously on, and had come quite close to the house before I could confirm that the figure waiting in my doorway was definitely not the revolutionary. I was just a few feet away when I saw the needle.

Some larger sense of defeat prevented me from mustering fear or anger, even though I could see the thin tube sticking into his arm. I took my key from my pocket and, as I unlocked the door, the junkie mumbled, barely coherent: 'Sorry.'

'It doesn't matter,' I said, letting myself into the house.

CHAPTER TWELVE
Which Are You? Quixote or Sancho?

Every few weeks our flat filled with the smell of religion. The combined perfume of candles and incense meant that Carmen would be standing at the stove in her dressing gown, heating a little saucepan of wax which she used to strip from her upper lip the hairs she thought were too dark. It seemed to me that she had no moustache to worry about – for Don Quixote, after all, long hairs on the lip are a sign of beauty. She seemed to enjoy the ritual, however, making hair-removal seem so straightforward that one afternoon I heated some wax with a view to doing the same for my underarms.

After watching the tablets dissolve in the pan, I left the mixture to cool for a few minutes before slathering it on with a wooden spoon. While I waited for the wax under one arm to cool to the right, elastic consistency, I put some wax under the other arm. For a few seconds I wandered around the flat, airing my arms, feeling rather pleased with myself. When the right arm's wax had reached its ideal consistency, I gave it a testing tug: it hurt. I pulled again and the pain was excruciating, a pinprick of blood appeared where one hair had been wrenched from its home. This was terrible: clearly it was not going to be possible to remove the wax without also removing part of myself.

The wax was hardening now and I could feel the skin under my arms becoming glued to my rib cage. Every slight movement of them was accompanied by agonising pain as another hair ripped out. I paced around the flat with my arms held rigidly away from my body like a penguin and started to panic – what on earth was I going to do? The doorbell rang. I shouted 'Who is it?' through the door, hoping that it was Carmen returning without a key. She would surely know what to do – she had once thought of training as a beautician. But instead a frail voice called back: 'I'm hungry, do you have any bread?'

'One minute.'

No one could have chosen a worse moment to come begging, but I was not about to turn a hungry child away from my door. I struggled painfully back into a T-shirt, pulling it over my head and as far up my arms as I could. I got the leftovers of our daily baguette and some cheese from the kitchen and opened the door to find a boy of about ten, very thin and pale. He took the food gratefully and shot me a curious look. Studying the peculiar lie of my shirt across my shoulders, he may have thought that I had some kind of deformity; it was not unusual in Spain. It crossed my mind, fleetingly, to ask the boy for his help but since he was a child, and male, he was sure to be inexpert. A fear of humiliation and of more pain decided me against that and the boy lolloped away. Back in my room I peeled off the shirt and spent the rest of the afternoon using warm water and scissors in an effort to remove the wax, but even a week later there were still traces of it and in lectures I felt the ravaged skin under my arms sticking gently to my ribs. From then onwards, the smell that accompanied Carmen's moustache-removal held less appeal.

∼ ∼ ∼

That was the only occasion that a beggar came to my door in Spain. While the gap between rich and poor widened inexorably in countries like Britain and the United States, Spain in the 1980s was actually closing it. Physical evidence of that change was inescapable. Younger Spaniards, born in more affluent times, were noticeably larger than their parents who had lived through the 'years of hunger' – the 1940s, when Spain's poverty was particularly acute and a United Nations trade blockade was in force.

While it was not unusual to see people in their twenties who had been crippled by polio, disability among children was much rarer. Nevertheless the legacy of Spain's poverty was still much in evidence. Huddled on the outskirts of major cities were the shanty towns. One of the most pitiful sights was that of a poor man or woman circulating the cafés or underground trains with a doctor's prescription for a sick child. Beggars on the street often sat beside handwritten signs bearing the long story of their misfortunes. Some had mutilations caused by accidents. Increasingly the signs referred to a new scourge. 'I have AIDS, please help.'

At one corner of a square near our house a disabled man sat in a wheelchair. Once I had seen him arrive in the morning by car. A frowning relative on his way to work, offloaded the wheelchair then lifted his charge into it with a disconcerting ease. The disabled man was small and soft and, like a rag doll with its yielding stomach and dangling legs, he could easily be folded into the wheelchair. He was not feeble: his muscular thighs gave way to strong knees but then, absurdly, petered out. Below the knee there was not even the social pretence of bone or flesh. Usually his trousers were rudely tied in a knot to stop them trailing in the dirt.

Until his relative returned from work, the man's job was to make as much money from his affliction as possible. In this respect he showed considerable spirit. Attached to one side of the wheelchair was a small but powerful microphone to which he casually raised his head, about once every twenty seconds, as though to make an observation to a neighbour at a dinner party. It would have made more sense for the microphone to be placed in front of him, but then it might have got in the way of his collecting box. Besides, there was nothing weary about the man's performance. Every time he raised his head to the microphone, and he must have done so thousands of times a day, it was to make the same, gentle suggestion: '*Una moneda*,' which, through force of repetition, had become something like a snatch of music, familiar to everyone who passed him, perhaps so familiar that they could hum or sing to it, but had forgotten what it meant, or how to respond to it. In quieter moments, the square's echoing walls endorsed and elaborated on his suggestion as if they were saying 'Give the guy a break, *una moneda* isn't much to ask for.'

∽ ∽ ∽

We had been on marches before, but this was to be the longest yet, an eighteen-kilometre walk to the NATO base at Torrejón de Ardoz, east of Madrid on the road to Alcalá de Henares. The march was taking place for the eighth year running, even though the seventy-two American fighter jets at Torrejón were scheduled to be removed and the site was going to be closed. As so often in Spain, the two campaign groups organising the demonstration could not agree about the motive of the march. One group was calling for the immediate demolition of the base and Spain's withdrawal from NATO, in spite of a referendum, held the year before, in which the majority of Spaniards voted in favour of the alliance.

The other group was less radical. It supported Spain's NATO membership, while demanding an undertaking that the government honour promises made at the time of Spain's entry: that all American bases would be withdrawn from Spain and that the country would play no part in the military structure of NATO.

The base, once vacated by US fighters, should be converted into a civilian airport.

The morning promised heat, and by the time Carmen and I arrived at the appointed meeting place, it was sweltering. Neither of us had strong feelings about NATO. Secretly we regarded the march as an opportunity to do some exercise and get brown. In my case, there was also the prospect of seeing the revolutionary.

We emerged from the metro to find thousands of people milling around, searching for the banners under which they were to march. The faces of those not yet reunited with their group looked strangely blank, as if waiting for expressions to be allotted to them, along with placards. The leaders themselves, men and women carrying loud-hailers, walked among the assembled ranks, practising chants and hustling their followers into columns.

Eventually the column set off in the direction of Torrejón. Some people had peace signs painted on their cheeks, or the symbol for anarchy. The Peruvians had brought pan pipes, and other groups had drums and whistles. We were a ramshackle army, mostly young and uniformed in denim.

It is a truism that Spaniards believe there is nothing more important than family life. In fact they would probably rather show allegiance to any kind of family than to the state. For most Spaniards, the need, outside the family, is met by the local bar, a place where one might spend at least an hour a day with friends. Close to my flat in Madrid there was a bar where transvestites met, most nights, to gossip and bandy insults. Ten years later, in Avila, I noticed that the same group of elderly ladies met for tea, at the same cafeteria table every day. Their husbands may well have been at a bar round the corner, playing dominoes. Most of the young people I knew while living in Spain belonged either to student unions, political parties or 'alternative' groups, such as the *okupas*. Spaniards love routine, sameness. Perhaps one legacy of Franco's long rule is a fear of change.

Young Spaniards often talk about the importance of 'solidarity', but they are probably too stubborn really to feel it – hence the rows and ruptures that have thwarted so many attempts to reach a consensus over the years. In his book *Modern Spaniards*, John Hooper quotes a classical musician who complains that the problem with tuning up in a Spanish orchestra is that 'Everyone has his or her own conception of "la".'

Yet for all their stubborn individualism, Spaniards like to unite, to protest – and to enact a kind of solidarity. So cheerfully we marched across the plain, banging, crashing, whistling, but most of all, shouting.

'We don't want your Yankee arms!' the woman with the loud-hailer would shout.

'You can stick them up your arse!' we shouted back.

After four hours of this, we limped into the main square of Torrejón, the town nearest to the NATO base. By now the heat was waning, bringing the relief of fresh air, but also licensing our limbs to set about aching. Having been walking with the sun constantly to the left of us, Carmen and I had achieved only half the tan we had been hoping for.

'What happens now?' I asked Arturo, who had kept me company the last few miles. 'Shall we go and get a drink?'

'This is where the march officially ends, which means that the police have told us to end it here,' he said.

'Why don't we do what the police say?' I hated breaking rules.

'If we carry on through the square and out the other side of the village, there's a field up to a main road. Beyond the road is the base. The idea is to cross the field and the road and get to the base. It isn't possible, of course: there'll be lots of police ranged along the road to stop anyone who tries to get near.'

'What if they don't stop us?'

'We storm the base!'

Having never stormed, nor had the desire to storm, anything, I was not enthusiastic about this plan – but felt a pressure to show solidarity. Most people who had completed the march were already making their way to buses parked in the station forecourt, or drinking water in the square, while others sat and rested, removing shoes to examine blistered feet. The few hardliners, of whom I now found myself an unwilling member, were continuing through the square and down a street which ended, as if by design, in a large expanse, fit for battle. The far side of this wasteland rose to a grassy bank, skirting a road. The bank was lined by police in full riot gear.

Once they reached the empty lot, as if obeying a telepathic command, the marchers scattered hither and thither, running towards the police, shouting and throwing stones. Up on the brow of the hill, the police deflected the stones with shields that gleamed silver in the sun. A trick of the light converted them into some medieval army.

'Move! This way,' Arturo shouted, and I found myself running with him towards a group of people who were standing chanting anti-nuclear slogans at the police.

'Bases out! NATO out!'

The policemen's eyes could not be seen beneath their visors, so it was anyone's guess what they would do. The chants became shorter and shriller, the better to goad our impassive adversaries. The sun had given me a bad headache and I felt slightly delirious. From where I was standing, the police, ranged against the setting sun, looked shinily ill-defined, but not malevolent; rather they seemed to be dancing, or waving at us in a friendly sort of way.

'Out! Out! NATO out!'

I scanned the field around me for the revolutionary, and saw him to my right, much closer to the police line, a lone figure hurling stones. His fury was strangely unaffecting. It seemed to be worn like a badge, along with the others he had pinned to his waistcoat.

Arturo jerked my arm – 'Run!' – and I looked up to see that the gleaming visors and shields were spilling down the hill, scattering the slogan-chanters in all directions.

'Why?' I heard myself protest. 'They won't do anything to us if we haven't done anything wrong.'

'The bastards are coming down! Run!'

George Orwell wrote that there are two principles, base wisdom and noble folly, residing side by side in every human being. 'If you look into your own mind, which are you, Don Quijote or Sancho Panza? Almost certainly you are both. There is one part of you that wishes to be a hero or a saint, but another part of you is a little fat man who sees very clearly the advantages of staying alive with a whole skin. He is your unofficial self, the voice of the belly protesting against the soul . . . it is simply a lie to say that he is not part of you, just as it is a lie to say that Don Quijote is not part of you either.'

Having shown ourselves quixotic on the battlefield, we now made a sanchoid attempt to get back home with our skins intact. Hundreds of people were struggling to make their way back up the street leading to Torrejón's main square. Like panicked animals, we pushed and trampled one another, and seemed hardly to advance at all. A scream at the back of the crowd made things worse.

Somebody said 'Cover your eyes'. I looked up and saw a helicopter circulating above us. Suddenly the air was filled with tear-gas. We were corralled on the ground and from the sky. We were very tired after the long march and that combined with stinging eyes made it hard to concentrate. Some people produced handkerchiefs, as if they had anticipated this attack.

The tear-gas did its stuff: the violence dissipated and the note of militancy dropped dead out of the air. Back in the main square, the remaining demonstrators wandered aimlessly, like ants deprived of the need to work, the blank expressions they had worn before the march restored to them.

In the railway station's forecourt, coaches were filling up with tired and demoralised demonstrators prepared to call it a day. The banners were being furled and, with the placards, stored away. A scrawny young man embarked half-heartedly on a chant, but no one joined him, and the slogan slipped away, incomplete.

We travelled back to Madrid on the train, crushed together like slaughter-bound sheep and when we arrived, though weary, dirty and limping, there was a reluctance to break up our gathering. It was as if we needed some time together to make sense of the day's experience.

Back at our flat, people collapsed as best they could on to the uncomfortable sofa and chairs. I dispensed aspirin and plasters while Carmen made tea. We compared the experiences of the day. Arturo had been chased down a dead-end street by several policemen, and beaten at the end of it. They had torn the film from his camera, which he was worried might be damaged.

I was surprised to find myself converted into one of the day's heroes: 'You should have seen the gringa,' Arturo told the others. 'Everyone else was getting ready to run, but she wanted to take on the police.'

He had misunderstood my questioning of the need to run: it was down to naïvety rather than courage. My gut instinct, as I explained to the others, was to believe that police would not attack civilians. Reading the papers the next day, we saw pictures of one or two people who had come off badly at their hands, especially a girl whose face had been hit by a rubber bullet.

The revolutionary had taken a bottle of wine into the kitchen to open it. A minute later we heard shouted swearing. I ran into the kitchen to find him clutching his thumb. He had tried to open a wine bottle by pushing the cork in with a knife and had broken its neck. Undeterred, he had made another attempt to push the cork down and cut his thumb on the jagged glass.

It was a bad cut and having staunched the blood, El Doc said he would sew it up himself. In a matter if minutes he had cleaned the thumb with alcohol. From somewhere he found a needle and thread and, in front of everyone, he stitched the wound there and then. The revolutionary, with no painkillers to call on, winced stoically. When El Doc had finished and bound the thumb up with a clean handkerchief, he sent the revolutionary and me to a pharmacist for various medicaments. As we walked through the centre of Madrid, I felt pathetically grateful to be alone with the revolutionary for the first time in several weeks.

We found a pharmacist that was on duty and bought the things El Doc had recommended, then set off back to the flat, past the statue of Don Quixote in the Plaza de España.

'Now I'll always have something to remind me of you,' said the revolutionary, ruefully. He indicated the bandaged thumb.

'It wasn't my fault!'

'I know, but perhaps you should invest in a corkscrew.'

We walked a bit further and he said, 'You're an affectionate person.'

'I suppose so. Why do you say that?'

'I'm not sure that I am.'

Whether this was an explanation or an apology, it sounded like an end point. There would be no reconciliation. We walked back up the Gran Vía as we had done after our first date at the cinema.

After the others had left, Carmen and I went into the kitchen and found the whitewashed walls were sprayed with tiny droplets of blood. The spray was amazingly far-reaching, and we had to scrub an entire wall to get it off before Alvaro came home. If I had still been in the first throes of love, I might have made a romantic equation of the blood with the revolutionary's heroic destiny. However I was beginning to realise that he was no more likely to involve himself in a revolution than any other idealistic student. He himself had told me that the nub of bone between his ribs was a defect he had been born with, not, as he had once said, an injury caused by police on the streets of Lima.

It did not make much difference to me. I still loved him, but I was resigned to the fact that nothing would come of it.

One weekend, some time later, I was sitting in my room, working on an essay when I heard Carmen scream.

It had been a glorious day, the sun shining fit to warp the hours, stretching the time. The park, where I had gone to do some reading, seethed with children dressed in bright new clothes. Reds and whites chased blues and yellows in and out of the crowd. The length of the boating pond was occupied by cross-legged tarot-readers and a clown stalked the area on stilts. Suddenly the colours had seemed to loom brighter against a sky that had become blackened and bruised. There had been a distant noise, like a groan of disappointment, then a loud roar of thunder that drew excited shrieks over on the other side of the boating pond.

The clown stumbled on his stilts, a wavering giant, before jumping back down to the human level. In a trice, the party was over. People around me started springing to their feet, shaking out blankets and snatching up the disarray of their picnics; bottles, plates, half-eaten bits of food were crammed back into the baskets from which they had been so ceremoniously unpacked, only a little earlier. Several babies, sensing an overturning of the adult order, set up a fearful wailing.

I was half-way to the park gate before the rain came down, and by the time I got to our street I was drenched. Back home, I dried my hair, then set to work on an essay. Then I heard the scream.

It is a cliché to talk of emotions or expressions coming 'straight from the heart', but there is a pain that seems to find its own voice, forcing the body to give it expression without the mediation of the mind. Such a pure cry is not touched by personality and that makes it frightening: it seems to be unworldly.

At first I could not make sense of the scream; it was like nothing I had ever heard before. As time slowed, almost to the point of stopping, I thought, impassively, that I would probably never hear anything so crucial again. I could not associate the noise with Carmen, although I realised that it was she who had screamed.

I felt my heart's heavy acceleration in the second's pause before I got off my bed and ran to Carmen's room. Next to it, the front door was still open where she had burst through it. She was lying on her mattress. Her crying was all the more terrible for its experimentation with pitch. Up and down the scales she went, as though seeking a new note to express a unique grief.

'What's happened?' I asked, but I think I knew before she told me that Miguel had died, another victim of Madrid's dangerous new passion for drugs. The birthday card she had been waiting to give him was still tucked into a corner of her mirror.

CHAPTER THIRTEEN
An Angel in Segovia

If only it were not for that hare. Don Quixote sees it streaking across the fields outside his village, chased by greyhounds and hunters, and knows that it is a bad omen.

Having been defeated by Bachelor Carrasco in a duel at Barcelona, Quixote has agreed to return to his village. His plan is to take a year off from knight errantry and spend it as a shepherd. He hopes to get the Priest, the Barber and Bachelor Carrasco to join him and Sancho Panza. The five of them will 'wander through the mountains, woods and meadows, singing here, lamenting there'. His name will be Shepherd Quixotiz and Sancho's Shepherd Panzino.

The news of Quixote's new career is sure to infuriate his niece, waiting at home. She has already expressed a fear, earlier in the book, that her uncle might take it into his head 'to turn shepherd and roam about the woods and fields, singing and piping and, even worse, turn poet, for that disease is incurable and catching, so they say'.

Quixote is looking forward to the pastoral interlude, until, as they are entering the village, he sees the persecuted hare. 'Malum signum! Malum signum!' cries Don Quixote.

Sancho tries to persuade him not to take the omen seriously, but soon afterwards Quixote falls ill and takes to his bed for six days. The Priest, Barber and Bachelor rally round. Those three men who have most strenuously opposed his madness now try to rekindle it. Carrasco says how keenly they are looking forward to their new lives as shepherds. He has already written an eclogue and bought two mastiffs to guard their flock. The attempts at encouragement fall on deaf ears: the doctor says that Don Quixote is dying, 'that melancholy and despondency were bringing him to his end'.

Don Quixote falls into a deep sleep then, six hours later, wakes abruptly and, with cries of gratitude to God, pronounces that he is once more sane. 'Congratulate me, good sirs, for I am Don Quixote de la Mancha no longer, but Alonso Quixano, called for my way of life The Good. Now I am enemy of Amadís of Gaul and of all the infinite brood of his progeny. Now all profane histories of knight erranty are odious to me. I know my folly now, and the peril I have incurred from the reading of them. Now, by God's mercy, I have learnt from my own bitter experience and I abominate them.'

The friends ought to burst out in applause and cheers. After all, this is what they wanted: Quixote's sanity. Instead they wonder – perhaps hopefully – if he has succumbed to a new bout of madness. Carrasco even begs him to *return* to his senses. 'Must you come out with that, Don Quixote, just now when we have news that the Lady Dulcinea is disenchanted? Now that we are on the point of turning shepherds to spend our lives singing like any princes, do you want to turn hermit?'

But the priest is convinced by Quixote's conversion. 'Truly he is dying and truly he is sane,' he says, as if sanity and death went naturally hand in hand.

Sancho is bereft. 'Oh don't die, dear master!' he cries. 'Take my advice and live many years. For the maddest thing a man can do in this life is to let himself die just like that, without anybody killing him, but just finished off by his own melancholy.'

Though he has often wavered in the past, this time Quixote is resolute. 'Let us go gently, gentlemen,' he says, 'for there are no birds this year in last year's nests. I was mad, but I am sane now. I was Don Quixote de la Mancha, but today, as I have said, I am Alonso Quixano the Good. May my sincere repentance restore your former esteem for me.'

Quixote lives three more days, fainting frequently, then, says Cervantes, 'he gave up the ghost – that is to say, he died.'

❧ ❧ ❧

It is one of the saddest scenes in literature. After a thousand pages of companionship, no one wants Don Quixote to die. Think of Nabokov totting up the melancholy knight's battles to show that he was not a failure, of Borges scrutinising those first twelve perfect words, of Baron Hartzenbusch and the royal Infanta printing off an edition in the dark cell at Argamasilla. Countless other readers have made their own investment in the novel, and feel the loss of its unheroic hero. Perhaps no other character in the history of literature has been so loved.

Cervantes makes it clear too, that the knight is not to be brought magically back to life in some sequel. He asks readers, if they chance ever to meet the rascally Avellaneda to pass on this warning: 'Leave Don Quixote's weary and mouldering bones to rest in the grave.'

In whatever century or country it reaches the recipient, news of Quixote's death is affecting. Ivan Turgenev felt his soul plunged into 'ineffable sadness'. Thomas Mann read of it on the last day of his voyage to the New World.

'Quixote's return to sanity rejoices us strikingly little,' he wrote in his journal, 'it leaves us cold, and to some extent we regret it. We are sorry about Don Quixote – as indeed we were sorry for him when affliction at his defeat stretched him out on his bed of death. For that is actually the cause of his demise; the doctor declares "that melancholy and vexation brought about his death." It is the deep dejection of seeing shipwrecked his mission as knight-errant and light-bringer that killed him . . . we share in his defeat.'

The following morning, as he watched the Statue of Liberty rise out of the mist of dawn, Mann realised that he had dreamed of Don Quixote. 'He looked different from the pictures; he had a thick, bushy moustache, a high, retreating forehead, and under the likewise bushy brows almost blind eyes . . . He was, now that I had him face to face, very tactful and courteous.'

As the ship prepared to dock in New York, Mann felt himself filled with 'pain, love, pity and boundless reverence' for the Knight of the Sad Countenance.

'But such thoughts are too European for my surroundings – they face in the wrong direction. Ahead out of the morning mist slowly emerge the skycrapers of Manhattan, a fantastic landscape group, a towered city of giants.'

Once you have read *Don Quixote*, you can see giants anywhere.

~ ~ ~

How could Azaña, an atheist, whose loathing for the church would play such a significant part in Spain's crisis, bear to think that Don Quixote had turned to God before his death? In 1930 he assured the women's literary group that Don Quixote does not die:

> The one who gives up and dies is Alonso Quixano. He recovers his reason, he ceases to be Don Quixote and he rejects the romances of chivalry. He dies of sanity. Nobody hates Don Quixote as much as

Quixano hates him, lying there on his deathbed. He wakes from his quixotism as one who wakes from a nightmare, he repents as if it had all been an aberration – he had been possessed by a bad spirit. But the manner of Alonso Quixano's death in no way diminishes the life of Don Quixote. Cervantes disassociates them, and it is Alonso Quixano who dies, a miserable vessel emptied of quixotism.

What passed through Azaña's mind as he lay dying ten years later in a French hotel can only be guessed at. He was sixty, a broken man, haunted by the horrors inflicted on his country in the last few years. At the height of the Civil War he had made a desperate appeal to future generations never to forget the damage that had been done in Spain by intolerance, hatred and destruction.

In retrospect, these words uttered about Don Quixote in 1930 look prophetic. 'No man can be sure', Azaña had said, 'that he too may not recover his reason on the brink of death, and be horrified by all the things he has done, and deplore the things he has not done, no longer sure of whether he was sane or mad when he did them.'

Did Azaña, like Quixote, also renounce his ideology before he died? A bishop was seen visiting him in his final hours. Later Azaña's widow gave conflicting accounts of his death to biographers, one of whom came away with the impression that the ex-Republican leader had indeed received the last rites and, disavowing his atheism, made a full confession before he died.

∽ ∽ ∽

When I left some beef on my plate at a small restaurant in Segovia, the cook came out personally to chastise me.

'Who left the meat?' she called out.

'I did,' I confessed, blushing in spite of myself.

'It was the best cut at the market,' she said. 'What did you think was wrong with it, out of interest?'

I was too embarrassed to start explaining, in front of all the other diners, that, because I was pregnant, I had to steer clear of any meat that was rare. So I mumbled something about not being very hungry and felt the full weight of the cook's disapproval decend on my shoulders.

Segovia was my last stop before returning to Madrid, and then to Britain. Either the hormones or the knowledge of my approaching departure made me moody. Motherhood was about to change my life for ever. I might never travel alone again, in the way I had, over the years, through Spain. From now on I would, indeed, be leading a double life.

I sat for about an hour on the steps beside the Roman adqueduct, the city's most impressive monument. Later I wandered around the Alcázar, the fantastically turreted castle that served as a model for California's own Disneyland castle. But I was more interested in people than architecture, and soon I found myself walking up to a gypsy encampment perched above the centre of the city.

There were two entrances to the area, both prowled about by dogs with teeth bared and tongues dangling. I managed to circumnavigate the dogs and found a man sitting outside the caravans. He looked suspiciously at me, but when I asked him where the residents' association was his expression eased. Just as Spaniards love to belong to an organisation, so they like outsiders to respect its authority. The man took me to one of the caravans and clapped outside it. Children's clothes were strung on a washing line between this caravan and its neighbour.

A short, extremely muscular man alighted from the caravan. He was wearing a red vest and jeans and had a tattoo on his arm which showed Jesus Christ with shaggy hair and a crown of thorns. The president of the residents' association examined me through narrowed eyes as I explained that I wanted to know more about his community. Marginalised and ostracised on the edge of Spain's cities, gypsies harbour a deep-felt mistrust of the non-gypsies they call *payos*. Perhaps pregnancy went in my favour. At any rate, the man decided to be hospitable.

'We send a lot of *payos* away,' he said, 'but I can see that you are sincere.'

He took me to a workshop that was full of finely crafted reproduction dressers and tables.

'This is an initiative that we set up to give our young men something to do, some way of involving them in society. There is a lot of prejudice against them and it's hard for them to get work. They end up turning to crime and drugs – these are our worst enemies. We needed something to restore their sense of self-respect.'

He was joined by a much taller friend who was wearing a pendant round his neck showing exactly the same shaggy, thorn-crowned Jesus.

'Do the authorities put pressure on you to integrate?' I asked.

'They're always talking about it, but they don't respect our ways. What they really want is to break up our community and disperse it around the city. We don't mind going to live in flats, but we want to live together and preserve our traditions.'

'What sort of traditions do you keep alive? Do you still have arranged marriages?'

My host smiled. 'Only last night, we were all together playing the guitar and singing. There were a little boy and girl there and their parents arranged an engagement between them.'

'Did the children understand?'

'Oh yes. They said they would like to get married.'

He accompanied me to the edge of the encampment, back past the slavering dogs. 'If you have any trouble with any of our people, let me know,' he said. 'I'll sort it out.'

That evening I went out to get something to eat. In a restaurant I ordered a 'summer salad' and was surprised to find that its main ingredients were boiled potatoes and raw onions. It was a constant source of surprise to me that Spaniards ate so much raw onion; their breath was not noticeably bad. A cassette-guide for blind Spanish tourists given to me by Miren advised that one should always try local specialities – 'You will surely never be disappointed.' Since I was travelling alone, and I had no one else to see that day, I went ahead and ate the onions, and it *was* a disappointment, but it made a change from double cheeseburgers.

Later that evening I was sitting in a bar having a coffee when a man of about fifty pulled up the bar-stool beside me. 'I think we're staying in the same hotel,' he said. 'My name's Angel.'

Angel worked as a psychoanalyst in Madrid, but he told me that he had just been presenting a paper at a literary conference. His lecture had been on Freud's attachment to Cervantes. 'He learned Spanish specifically to read Cervantes,' said Angel. 'He even corresponded with a friend in seventeenth-century Spanish to improve his understanding of the novel. They called themselves the "Castillian Academy". Freud studied Spanish secretly so that his parents wouldn't think he was taking time off school work.'

I was fascinated to hear this, so when Angel suggested a walk around the old centre of Segovia I agreed. It was getting on for eleven o'clock and dark, but at the height of a Spanish summer that is when the streets are at their busiest.

Angel told me that Freud and his schoolfriend Silberstein had read one of Cervantes' exemplary novels, *The Dialogue of the Dogs*, written in 1612, and adopted the two characters' names. In the story, one of the dogs, Cipión, expresses a great desire to talk about his life and his memories while the other, Berganza, encourages him. 'I shall listen with great pleasure without interrupting you unless I see that it is necessary,' he says. Cipión says that some of his fantasies are so strong they seem real to him. Berganza encourages him to examine his beliefs to see if they are really true.

'It's the precursor,' said Angel, 'of what would become psychoanalysis. The relationship between Cipión and Berganza is clearly that of analyst to patient. The story is even called a "dialogue". Sometimes Freud described psychoanalysis as a "dialogue".'

The main square was full of strolling couples and children kicking footballs; Angel and I sat on a bench.

'What about Don Quixote? If he were one of your patients, and you had him on the couch, how would you diagnose him?'

Angel took this frivolous question very seriously indeed. After thinking for a few moments, he said, 'The consensus is that Don Quixote goes mad from reading too many books of chivalry. I think his illness is caused by his domestic situation. He lives alone with two women, a housekeeper and his niece. They emasculate him. You see it happen in Spain all the time. Look at them,' he pointed at an old lady who was crossing the square with her middle-aged son. 'That man's probably never left home,' said Angel. 'He's been sucked dry by his mother.'

I was taken aback by the bitterness contained in this observation, though it was true that Spanish mothers could be domineering. Unamuno, on the other hand, thought that Quixote needed more women in his life, a wife, specifically, to curb his desire for adventure. If he had to assume responsibility for a family, he would have less freedom to go off.

'Don Quixote isn't entirely alone with the women,' I said. 'There's the boy who saddles his horse for him.'

'He doesn't live in the house though, does he? Anyway, it's clear that the women both have very strong characters – they preside over the burning of his books.'

'The idea for the book-burning comes from the priest and the barber, Quixote's closest friends,' I said. 'The niece and the housekeeper are only trying to protect Quixote. They're frightened by his behaviour. Remember that he's selling off all his land, and he's capable of thrashing around, deliriously, for days on end. They have a right to safeguard the furniture, if nothing else.'

All the same, it was true that Quixote's niece had a cruel streak. She often taunted her uncle with being old and foolish, pouring scorn on his literary ambitions.

Angel seemed to be preoccupied by women's influence on men generally, not just on Quixote.

'Motherhood is potentially very dangerous,' he said. 'If you have a boy you'll have to be careful. You could have a powerful effect on him.'

I was beginning to feel irritated by Angel's pronouncements. 'I'm not sure Freud was right about everything.'

'Are you Jewish?' Angel asked.

'No.'

'Shame. A very fascinating people. This used to be the Jewish quarter of Segovia, before the expulsion. Up until then, Spain had the biggest Jewish community in the world. What a damage was done to our national spirit.'

'I wonder what it was like to walk around these empty streets in the days after they left.'

He led me into the narrow winding streets that make up the oldest part of the city. It was about midnight now and the cafés and bars were thronged with people. We passed a bar that was blaring out music and Angel, suddenly infused by the spirit of youth, wondered if I would like to go dancing. I felt, on reflection, that I would not.

Children were chasing each other up and down the steps. There were plenty of people in the streets, no reason not to continue our meander through the ever narrower streets of old Segovia. Even so, perhaps I should have known better than to follow a Freudian up an alley. Angel chose one of the skinnier stretches of an ancient pass to make his own pass at me. He knew that I was married and pregnant, and by now he was also close enough to know about my experiment with the onion salad. In spite of all this, he made a clumsy attempt to kiss me. We tussled awkwardly for a few seconds, then continued up the alley in an embarrassed silence.

'I think I'd better go back to the hotel,' I said.

'So had I,' said Angel – then we remembered that we were staying in the same place. We walked together to the hotel, through the crowed streets, without exchanging a word.

Before we parted at the lifts, Angel apologised. 'I thought perhaps you understood me,' he said forlornly. He was fiftyish, bookish, and a bit of a dreamer.

Borges believed that there was such a thing as a 'perfect page', in which every word was vital and nothing could be altered without harming the whole. By such a token it would be impossible ever to translate a book into another language without betraying its author.

In every century there have been rows about the real meaning of *Don Quixote*, a book Milan Kundera has described as 'ungraspable'. Shortly after its publication in English, *Don Quixote* was already engaging scholars in heated debate about the meaning, not just of the work itself, but even of specific words and phrases. Curious and envious critics picked over the book. One particularly fussy seventeenth-century reader queried the fatness of the Innkeeper, because 'most travellers have declared that a fat man in Spain is seldom, if ever, met with'.

In the summer of 1789, differences of opinion about Cervantes' novel even became caught up in a murder case. The defendant was

Joseph Baretti, an Anglo-Italian scholar of Spanish literature who was put on trial for a fatal stabbing in London. Baretti had escaped hanging, thanks partly to the evidence of Dr Samuel Johnson, who testified that he was not a drunkard, nor given to picking up prostitutes and that, in any case, he was too short-sighted to stab accurately. Johnson's involvement in the trial added to its high profile, but afterwards letters were sent to four different gentlemen's magazines alleging that the wrong verdict had been handed down. The letters claimed that Baretti had brow-beaten Johnson, who was not well, into giving false evidence. Enraged by the letters, Baretti believed he knew who was behind this campaign to blacken his newly cleared name.

The perpetrator was none other than the Reverend John Bowle, a respectable clergyman and an eminent Hispanist. The motive was revenge: Joseph Baretti had publicly mocked Bowle's edition of *Don Quixote*, a labour of love that had taken some fourteen years to complete and could claim to be unique in the world.

Bowle's *Don Quixote* was not a translation, but an edition in Spanish, authorised by the Royal Academy of the Spanish Language, with two thousand notes, a glossary and a biography of Cervantes. Bowle had gone about his research with extraordinary industry. In 1769 he had set about reading *all* the chivalric literature Don Quixote might have come across, starting with Amadís of Gaul. It took seven years and made him, not mad, but very bored. He had also studied medieval treatises on knight-hood, and discovered one or two cases where Quixote's behaviour constituted 'flagrant violations' of them.

The most revolutionary aspect of Bowle's edition, perhaps, was that it made use, for the first time, of a form of spelling that has since been standard in Spanish. This seems to be the bone of Baretti's contention: he did not believe that Russia should be spelt with only one 's', as is the case in modern Spanish, nor that

'Philosophy' should be spelt with 'f's as in 'Filosofia'. He poured scorn on Bowle's glossary, and pronounced 'a pox' on his preface.

In a 500-page diatribe about Bowle's *Don Quixote*, Baretti invited his rival to make a bonfire of his edition in the yard and set fire to it. The reverend was apparently so upset by Baretti's attacks he started running around Wiltshire with his wig awry stopping people in the street to rage against Baretti, and scheming his 'utter annihilation' as a man of literature.

Baretti declared himself so infuriated by the whole *Don Quixote* débâcle, he felt like throwing his slippers in the Thames, and was resorting to snuff to calm himself down. 'I have on my side taken such a dislike to you,' he told Bowle, 'that you are now as odious to me as the fiddle of an old footman whom I hear from morn to night scrape and scrape in my next neighbour's kitchen ... Thou hast dragged me out of that quiet obscurity, in which I promised myself to live the short remainder of my days, and must take the consequence, if I am now as mad as Don Quijote.'

~ ~ ~

But supposing Don Quixote were not mad at all? What if the enchanters and the giants were only a hobby, an excuse, as Angel hinted, to get away from the women in his life?

For Samuel Taylor Coleridge, in a lecture given in 1811, this was at least a possibility. He identified five different kinds of madness, but could not conclude that Quixote was suffering particularly from any one of them. This, he thought, was a case of an under-employed genius who needed to get away from the *pueblo* to find some stimulation.

An essay by W. H. Auden points out that Quixote 'never sees things that aren't there (delusion) but sees them differently, e.g. windmills as giants, sheep as armies, puppets as Moors, etc.' Rather than a delusion, says Auden, Quixote's way of seeing is therefore a kind of faith. 'The relation of faith between subject and object is unique in every case. Hundreds may believe, but each has to believe by himself.'

Many readers, before and since Auden, have seen Quixote as a man of faith, of mission. Cervantes' contemporaries thought they recognised a portrait of Saint Ignatius Loyola, the founder of the Jesuits, in the melancholy knight. Turgenev thought he was 'soaked through and through with love of the ideal'.

There certainly are religious parallels in *Don Quixote*. The most striking of them comes towards the end of the book, when Quixote is taken riding through the streets of Barcelona by his host, wearing a gown that has been embroidered with the words 'This is Don Quixote de la Mancha'. The poor knight is delighted and amazed to find so many people addressing him by his name. Nabokov seethed at the cruelty of the scene.

But Quixote would not be half as interesting as a character if he really were the man of conviction that Auden and others describe. The truth is that Quixote is not positively certain of anything. Rather he clings to the *idea* of certainty, which is partly why he gets so angry with people who disagree with him. Quixote knows that the world is terrifyingly complex. How do you cope with life's uncertainties? One way is to create a philosophy, a pattern, and force yourself to follow it. If others reject it, so much the better – you can consider yourself misunderstood, but in the right. Don Quixote's delusions make him staunch; they give him something to hold on to.

Cervantes, in providing the world with its first novel, gave it a powerful work of psychological investigation. It is one of the reasons that Freud found a better description of delusions and wish-fulfilment in *Don Quixote* than he did in his Psychiatry studies. In August 1883 he wrote to his fiancée, Martha, 'I now possess *Don Quixote* . . . and concentrate more on it than on brain anatomy.'

It befits literature's first modern hero to have been present at the birth of psychoanalysis.

Towards the end of the novel, the Duke and Duchess, in search of ever crueller tricks to play on Quixote, decide to send him and Sancho on a 'magic horse' to a faraway land. There, among other things, the pair are going to disenchant a group of damsels who have grown beards. Blindfolded, Sancho and Quixote climb on to a rocking horse with fire crackers attached to its tail. They 'fly' briefly – while servants stand around them puffing bellows – then are thrown to the ground, apparently having accomplished their mission.

Afterwards, Sancho waxes quixotic about the experience of flight. He has seen the earth, 'no bigger than a grain of mustard seed, and the men walking on it little bigger than hazelnuts. So you can see how high we must have been then.' Don Quixote, for a change, is not convinced by the so-called magic horse. He says Sancho must either be lying or dreaming.

He is, however, willing to strike a deal: Quixote promises to believe Sancho's account of what happened on the magic horse, if Sancho will believe his earlier claim to have met Dulcinea when he was the guest of the sorcerer Montesinos in an underground cavern. This will be their bond, a mutual belief in impossible things. Sancho, wavering, accepts the deal. In a sense, this is the culmination of an experiment in which the knight and his squire have tried to recast reality in their own mould. If they cannot fool other people, can they at least fool themselves?

Quixote's hope is that you can make things true by believing in them hard enough, but in the end he is unable to sustain the delusion. Doubt is the giant that pursues Quixote. The battle to keep it at bay can be seen in these, perhaps the most important lines in the book:

'God knows whether there is any Dulcinea in the world, or whether she is imaginary or not imaginary,' Don Quixote tells

Sancho. 'These are things the proof of which must not be pushed to extreme lengths.'

Back in London, my journey around Castile over, I opened a copy of *El País* one day to find an article full of Quixote's shortcomings. 'He always wanted to be in the right and he never paid for his drinks', complained its author, Manuel Vincent. 'The history of Spain, the conquest of America and Castilian literature would all have been much better if we had taken as our example Sancho Panza, with his irony, pragmatism and the enjoyment of simple pleasures, instead of that lunatic stuck in the past.'

CHAPTER FOURTEEN
New Life in Castile

We parked the car in one of the winding streets close to the church, and took the baby from the back seat. It was another incredibly hot day, in a small Castilian town. During the fifteen years since I first visited Spain, I had known innumerable little towns like this, and suffered untold days of heat, but this was the first time I had travelled abroad with a six-month-old baby – my son. So far it had not been a pleasant experience. The baby had spent most of the night crying, apparently in great pain, and in the early hours of the morning my husband and I had taken him to a hospital in Bilbao. A stern paediatrician and her assistant stripped and examined him while he howled and struggled. I watched, biting my nails and hating myself for bringing him to Spain.

The paediatrician's diagnosis was short and to the point.

'*Gas.*'

We took our small charge back to the hotel, encouraged him to break wind like Sancho Panza and when finally he was restored to good humour we put him in the car and set off across the fields south-west to the town of Castrillo de Murcia, in the region of Castilla y León.

In Cervantes' time it took six days to cross La Mancha on horseback. Today you can leave London in the morning and arrive at the smallest, most ramshackle Castilian town in time for a pre-lunch plate of piglet's ears and a glass of chilled sherry. The world is a smaller place, yet Spaniards, for all their fears of losing 'Spanishness', are unique – as the very nature of the event we had come to witness proved. Later in the day we were going to join hundreds of locals in watching a man dressed up as a kind of court jester run around the town jumping over dozens of babies – including ours.

The annual ritual of El Colacho has taken place on the Sunday after Corpus Christi since 1621. El Colacho, a folkloric figure who crops up in other guises, at other fiestas, is said to represent the devil fleeing from the sight of the Eucharist. Babies born in the previous twelve months are dressed in their finest clothes and laid on mattresses over which El Colacho leaps. The jumping is meant to protect the year's crop of newborns from serious illness, especially hernias. To get extra coverage, pushier mothers ask El Colacho to jump again, and he may return to the same mattress several times. There is something in the ritual for unmarried women too – another get-hitched-quick deal: if they can be the first to pluck a baby from the mattress after El Colacho has jumped it, they will marry within the year.

The main square of Castrillo was dominated by an over-sized church topped with the ubiquitous stork's nest. Storks and churches are inseparable in Castile. Arturo once told me that was because storks were anarchists, occupying and using churches for their own purposes, like the 'reds' at the start of the Civil War. But I had also heard that they were reincarnated priests, returning to their parishes. It goes to show that you can never be sure of your facts.

In the absence of churches, the birds will settle for other beautiful, ancient buildings. Walking in Salamanca to meet the private detective once, I had felt a large stick drop on my head.

Looking up ready to tick off some child on a balcony, I saw an ungainly stork flying towards its half-made nest on top of one of the old faculties.

Outside the church people were milling about with an air of expectancy. El Colacho was already at large in the streets, chasing the local children with a stick and a horse's tail. Hooded, he wore a medieval yellow and red costume and a devilish carnival mask. The children, as tradition demands, hurled abuse at him, both personal and folkloric. It is traditional to mock El Colacho for knowing 'no Castilian, only Latin', because once it was the parish priest who took his role, and did all the jumping. Otherwise modern insults, along the lines of 'big nose', or 'baldie' do just as well, but El Colacho is entitled to thwack anyone who comes near enough.

The *cofradía*, or brotherhood, that accompanies El Colacho on his rounds, is drawn from local townsmen. Each brother must accept his nomination or risk being fined whereas El Colacho can pay someone else to take his place, if he cannot face the jump. Every year he is accompanied by an apprentice, a kind of trainee devil who also jumps over the mattresses, though perhaps less expertly.

～ ～ ～

No country rivals Spain for the variety and colour of its fiestas, of which there are about eight thousand a year. Every town holds some kind of annual celebration, to mark religious events, the harvest, the annual slaughter of animals or historic victories.

One fiesta day in Madrid, during the time I was a student there, a number of army trucks trundled into the main square, the Plaza Mayor. This was not the beginning of a revolution, however, but of a massive peace offering. Vast cauldrons appeared and soldiers set to work cooking huge quantities of the city's favourite dish, *cocido madrileño*, a stew made from beef, ham, chicken, chickpeas and vegetables. *Cocido* is an economical dish because the one stew provides three courses: first the broth is served, then the chickpeas and lastly the meat. As the Plaza Mayor filled with the smell of simmering chickpeas, young conscripts doled out *cocido* in military rations. It was like something out of a magical realist novel, one of the most beguiling sights I had ever seen.

But few things are stranger than a Spanish fiesta. There are towns where giants teetering on stilts are chased through the streets; where locals throw tomatoes at one another. In Cáceres, women march, once a year, to the mayor's house and demand a bull to fight. The third time they ask him, he sends one down to the bullring and, once they have fought it, their boyfriends have a go. In a town near Alicante every year the locals dress up as Moors and Christians and enact a battle (the Christians always win it).

During the *Fallas* of Valencia, massive sculptures made of wax are set ablaze to the chants of a hyped-up crowd. The huge totems caricature celebrities, fictional characters and local politicians – especially corrupt ones. According to one description, the event is supposed to provoke a 'catharsis by fire' – and there is something in that. Carmen and I once went to *Las Fallas* with a couple whose relationship was in trouble. During the night, as the city blazed and crackled, we kept seeing them on one street corner or another, arguing furiously, fire crackers going off all around them. By dawn, they had decided to separate.

Some of the fiestas have changed little over the centuries. When Quixote and Sancho come across a band of hooded penitents carrying a statue of the Virgin Mary on a bier, the deluded don thinks they are bearing off a damsel, and orders them to stop chanting and listen to what he is going to say. 'Say it quickly,' says a priest, in one of the novel's many Pythonesque moments, 'for these brethren of ours are lashing their flesh, and we cannot possibly stop to hear anything, unless it is so brief that you can say it in two words.' Another fight ensues, and this time, as Nabokov would have recorded in his tally, Don Quixote comes a cropper.

Four hundred years later, Holy Week processions of hooded brethren still follow the statue of that parish's Virgin, or Christ, on a bier bedecked in flowers. Penitents, sometimes shackled, and wearing real crowns of thorns, carry crosses in imitation of Christ. They may be prisoners earning an early release by this penance. Others flagellate themselves until their backs bleed, or shuffle on their knees until they bleed, or bang drums, making their fingers bleed. Whatever the tourists may think, fiestas are not always fun.

In a little village of Galicia, families make an annual pilgrimage to the shrine of Saint Marta carrying any family members who have been seriously ill, or otherwise cheated death, in the coffin that was so nearly theirs. It is an eerie kind of resurrection, a procession of coffins with no corpse in sight. The grateful living, many of them children, stare out of the coffins they might have occupied, with expressions of bewilderment.

In Castrillo, the mounting anticipation was like that preceding a match or a race. We stopped for a sandwich in a bar and my husband asked someone what the best strategy was for the afternoon's proceedings. She said that we should get our son registered as a participant at the Town Hall. The baby hiccuped gently against his father's shoulder, unaware of the ordeal in store.

'What about the mattress? Are you supposed to bring your own?'

'You can use any of the mattresses you want, but some of them are more popular than others, so you have to be ready to grab one.'

In fact mattresses were beginning to appear in the streets, huge floppy squares that had given uncomfortable nights to generations of Spaniards, cushioning the conception and birth of their offspring. Families staggered under the weight of them. Young men trotted in formation down the streets with them. They were laid down around the town in a circuit, then covered in lace counterpanes and pillows and made to look so refined that Dulcinea herself would have been happy to recline on one.

'Babies wherever you look!' I remarked to an old lady standing in a doorway behind me.

'This is nothing,' she said with a dismissive tut. 'There used to be thousands of them, they came from all over the place. Now no one has children any more.'

The low birth rate had come to be such a motif during my journey round the two regions of Castile that I half expected it to be used as an excuse for anything, from the shortage of nuns, to the unavailability of ice cream. It made this ceremony seem all the more important, as if the participating babies were a scarce resource.

Months previously I had visited the Association for Numerous Families and met the daughter of its president. She told me that there had been a revolution in Spain, but what she was talking about was really an implosion. Spain had the lowest birth rate in Europe, the second-lowest (after Japan) in the world. A survey suggested that financial worries stopped people having larger families. What really made the difference was that Spanish women were particularly reluctant to abandon their careers for mother-hood, because their arrival in the workplace was so recent.

'Spaniards have become selfish and greedy,' this girl told me. 'They look for personal fulfilment at work instead of in the home and tell themselves they would rather have a yacht than a child.'

'There can't be *that* many yachts!'

'I'm not kidding. There is an advertisement on television in which a couple are buying a flashy, big car. They wonder how to fill the extra space. The woman says, "I know – let's get a dog!" '

Such reckless frivolity sounded quite appealing in a country where women had for so long been slaves to home and family. I liked to think of the archetypal Spanish grandmother, in black dress and support stockings, sailing a yacht with her face to the wind, or behind the wheel of a flashy car. But the girl said she was shocked by the change in values. At twenty-three, she was already planning a large family.

Her mother, remarkably youthful for someone with thirteen children, was buzzing around the office, making phone calls, receiving faxes. The association she headed had just held a convention at which a gigantic paella was served for 2,500 people. Did she never feel the lack of privacy, with all these children?

'Once', she said after some thought, 'I did feel like crying about something and I thought there's nowhere in his house for me to be by myself. Then I realised what a marvellous thing that was! You can never be lonely in a large family.'

'The traditional Spanish family is breaking down,' said her daughter. 'Toy factories are having to close because there are so few children.'

It was a terrible image to take away. Spain, a country that once seemed built on families, reduced to closing down factories because there was no one to play with the toys.

A truckload of toys would not have gone amiss in Castrillo de Murcia, where babies were now starting to emerge from all corners of the town. They arrived in prams, pushchairs, carrycots, dressed in their best clothes, lace-bonneted and cosseted by doting parents and grandparents. Wherever you looked there were parked prams and frilly parasols. The streets filled with a gurgling and cooing. Babies, patted, dandled, kissed and cuddled, started to take over. Nearly one hundred of them would be taking part in the ritual.

Mattresses, thrown down from windows, walked across the

square on six or eight feet like those geometric creatures in Miró's paintings. One flabby rectangle struggling across the plaza could barely contain its springs. Watching it brought to mind uncomfortable nights spent in Spanish boarding houses years ago, when the beds were always jumping with bugs and there was never any hot water. Spain had changed so much, and so quickly.

In 1989 the association of Spanish mattress manufacturers announced an increase in the length of the standard size. A good diet and better health care has made Spaniards substantially taller – you need only observe their enthusiasm for basketball. Spain has changed shape in many other ways since 1964, the year when the United Nations removed it from the ranks of developing countries.

The image of a poor, rural and Catholic country is long out of date. Spaniards of all backgrounds are richer than they used to be, often with a greater purchasing power than their contemporaries in Britain. Most of them live in cities; fewer than half are practising Catholics.

Some things do not change: though they may live in cities, Spaniards retain affection for the pueblo and always go back for the fiesta. They love their families, to the point of a tremendous reluctance to leave home. Two-thirds of Spaniards under the age of thirty live with their parents and Spain has the lowest marriage rate in the European Union, but then it also has the highest life expectancy – so perhaps they are on to something.

Beer and double cheeseburgers will change the shape of the next generation. Young Spaniards have taken to fast food and alcohol only recently, but they are catching up with their fatter peers in the north. Indeed they are reckoned now to have the highest cholesterol intake in the European Union, so the mattresses of the future may need to be stronger, as well as longer.

'Spanish society today is much more competitive, aggressive, and stressful,' Rosa Montero, a journalist and novelist, has written. 'We have lost much of that unhurried love of the present moment that was disastrous for business but made life pleasant, without – it seems – an equivalent gain in efficiency.'

For those people who cannot honestly find their way in Spain's new business world, there are still lucrative loopholes. Corruption scandals dogged the socialist government in its last years and ensured a victory in 1996 by the cleaner-cut right-wing Partido Popular.

By the time I left Spain, in 1988, it seemed that most of the people I knew were running illegal telephone services. Even El Doc, the high-minded Peruvian paediatrician, had abandoned his studies and his thoughts of going back to Peru, to get in on the scam. His argument was that he had to make money while he could, to finance a poorer future helping children in Peru, but he knew it was a cop-out.

However, the days of the *locutorios* were numbered. Rufus had found out that the police were tapping one of his lines in the hope of hearing information about drugs deals from the Colombian clientele. Plain-clothes detectives had been spotted lingering outside one of the flats. Not long after I left Spain, Carmen sent me a cutting from *El País* showing that one of the *locutorios* had been raided, but somehow Rufus, always light-footed, avoided arrest. He used the money he made out of the *locutorios* to buy a small boarding house.

Arturo was perhaps the only friend who remained true to his ideals. I saw him on various occasions in the years after I left Madrid, and he never missed an opportunity to lecture me about anarchism. Carmen, by now, was living in the Canary Islands in an old farmstead with no electricity. Another friend had become an international guano merchant, a job description that entertained him as much as it did everyone else. Whenever he was asked how he was, he answered, with great hilarity: 'Deep in shit!'

As for the revolutionary, he returned to Peru some years ago – but there is still no word of the revolution.

❧ ❧ ❧

Once all the mattresses were down, they were swooped on by parents. The more popular ones turned out to be in the main square, perhaps because El Colacho had a good run up from the church steps, and therefore a better chance of clearing the babies without mishap, or maybe it was simply felt to be a location closer to God.

I was too much of a new mother. Everything about the day made me nervous: the wasps, the heat, the possibility of another painful bout of wind afflicting my son. More than anything I was worried that the devil would land on him. What if that year's Colacho were a bad jumper, or drunk, or accompanied by a useless apprentice?

There is a photograph, from 1934, showing El Colacho jumping over that year's mattressful. His feet are a blur of movement, seeming barely to skim the curly heads beneath him. Like the babies, the men and women surrounding the mattress are dressed in their best clothes; the men wear bow ties, the babies' faces protrude from ruffles and bows, but they look as sombre as their parents, because this was a serious occasion. The families were poor, and in 1934 infant mortality was high. They were *really* hoping that El Colacho could do them a good turn.

Nowadays, when there was less excuse to be superstitious, did the people of Castrillo really believe El Colacho could protect their children? It would be such a relief to think that one acrobatic leap could wipe away the threat of serious illness for ever.

'Do you think it works?' I asked a fellow mother. She shrugged and said, 'It's a tradition' – which was no kind of answer.

Perhaps sometimes, through the force of belief, you can make things real. At Campo de Criptano, site of the famous windmills that Don Quixote took for giants, one of the guides was regularly asked which of the windmills it was the knight had attacked. She always explained that Don Quixote was a work of fiction – there had been no battle with imaginary giants. The tourists were inevitably disappointed and one group returned quickly to the tour bus, visibly crestfallen. From then on, the guide decided to change her policy. Now, when people ask her which windmill Quixote fought, she tells them.

~ ~ ~

The mattresses were filling up with babies, and we had found one that looked inviting: it would be the fifth to be jumped, so El Colacho would be practised, but not too tired; its suspension was good. I put my baby down, and he seemed happy enough with the company. After the morning's drama, he looked reassuringly robust compared to the tiny creature lying next to him. 'Only six days old, poor mite,' said this one's mother, with an air of detachment, as if the baby were not really anything to do with her. By the time our mattress was full there were eight infants, lying on their backs, looking at the Castilian sky.

It was not long now until the ceremony began. From the main square, two couples came running down the street with their arms full of bundles. We watched them being turned away from the mattress up the road.

They ran on down towards our mattress, but there was no charity to be had from us, either.

'No! Full up!' cried the mothers, like innkeepers in Bethlehem. 'You have to leave enough room for the babies to roll,' somebody muttered, by way of justification.

The parents hurried to see if they could squeeze on to the next mattress further down the road.

'They should have been better prepared,' said a mother. 'It's just about to start.'

Soon we could hear the proceedings beginning in the main square. There was a distant banging of drums, a tinkle of bells.

Everyone strained to listen, like people outside a church where a wedding is taking place. The babies who knew how began to essay a few basic manoeuvres. Those confined to their backs waggled their arms and legs. One or two cried, and were plugged with dummies. As the noise grew louder, the front of the procession appeared at the top of our street; now I could make out a group including a priest walking under a canopy supported by six suited dignitaries. Behind them came the white-cassocked members of the brethren. Evidently it was the locals' habit to follow the procession to each mattress – there were so many people gathered around the babies up ahead that we could barely make out El Colacho's jump, just a rush of red and yellow amid the crowd.

Now it was our turn: the procession, villagers and visitors squeezed a way down the narrow street towards our babies. At the front were traditional dancers with bells attached to their ankles who pranced and jingled around the mattress. Then came the bespectacled priest, looking faintly absurd under a canopy that required so many people to carry it.

'Make way!' shouted men flanking the procession and suddenly I was manhandled off the route, separated from husband and child, by someone who looked like a Barcelona nightclub bouncer. I heard myself shout above the racket that I was a *mother* – and perhaps for the first time it came home to me that I really was – I needed to stay close to the mattress. It made no difference: I was swallowed into the crowd. For a few minutes I could not see my boy at all.

The din produced by giant drums, the dancers' bells and cymbals was overwhelming and the crush frightening. I remembered other occasions of crush and din, at other fiestas in Spain and it crossed my mind that the fear, in a sense, was part of the deal. There is always a moment at one of these events when you would do anything to get out – the noise and the people are suffocating – yet afterwards everyone will claim to have had a wonderful time. It occurred to me that Spaniards cannot get away from the drama of religion, from a love and hatred of it.

A few yards away from me, the priest stopped at a makeshift altar, set up outside someone's house. There was a moment's quiet, while the priest held the Eucharist aloft, and blessed the occupants of our mattress. Children watching from a window above the altar dropped rose petals on to the priest's shining pate. Then half a dozen little girls dressed in starched white dresses stepped forward to scatter more petals over our bemused babies, turning them into players in some strange piece of theatre.

From my vantage point I could occasionally see my baby's yellow leggings paddling the air, but I did not know if the paddling indicated distress or contentment. The clanging noise set up again and it was El Colacho's turn to jump. As he walked around the mattress, swishing the horse's tail, he seemed to be sizing up the leap it would be necessary to make. He had removed the mask now, perhaps to reassure the babies, revealing a dark-skinned face with thoughtful eyes. He was thin, scrawny even, and I noticed that he was wearing high-tech, pneumatic trainers – so much the better for us. Then he retreated some paces, took a run up and made his leap.

Holding a camera above the crowd, I snapped a picture that caught him in the air, one foot pushing forward, the other stretched back, the horse's tail swishing in his hand behind him. Veins stood out in his neck with the effort of the jump. The faces in the crowd behind him were suspended in anticipation. A quota-filling nun I had not noticed before, had crept into the picture to supply an ethereal smile.

El Colacho hung in the air and the babies, covered in rose petals, looked curiously up at him. None of them cried, but rather they seemed intrigued. In their short lives they had seen many entertaining objects rattled and waved above them, but nothing as extravagant as this. Eight pairs of eyes watched as the devil passed swiftly overhead.

It took a second, the space of a heartbeat – and a new generation set out into an uncertain world.

FURTHER READING

Azaña, Manuel, *La Invención del Quijote* (Madrid, 1934).

Azorín, *La Ruta de Don Quijote* (Madrid, 1915).

Baretti, J., *Tolondrón: Speeches to John Bowle about his Edition of Don Quixote* (London, 1786).

Bloom, Harold, *The Western Canon* (London, 1996).

Borges, Jorge Luis, *The Total Library, Non-Fiction 1922–1986* (London, 2000).

Borges, Jorge Luis, *Fictions* (London, 1985).

Canavaggio, Jean, *Cervantes* (New York, 1990).

Carr, Raymond (editor), *Spain: A History* (Oxford, 2000).

Cervantes Saavedra, Miguel de, *Don Quixote*, translated by J. M. Cohen (London, 1950).

Coleridge, Samuel Taylor, *Lectures on European Literature* (London, 1818).

Gibson, Ian, *Fire in the Blood: The New Spain* (London, 1992).

Graham, Helen and Jo Labanyi (editors), *Spanish Cultural Studies: An Introduction* (Oxford, 1995). I found the chapter on censorship particularly useful.

Greene, Graham, *Monsignor Quixote* (London, 1982).

Hooper, John, *The New Spaniards* (London, 1995).

Johnson, Carroll, *Madness and Lust: A Psychoanalytical Approach to 'Don Quixote'* (Berkeley, 1983).

Kafka, Franz, *Shorter Works* (London, 1973).

Kamen, Henry, *The Spanish Inquisition: An Historical Revision* (London, 1998).

Kundera, Milan, *The Art of the Novel* (London, 1990).

Martín Gaite, Carmen, *Usos Amorosos de la Postguerra Española* (Barcelona, 1987).

Morris, Jan, *Spain* (London, 1982).

Madariaga, Salvador de, *Don Quixote: A Psychological Study* (London, 1934).

Nabokov, Vladimir, *Lectures on Don Quixote*, ed. Fredson Bowers (New York, 1983).

Nelson, Lowry, *Cervantes: A Collection of Critical Essays* (London, 1969). Includes essays by Thomas Mann and W. H. Auden.

Ortega y Gasset, José, *Meditations on Quixote* (New York, 1963).

Preston, Paul, *¡Comrades! Portraits from the Spanish Civil War* (London, 2000).

Riley, E. C., *Cervantes' Theory of the Novel* (Oxford, 1962).

Robbins, Jeremy, *The Challenges of Uncertainty: An Introduction to Seventeenth-Century Spanish Literature* (London, 1998).

Rodgers, Eamonn (editor), *Encyclopedia of Contemporary Spanish Culture* (London, 1999).

Thomas, Hugh, *The Spanish Civil War* (London, 1990).

Unamuno, Miguel de, *Vida de Don Quijote y Sancho* (Madrid, 1998).

INDEX

Alcalá, University of, 144
Alcalá de Henares, 6, 82, 155, 197
Alcázar (Segovia), 211
Alcázar (Toledo), 142
Alemán, Mateo, 92
Alfonso VI of Castile, 141
Alfonso XIII, King of Spain, 155
Almodóvar, Pedro, 179
Andalusia, 167, 169, 183
Aragón, 170
Argamasilla del Alba, 184–8, 208
Army of Africa, the, 158
Association for Numerous Families, the, 227
Astray, General Millán, 171–2
Asturias, 170
Auden, W. H., 219–20
Avellaneda, 9, 38
Avila, 91–105
Azaña, Manuel, 4, 154–8, 209–10

Barca, Calderón de la, 92
Barcelona, 180
Barefoot Trinitarian Sisters, 2, 10–11
Baretti, Joseph, 217–18
bars, number of, 17
Basque Country, the, 164, 169, 171; see also ETA
Beckett, Samuel, 178
begging, 195–7
Bible, Polyglot, 82
Bilbao, 222
birth rate, 3, 227–8
Borbón, Juan Carlos de see Juan Carlos I, King of Spain
Borges, Jorge Luis, 8, 38, 181–3, 208, 216
Bowle, Reverend John, 217–18
Britain see Great Britain
Buñuel, Luis, 166
Burgos, 160–70
Byron, Lord, 130–31

Cáceres, 225
California, 24
Campo de Criptano, 213
Canalejas, Jose, 22

Carrero Blanco, General Luís, 41
Carrillo, Santiago, 160
Castile, 2, 168–71, 222–35; see also
  Castilla y León
Castilla Libre movement, 170
Catilla y León, 162, 222; see also
  Castile
Castilla-La Mancha, 183
Castrillo de Murcia, 222–35
Catalonia, 164, 169, 174
Cela, Camilo José, 180; The Family
  of Pascual Duarte, 84
censorship, 176–81
Cervantes Saavedra, Miguel de:
  memorial mass for, 1–5, 55; life,
  6–11, 82; works in Italy, 6–7;
  author's interest in, 21; seeks job
  in New World, 24–5; nickname,
  86–7; and chivalric literature,
  91–3; and lack of moralising,
  130–31; as bureaucrat, 135; and
  Muslims, 138–40; favours clear
  writing, 181; Freud and, 213; and
  psychological investigation,
  219–21; The Dialogue of the
  Dogs, 213–14; La Galatea, 8;
  Persiles and Sigismunda, 10; see
  also Don Quixote; Dulcinea;
  Sancho Panza
Cid, El (Rodrigo Diaz de Bivar),
  141, 162, 167
Cisneros, Grand Inquisitor Cardinal
  Ximenez de, 82, 144
Civil War see Spanish Civil War
Cohen, J. M., 93
Colacho, El (annual ritual of),
  223–35
Coleridge, Samuel Taylor, 218
Columbus, Christopher, 134
Complutense University, 82–5
Confederation of Deaf People, 129
Constitution (1932), 156
Cortés, Hernando, 91
Council of the Indies, 24

Cuba, 62

Daily Express (newspaper), 22
Day of the Hispanic Race, 171
Diario de Burgos, El, 162
Dickens, Charles, 37
divorce, 58–9
Don Quixote: as Spain's most
  famous book, 5; Cervantes' state
  of mind when writing, 8; success
  of, 8–9; author re-reads, 21; Don
  Gregorio on, 22–5; Rocinante in,
  26; opening chapter, 28–9;
  responses to, 30–32, 181–3,
  188–90, 216–19; nature of, 32–9;
  Picasso's illustrations of, 40; and
  Maritornes, 56–7; Unamuno on,
  61–4; Sansón Carrasco in, 65;
  and the nature of reality, 71–3;
  Cervantes' purpose in writing,
  91–3; non-stop reading of,
  129–33; Muslims in, 138–40;
  Inquisition censors, 146; Morisco
  translation of, 147; Azaña on,
  154–8; Republicans claim
  allegiance to, 158–9; priest
  'purges' books in, 176–7;
  beginnings of, 183–5; ending,
  206–8; see also Cervantes
  Saavedra, Miguel de; Dulcinea;
  Sancho Panza
Doré, Gustave, 35
Dostoevsky, Fyodor, 5, 32, 189
drug-dealers, 50–1, 73
Dulcinea, nature of Quixote's
  relationship with, 35

El Cid see Cid, El
El Greco see Theotokopoulos,
  Domenikos
Engels, Frederick, 5
England see Great Britain
English Language News Bulletin of
  the International Brigade, 159

Erasmus, Desiderius, 6, 135
eroticism, 179–81, 188
ETA, 41, 166; *see also* Basque
Country, the
European Economic Community,
166
European Union, 167, 229

Falla, Manuel, 166
Fallas, Las, 225
fast food, 61
Ferdinand V of Aragón, 144
Fielding, Henry, 38
Flaubert, Gustave, *Madame Bovary*,
34, 188–9
France, 82, 134
Franco, General Francisco: death,
16, 40–41, 65, 79; undoes
Republican anti-clerical reforms,
20; headquarters during Civil
War, 57, 171; liberates captives
from Alcázar, 142; insistence on
Roman Catholicism, 150; and
Azaña, 156; and military coup,
158; Burgos seat of military
operations of during Civil War,
162; régime of, 163–6, 176–81;
orders Unamuno's execution,
172; legacy, 198
Freud, Sigmund, 5, 213, 219

Gaite, Carmen Martín, 163
Galicia, 169
Gayton, Edmund, 34, 91
Germany, 66, 82, 134, 189
Gibraltar, Straits of, 133
Gibson, Ian, 160
González, Felipe, 40
Gorbachev, President Mikhail, 175
Granada, 136, 144
Grandes, Almuneda, *The Ages of
Lulu*, 179
Great Britain, 82, 134–5, 196
Greene, Graham, *Monsignor

Quixote*, 187–8
Guevara, Ernesto (Che), 174
Guijarro, Cardinal Martínez de,
144
gypsies, 211–12

Hartzenbusch, Baron, 185–6, 208
Hemingway, Ernest, 86
Hogarth, William, 35
Homer, 38
Hooper, John, *Modern Spaniards*,
199
Huarte, Juan, *Un Examen de
Ingenios*, 35

immigrants, 133–4
Inquisition, the, 143–6
International Brigade, 82, 159
Isabella of Castile, 144
Italy, 6–7

Japan, 160, 227
Jews, expelled from Spain, 6
John Paul II, Pope, 160
Johnson, Carroll B., 181; *Madness
and Lust*, 35
Johnson, Dr Samuel, 217
Juan Carlos I, King of Spain (Juan
Carlos de Borbón), 41–2, 150

Kafka, Franz, *The Truth about
Sancho Panza*, 189
Kundera, Milan, 216

La Mancha, 183–90
Law of Political Responsibility
(1939), 176
Lenin, Vladimir Ilyich, 174
Lepanto, Battle of, 7, 21, 137
life expectancy, 59
Llosa, Mario Vargas, 180
Lope de Vega *see* Vega Carpio,
Lope Felix de
Lorca, Federico García, 66, 166

Loyola, Saint Ignatius, 219
Luther, Martin, 135, 146

Madariaga, Salvador de, 159
Madrid: funeral mass in, 1–5;
    Cervantes born near, 6; Chueca
    district in, 11–16; author arrives
    in, 18; Calle Huertas, 21; Puerta
    del Sol, 22, 26; Gran Vía, 23–4,
    26; author first stays in, 25–9,
    73–82; Santa Bárbara, 26; Cuatro
    Caminos, 26; fall of, 159; fiesta
    in, 224–5
Málaga, 41
Mann, Thomas, 32, 189–90, 208–9
Marx, Karl, 5, 174; Das Kapital,
    176
Mendicutti, Eduardo, 180–81, 188
Mohammed, Emir, 150
Mola, General, 22, 82
Molière, 9
Montero, Rosa, 229–30
Morocco, 158, 171
movida, la (post-Franco backlash),
    77–8
Muslims, expelled from Spain,
    6

Nabokov, Vladimir, 30–31, 34, 36,
    71, 93, 139, 208; Lolita, 189
National Organisation of the
    Spanish Blind (ONCE), 73,
    146–7, 149–50
NATO (North Atlantic Treaty
    Organisation), 197–201
New World, 24–5, 34; see also
    South America
New York Post (newspaper), 163
nicknames, Spanish use of, 86–7
noise, 160–61
nuns, 18–20, 67–70; see also
    Barefoot Trinitarian Sisters

ONCE see National Organisation

for the Spanish Blind
Ortega y Gasset, José, 63
Orwell, George, 25, 38, 172, 201

paeso, el (the evening stroll), 18
País, El (newspaper), 134, 173
Patagonia, 24
Peru, 80, 87, 152, 230
Philip II, King of Spain, 6, 135–6,
    164–5
Philip III, King of Spain, 138
Picasso, Pablo, 35, 40, 166
Pinter, Harold, 178
Portillo, Luis, 171
Portillo, Michael, 171
prostitution, 59–60, 75
protest march, 197–204
Proust, Marcel, 38
Purity of Blood Statute, the (1547),
    144

Rains of Ranchipur, The (film), 178
Réage, Pauline, The Story of 'O',
    179
Regenerationists, the, 155
religion, 134–46
Rivera, Primo de, 155
Rocinante: Don Quixote leaves fate
    to, 26; appearance, 36; and Don
    Quixote's clothing, 37
Royal Academy of the Spanish
    Language, 3

Sade, Marquis de, 100 Days of
    Sodom, 179
Salamanca, 55–70, 88–90, 223
Salamanca, University of, 171
Sancho Panza: appearance, 35–7;
    and Quixote's misinterpretations,
    71; effect of fear on, 72; and
    Quixote's death, 206–8; and
    experience of flight, 220
Scott, Sir Walter, 92
Second Republic, the, 22

Second World War *see* World War II

secularisation, 20

Segovia, 210–16

Segura, Cardinal, Archbishop of Toledo, 156

Seville, 135

Shakespeare, William, 9, 10, 34; *King Lear*, 34

Silva, Feliciano de, 33

South America, 80, 134–5; *see also* New World

Spanish Civil War: and author's flat, 14–15; Franco victorious, 20; and *mutilados*, 21; General boasts he will take Madrid during, 22; Don Gregorio on, 24; Orwell on, 25; fall of Salamanca in, 57; anarchist activity before, 66; Complutense University during, 82–3; and 'two Spains', 135; Toledo during, 142–3; Burgosa nationalist stronghold during, 162; executions following, 164; Argamasilla's church sacked during, 186; Azaña makes appeal during, 210

Spanish Foreign Legion, 171

Swift, Jonathan, 38

Tenerife, 134

Tenochtitlán, 91

Theotokopoulos, Domenikos ('El Greco'), 87, 140

Thatcher, Margaret, 166

Thomas, Hugh, 82–3

Toledo, 139–51

Torquemada, Tomás de, 144–6

Torrejón de Ardoz, 197–9, 201

tourism, 41, 231–2

transvestites, 50–51, 76, 198

Tuna, the (strolling minstrels), 57

Turgenev, Ivan, 208

Unamuno, Miguel de, 31, 61–5, 130, 171–2, 214; *The Life of Don Quixote and Sancho*, 61, 64

United Nations, 165, 196, 229

United States of America, 196

Valencia, 133, 225

Valencia, Pedro de, 'A Treaty on the Spanish Moriscos', 136–8

Valladolid, 135

Vega Carpio, Lope de, 8–9

Wilkins, George, 9

Woolf, Virginia, 5, 93, 130; *Jacob's Room*, 189

World War II, 83

Zaragoza, 156

Zocódover, Plaza de (Toledo), 140–42, 146